Architectural Design
March/April 2008

Versat

Performa

Guest-edited
Michael Hensel and Achim Menges

M000312746

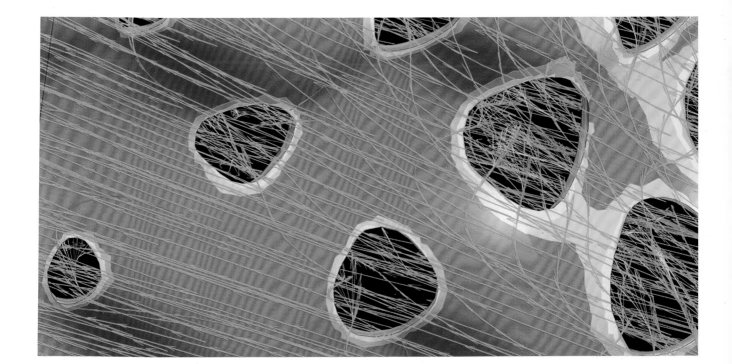

WILEY
wiley.com

ISBN-978 0470 51687 4
Profile No 192
Vol 78 No 2

Editorial Offices
International House
Ealing Broadway Centre
London W5 5DB

T: +44 (0)20 8326 3800
F: +44 (0)20 8326 3801
E: architecturaldesign@wiley.co.uk

Editor
Helen Castle

Production Editor
Elizabeth Gongde

Project Management
Caroline Ellerby

Design and Prepress
Artmedia Press, London

Printed in Italy by Conti Tipocolor

Advertisement Sales
Faith Pidduck/Wayne Frost
T: +44 (0)1243 770254
E: fpidduck@wiley.co.uk

Contributing Editor
Jayne Merkel

Front cover: Performative branching structure of
the competition design for the New Czech
National Library in Prague (2006) by OCEAN and
Scheffler + Partner Architects. Image © Achim
Menges, OCEAN and Scheffler + Partner
Architects.

Requests to the Publisher should be addressed to:
Permissions Department,
John Wiley & Sons Ltd,
The Atrium
Southern Gate
Chichester,
West Sussex PO19 8SQ
England

F: +44 (0)1243 770620
E: permreq@wiley.co.uk

Subscription Offices UK
John Wiley & Sons Ltd
Journals Administration Department
1 Oldlands Way, Bognor Regis
West Sussex, PO22 9SA
T: +44 (0)1243 843272
F: +44 (0)1243 843232
E: cs-journals@wiley.co.uk

[ISSN: 0003-8504]

_D_ is published bimonthly and is available to
purchase on both a subscription basis and as
individual volumes at the following prices.

Single Issues
Single issues UK: £22.99
Single issues outside UK: US$45.00
Details of postage and packing charges
available on request.

Annual Subscription Rates 2008
Institutional Rate
Print only or Online only: UK£180/US$335
Combined Print and Online: UK£198/US$369
Personal Rate
Print only: UK£110/US$170
Student Rate
Print only: UK£70/US$110
Prices are for six issues and include postage
and handling charges. Periodicals postage paid
at Jamaica, NY 11431. Air freight and mailing in
the USA by Publications Expediting Services
Inc, 200 Meacham Avenue, Elmont, NY 11003
Individual rate subscriptions must be paid by
personal cheque or credit card. Individual rate
subscriptions may not be resold or used as
library copies.

All prices are subject to change
without notice.

Postmaster
Send address changes to 3 Publications
Expediting Services, 200 Meacham Avenue,
Elmont, NY 11003

CONTENTS

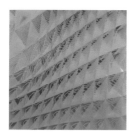

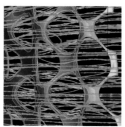

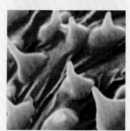

Editorial

With *Versatility and Vicissitude*, guest-editors Michael Hensel and Achim Menges have given us a curiously Jane Austen-like title for an issue of *AD*. Like *Sense and Sensibility* or *Pride and Prejudice*, alliteration is combined with two differing if not entirely opposing characteristics. By pairing up two words that, at least initially, sound alike, we are forced to decode what is being communicated to us. There is nothing obvious or self-evident about the notion of versatility or vicissitude in an architectural context. The title invites enquiry. It begs us to do a double take, think again, if not rush to the dictionary for a definition.

The approach of the title is analogous to Hensel's and Menges' approach to architecture. It requires a level of serious engagement. There is no all-encompassing soundbite to sum it up. It is founded on the notion that it can only be realised through a long-term investment in design research that draws on the knowledge of a broad range of experts, whether it is material scientists, structural engineers or manufacturers. (Both Hensel and Menges are directors with Michael Weinstock of the Emergent Technologies in Design MSc/MArch programme at the Architecture Association, where they draw on the regular expertise of the design engineer Nikolaos Stathopoulos from Buro Happold and Professor George Jeronimidis of the Centre for Biomimetrics at Reading, in addition to visiting specialists from other disciplines.)

In the first paragraph of their introduction, Hensel and Menges outline their aim to seek out an alternative approach to sustainable design. This might sound like the holy grail of many other contemporary architects, but to them it is one that can only be realised through a radical new way of thinking about design. Steering away from such words as 'green', 'ecological' or 'sustainable', they make us think about the word 'ecology' from afresh, as 'the relationship between an organism and its environment' (p 7). This emphasis on the subject and its environment underlines the importance of a dynamic relationship between people and the built environment, which realised through new technologies can more easily be likened to the natural world with its own dynamic processes in place.

Versatility and Vicissitude is both a sequel and a one-off publication. It is the third publication that these two guest-editors have worked on together; the previous two were compiled with the collaboration of Michael Weinstock. As a sequel, we can perceive a development of ideas: the first issue *Emergence: Morphogenetic Design Strategies* (*AD*, No 3, Vol 74, 2004) advocated emergence as a new model of thinking and design in architecture (emergence being, in the sciences, system theory and philosophy, the way complex systems and patterns arise out of a multiplicity of relatively simple interactions); the second, *Techniques and Technologies in Morphogenetic Design* (*AD*, No 2, Vol 76, 2006) started to play with how these might come about. Here, the new emphasis on performance in a dynamic architectural context casts architecture not only potentially as part of a greater natural ecology, but starts to suggest what this might offer the end user in terms of 'intensified spatial experiences' and 'microclimatic conditions'. Architecture is as much about human habitat as new technologies. *AD*

Helen Castle

Defne Sunguroğlu, Complex Brick Assemblies, London, 2006
Airflow analysis of a porous double-curved brick assembly.

Versatility and Vicissitude

An Introduction to Performance in Morpho-Ecological Design

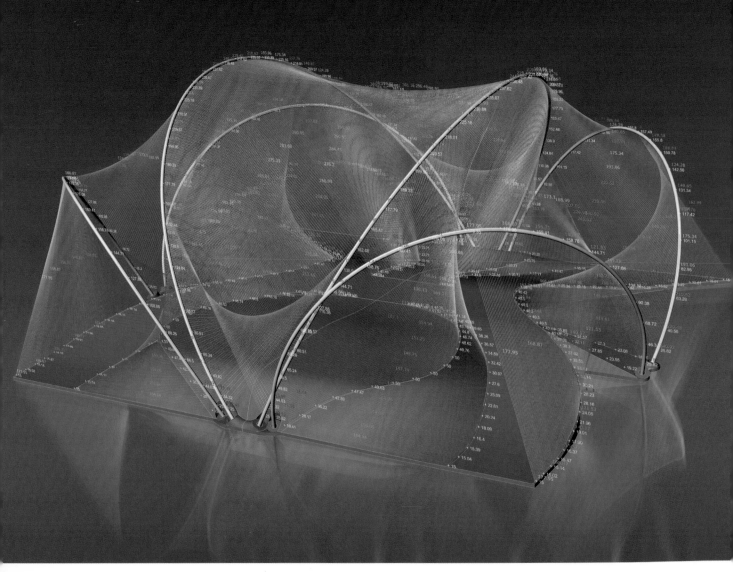

The dictionary explanation of 'performance' is to 'carry out an action' or 'to fulfil a task'. Invariably, this definition seems to invoke a tired utilitarian debate on the correlation between form and function. Here, **Michael Hensel** and **Achim Menges** explain how in this issue of *AD* they aim to move the debate on entirely. In so doing, they redefine form not as the shape of a material object alone, but as the multitude of effects, the milieu of conditions, modulations and microclimates that emanate from the exchange of an object with its specific environment – a dynamic relationship that is both perceived and interacted with by a subject. Performance evolves from the synthesis of this dynamic, while morpho-ecological design concerns an instrumental approach, making form and function less of a dualism and more of a synergy that aspires to integral design solutions and an alternative model for sustainability.

Complex roof structure of the BMW Welt building in Munich by Coop Himmelb(l)au architects and Bollinger + Grohmann structural engineers. See 'Form, Force, Performance: Multi-Parametric Structural Design' on page 20.

Versatile adj. capable of or adapted for many different uses, skills, etc.
Vicissitude n. variation or mutability in nature or life

Today, many make grand claims with regards to sustainability, but if one looks closely such claims all too often serve either mere public-relations and fund-raising purposes, or boil down to an ever greater division of exterior and interior space through ever thicker thermal insulation combined with reductions in energy use of electrical heating, cooling, ventilation and air-conditioning devices. When passive methods of environmental modulation are mentioned, it is often in an apologetic tone, assuring that the aim is not to promote a move back towards outmoded means that might sacrifice contemporary levels of comfort. Several questions arise from this. Can one offer alternatives to the currently prevailing approach to sustainability? Can passive means that utilise material and spatial strategies be updated so as to make redundant entire energy cycles currently involved in sustainable design? Can such an alternative approach evolve and carry its own beauty and aesthetic without devolving into superficial metaphors? Can such an approach promote a rethinking of currently prevailing modes of inhabiting space together with its related social formations, and thus become socially and culturally sustainable and robust?

The aim of this issue of *Architectural Design* is to let these questions remain implicit rather than explicit through the various investigations and discussions. We seek to encourage the rise of further questions, thoughts and approaches, instead of pretending that there already exists a fully developed paradigm. On the contrary, we wish to show some potential beginnings that might eventually lead to a fully developed paradigm that we generally refer to as performance-oriented design, the more specific basics of which we have attempted to outline in our book *Morpho-ecologies*.[1] This publication therefore aims to trace historical precursors and precedents and also to present the current state of the art of morpho-ecological design.

Within this context, 'versatility' entails the notion of the behaviour and performance of an organism or artefact within its specific context, while addressing both the object and the subject. 'Vicissitude' entails the differentiation of the object and the dynamic of the environment. The notion of 'ecology' addresses precisely this: the relationship between an organism and its environment. Ecology is in this way a central concept for morpho-ecological design. Thus this approach commences with a high degree of articulation of the built environment as a substrate and catalyst of motile, mutable and feedback-based relations between habitat and inhabitants that yield diverse and intense social interactions. Here, inhabitants' activities can be understood as emergent real-time matches between individual and collective itineraries, with provisions made and conditions yielded by highly differentiated spatial organisation and material systems. This notion of spontaneously emerging

The relationship between form, material and performance is the key driver in the design process of OCEAN's German Pavilion for the Prague Quadrennial International Exhibition of Scenography and Theatre Architecture 2007, as presented in 'Designing Morpho-Ecologies' on page 102.

As part of the Freeform Construction research project at Loughborough University, the morphology of a Macrotermes michaelseni termite mound is scanned. See 'Manufacturing Performance' on page 42.

Responsive surface structure that instrumentalises moisture-content activated shape changes of timber components. See 'Material Performance' on page 34.

The transition from space-frame to surface morphology within one system offers a range of performative capacities through related changes of porosity. See 'Inclusive Performance: Efficiency Versus Effectiveness' on page 54.

activities and their migration and mutation in relation to morpho-ecological dynamics can then serve to speculate about alternative notions of the social and cultural sustainability of the built environment.

Performance capacity of the synergy between spatial organisation and material assembly thus becomes a driver of morphogenesis. This marks a most significant shift in design approach and production towards levels of effects and performativity not previously considered. Bringing these concepts together has potentially tremendous consequences for the future of our human environment.

The first section of this issue outlines significant changes over the last century in the way performance has been understood and instrumentalised with regards to the correlation between stimulus or force, material response or form and the performative capacity that ensues from this dynamic relationship. This threefold correlation between force, form and performance is elaborated through a historical account, a contemporary approach and a visionary outlook in this section. The issue begins with Professor Remo Pedreschi's examination of the works of exceptional 20th-century structural engineers and their developments of form-active structures within the context of methodological and technological progress. The design approaches of Robert Maillart, Pier Luigi Nervi, Eduardo Torroja, Felix Candela, Eladio Dieste and Heinz Isler are presented as a multifaceted lineage, aiming for a more integral understanding of form, material, structure and the resultant structural behaviour. In the following article, Professor Klaus Bollinger, Professor Manfred Grohmann and Oliver Tessmann challenge the common classification of structural typologies that were central to 20th-century engineering design and the related ethically loaded concepts of 'building correctly'. Considering each structure as an individual case with inherently complex behaviour, rather than a particular variant of an established archetype, they discuss their approach to design engineering, the relevant methods, generative techniques and the respective consequences of the relationship between force, form and structural performance along a number of their recently completed projects.

Michael Weinstock's article, entitled 'Metabolism and Morphology', then looks at an approach based on metabolism, highlighting the consequences for performance-oriented design. In the natural sciences, metabolism refers to all energy transformations, the sum of the complex chemical and physical changes that take place within an organism and promote growth, sustain life, and enable the processes of living organisms. Weinstock presents an account of the thermodynamics of mammalian, marine and plant metabolisms and their relationships to morphology and scale, to behaviour and to the environment. The relationships between living organisms and their environment are analysed in terms of the vectors of energy and material flows in populations, habitats and ecosystems. He also sets out a new model of metabolism for buildings

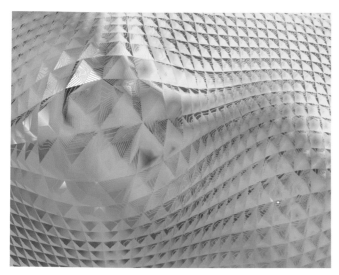

Computer fluid dynamics can be instrumentalised to explore and strategise the performative effects of material systems. See 'Inclusive Performance: Efficiency Versus Effectiveness' on page 54.

In the following article, 'Manufacturing Performance', Menges describes how advanced computer-controlled manufacturing processes can provide key design parameters for the development of performative structures. He investigates and explains the work of the Rapid Manufacturing Group at Loughborough University, which is at the forefront of developing rapid manufacturing technologies for various fields and is currently developing additive manufacturing processes at the construction scale. Aiming to instrumentalise so-called 'quasi composite material', that is, materials that can acquire a wide range of physical and mechanical properties through multiscalar variations in the manufacturing process of a single material, the group not only focuses on the development of related manufacturing technologies, but also undertakes in-depth studies of the versatility and performance of natural, single material systems. Menges discusses this research as an example of an emerging kind of computer-controlled manufacturing technology that may fundamentally challenge not only the way we build, but also the way we envisage performative architectural design.

The final section leaps into a more inclusive understanding of performance-oriented design as outlined above. In 'Performance-Oriented Design: Precursors and Potentials', Michael Hensel examines and systematises selected historical precursors to performance-oriented design, with particular focus on passive means of environmental modulation and the opportunities that arise for inhabiting space and rethinking the strict division between exterior and interior, as well as the fear of loss of comfort that underlies current approaches to sustainable design.

In 'Efficiency Versus Effectiveness', Hensel and Menges elaborate their morpho-ecological design approach. Based on an understanding of material systems, not as derivatives of standardised building systems and elements, but rather as generative drivers in the design process, this approach seeks

and cities that unfolds concepts, systems and relationships for groups of environmentally intelligent buildings, with interlinked systems of material and energy flows.

The second section presents changes in the way we may understand material performance and related manufacturing logics. In the first article, 'Material Performance', Michael Hensel and Defne Sunguroğlu ask why not all materials are considered 'smart' and test this label on wood to demonstrate that performance-oriented design would have a lot to gain from utilising the capacity of all materials, whether long in existence or new, to respond to extrinsic stimuli. Later in the same article, Achim Menges discusses a research project that demonstrates the potential consequences of this approach to material performance and the integral relationship between formation and materialisation processes.

Digital form-finding of a complex membrane system. See 'Membrane Spaces' on page 74.

Differentiated membrane component system. See 'Membrane Spaces' on page 74.

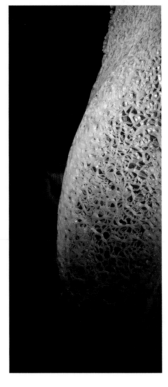

Full-scale prototype of a 3-D spacer-textile composite surface. See 'Environmental Intensifiers' on page 88.

Full-scale prototype of a glass-fibre band component surface. See 'Environmental Intensifiers' on page 88.

that instrumentalise multiparameter form-finding processes. A membrane is a thin, synthetic or natural pliable material that separates two environments and constitutes the lightest elements available for spatial organisation and environmental modulation in architectural design. The membrane expert Klaus-Michael Koch once posited that 'building with membranes is emerging from the shadow of the early pioneering achievements. Several decades of practical experience have led to a technology that is future oriented and that deserves to be more widely established.'[2] In this article the emphasis is on an understanding of membranes as inclusive systems that are form found as the equilibrium state of internal resistances and external forces, while at the same time anticipating a wide range of interactions with environmental influences.

An even more radical departure from established design and construction strategies is discussed, again by the guest-editors, in the article entitled 'Aggregates', which are loosely compacted masses of particles or granules. While an abundance of construction applications of bound aggregates exists (for example, concrete and asphalt), the authors argue that research on loose aggregates requires a fundamental rethinking of architectural design and its preoccupation with element assemblies as aggregates are formed not through the connection of elements by joints or a binding matrix, but

to develop and employ computational techniques and digital fabrication technologies to unfold innate material characteristics and specific latent performative capacities. Extending the concept of material systems by embedding their material characteristics, geometric behaviour, manufacturing constraints and assembly logics within a computational model, the systems manipulations can be recurrently evaluated in relation to structural and environmental performance. In doing so, the article focuses on the possibilities of rethinking the prevailing notion of efficiency through the effectiveness of material systems.

In order to further elaborate and exemplify the morpho-ecological design approach, a variety of projects and material systems are presented and discussed in greater detail in the following articles.

Defne Sunguroğlu introduces her approach to brick – one of the oldest building materials of humanity. Two aspects are of interest here: first, what are the innovations that one might wish to draw upon, and second, what are the unexplored possibilities of building with brick. The article offers a short historical inquiry into specific lineages of the innovative use of brick, with particular focus on the work of Rafael Guastavino and Eladio Dieste, as well as an introduction to Sunguroğlu's current research project entitled, like the article, 'Complex Brick Assemblies'.

In 'Membrane Spaces', the guest-editors discuss recently developed approaches to designing with membrane systems

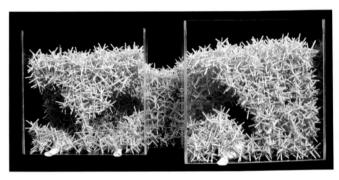

Cavernous spaces emerging from the self-stabilising process of aggregates. See 'Aggregates' on page 80.

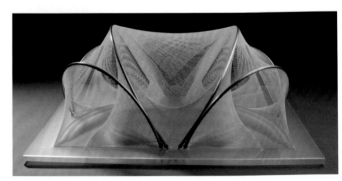

A 1:20 scale model of OCEAN's German Pavilion for the Prague Quadrennial International Exhibition of Scenography and Theatre Architecture 2007 was employed to test different intensities of transparency, reflection and density that provide a space of various microconditions. See 'Designing Morpho-Ecologies' on page 102.

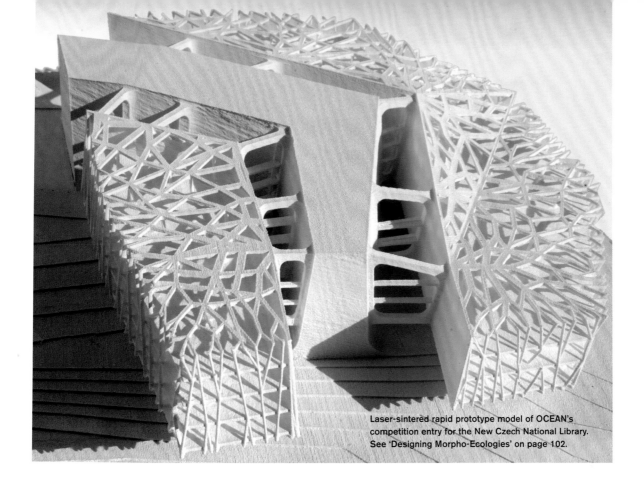

Laser-sintered rapid prototype model of OCEAN's competition entry for the New Czech National Library. See 'Designing Morpho-Ecologies' on page 102.

through the loose accumulation of discrete elements. This offers a different inroad to the design of performative structures, based on design understanding of the processes of self-organisation of systems interacting with the environment rather then the fully controlled, precise geometric definition of the still prevalent tectonic element assemblies. A number of related research projects are introduced alongside the article.

In 'Environmental Intensifiers', Aleksandra Jaeschke examines the work undertaken by the Department of Form Generation and Materialisation at the Hochschule für Gestaltung (HfG) in Offenbach, Germany. The research projects presented here focus on design processes that instrumentalise the inherent possibility for differentiation in fibre composites. Driven by exploration and parameterisation of innate material constraints, elaborate morphologies with complex, internal fibre architectures can be articulated in response to structural forces and environmental influences. These projects are discussed as possible modes of integrating form-generation and materialisation processes in deep, performative skin structures that intensify the surface's interaction with the environment and the body of the user.

Peter Trummer speculates about the possibilities and potential repercussions of 'engineering ecologies' inherent to a change from physics to biology as the underlying paradigm of engineering, and eventually the discipline of architecture. Shifting from the micro-ecological scale of product design elaborated in the previous article to the macro-scale of landscape, he investigates a broader palette of disciplines with regards to design aiming for careful

modulations of environments and ecologies. Based on the introduced morpho-ecological design approach and the corresponding understanding of optimisation, efficiency and redundancy in relation to multiperformative material and construction systems may indicate a very different take on spatial organisation, environmental modulation and, ultimately, social formation.

In the final article, 'Designing Morpho-Ecologies', Michael Hensel and Achim Menges discuss a number of recent projects by OCEAN: the competition entry for the New Czech National Library and a design study of a pavilion in Prague. Set within considerably different contexts and with different scales, the projects explore a high degree of articulation of the material and tectonic systems that yield diverse and intensified spatial experiences and microclimatic conditions. Furthermore, they highlight the importance of the designer in an alternative role, one that is central to enabling, moderating and influencing integral performance-oriented design processes that require novel skills and methods to achieve synthesis of versatility and vicissitude. Δ

Notes
1. Michael Hensel and Achim Menges, *Morpho-ecologies*, AA Publications (London), 2006.
2. Klaus-Michael Koch, *Membrane Structures*, Prestel (Munich, Berlin, London and New York), 2004.

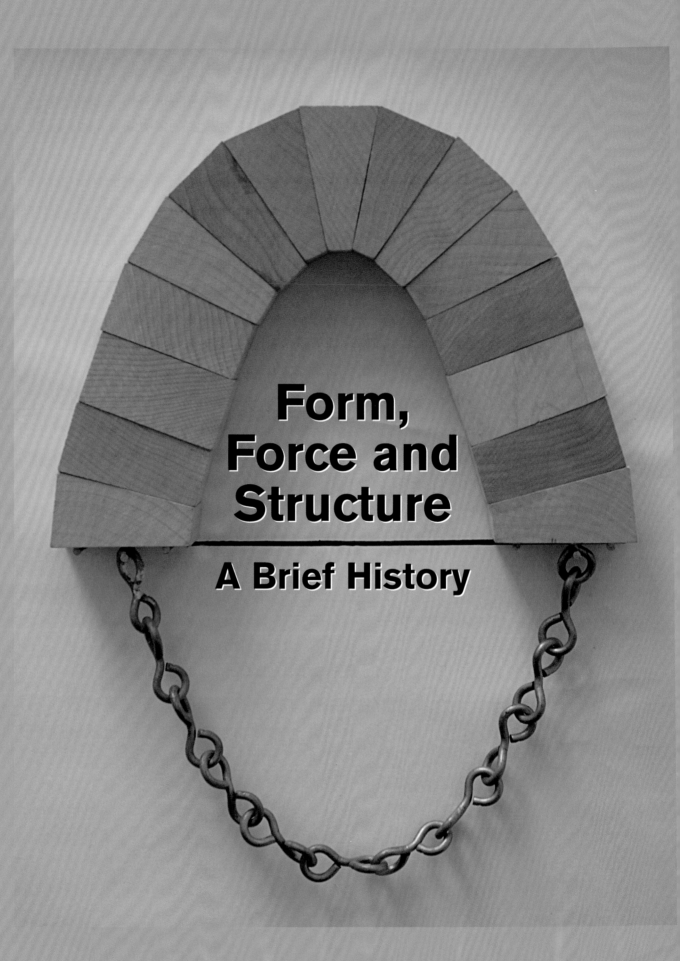

Form,
Force and
Structure

A Brief History

Over the last century, engineers' and architect-engineers' approach to the relationship between form, force and mass has changed significantly, both on a conceptual and methodological level. It is a shift only made possible by the collaborative efforts of design, engineering and construction expertise. Professor Remo Pedreschi discusses the work of Robert Maillart, Pier Luigi Nervi, Eduardo Torroja, Felix Candela, Heinz Isler and Eladio Dieste to illustrate the important changes and contributions that have taken place and how they influence the way we think about performance from an engineering point of view today.

The beginning of the 20th century was a special period in the history of structural and architectural form during which reinforced concrete, a material that would become one of the defining aspects of the century, came to the fore. Although concrete had been discovered by the Romans in the form of pozzolanic cements, contemporary reinforced concrete was a product of the late 19th century, particularly following François Hennebique's patent for fireproof framing in 1892.[1] Such was Hennebique's business acumen that by the turn of the century, with licence agreements throughout Europe, more than 1,200 projects in reinforced concrete had been completed.[2] Initially, structures using reinforced concrete mimicked the iron- and steel-framed buildings of the 19th century. However, designers very quickly saw the greater potential offered by the formless or, more precisely, form-finding qualities of plastic-liquid concrete. Thin, double-curved concrete surface structures with little historical precedent evolved. As designers studied the new material, many incorporated a strong desire for structural expression and structural efficiency – to make virtue out of economy. Thus they drew together form, force and architecture.

Following is a very brief review of the work of a number of designers of the early to mid-20th century, all of whom sought expression in new materials and the opportunities to create structural forms. Much of their work has come to symbolise 'structural art', as defined by David P Billington:

> The disciplines of structural art are efficiency and economy, and the freedom lies in the potential it offers for the expression of a personal style motivated by a conscious aesthetic search for engineering elegance.[3]

'Economy' in this sense is most often concerned with 'an economy of means', to use the minimum of materials, obtained by the efficiency of a structure in resisting forces imposed on it. The majority of the designs used concrete as a 'tectonic compact',[4] where its qualities go beyond the purely structural to become shelter and skin. F Angerer proposed a new classification for these structures particular to the 20th century: 'surface structures', differentiated from the historical classification of the solid or the skeleton and skin, themselves a progression from their prehistoric comparators, the cave and the tent to mass masonry construction and the frame.[5] The defining characteristic of surface structures is the coincidence of the inner space and external form being almost identical; the form can be read from both inside and out.

> Shell construction is the most truthful of all building forms, since the shell expresses space most closely.[6]

The refinement of form depends on a heightened sense of structural behaviour, employing both a conceptual and mathematical understanding of structural action. It is worth considering the development of structural mechanics in the two centuries preceding the 20th century. Prior to this time, structures were designed in a primarily empirical way based on experience and observation. Mainstone describes three forms of intuition that have guided structural innovation:

Intuitions of structural behaviour:
a spatial or muscular sense of the actions of force and stability, that an arch may spread if the abutments are not sufficient to push against the thrust or that a tall slender column is less stable than a short broad column.

Intuitions of structural action:
a deeper understanding of structural behaviour, supported by careful observation that led to more precise ideas of force, moment and equilibrium; the start of a quantitative understanding of structure.

Intuitions of structural adequacy:
a perception of the adequacy of a generic structural form for a particular application, conditioned perhaps by the significance of changes in scale and proportion.

He argues that there is a continual interplay between such intuitions, and his analysis provides a useful backdrop to many of the innovations of the early 20th century: 'Intuitions of behaviour and action also merge into intuitions of adequacy when a new structural form, sought initially in terms of the abstractions of behaviour and action, is conceived in more concrete terms as adequate for a specific purpose'.[7]

Remo Pedreschi, The catenary and the arch, 2007
A model showing an arch using timber voussoirs. The arch is in compression under its self-weight. The geometry of the arch can be determined from the catenary form of the steel chain in tension under its own weight.

The Relationship Between Force, Form and Geometry

The study of the relationship between structural form and force began, in the 17th century,[8] with the understanding of the catenary and its correspondence to the arch. The catenary is the natural curve that a cable or chain will adopt if suspended by its two ends. Under this condition the cable is subjected only to axial tension. If the curve of the cable is flipped around its anchor points, the resulting geometry is the corresponding ideal form for an arch resulting in uniform axial compressive forces.

The Italian mathematician Poleni used the catenary to examine the stability of the dome of St Peter's in Rome in 1742.[9] Thus the relationship between structural form and force, of structural action, was established. A major step occurred with the development of graphic statics[10] by Karl Culmann, a professor at the Federal Technological Institute in Zurich. The method was based on a graphic representation of the force in a structure, both in magnitude and direction, a graphical representation of Newton's third law. According to Addis: 'It would be difficult to overestimate the impact of graphic statics on the world of structural engineering: it was certainly no less significant than the impact of the computer in the late 20th century'.[11]

The graphic method provides direct correspondence between the forces in a structure and the geometry of the structure itself. It became a design tool allowing the rapid development and refinement of the form to either control the forces themselves or to manipulate the geometry of structure itself.[12]

Robert Maillart

The Swiss engineer Robert Maillart graduated in engineering from the ETH in Zurich, and in 1902 formed his own design and construction company. His work, his designs and constructions are remarkable given that they began very shortly after Hennebique's promotion of concrete. It is therefore worthwhile briefly considering the conditions under which Maillart operated, as most of those who came after him faced similar situations.

Reinforced concrete was first introduced to Switzerland via an agent of Hennebique, in 1895. There was considerable resistance towards its introduction, a reluctance to accept both its technical efficacy and its aesthetic merits.[13] Maillart's first project was the design of the Stauffacher Bridge in Zurich (1899). Although the bridge was constructed in concrete, its form was based on traditional stone bridges and incorporated stone sidewalls to support the fill for the road surface above. Using traditional forms and details with a new material was quite common; for example, a century earlier Darby had used cast-iron dovetail joints, modelled on timber construction, in his iron bridge (1779) in present-day Ironbridge, near Coalbrookdale in Shropshire. Maillart was clearly dissatisfied with this early bridge, and he therefore pushed and developed new forms of concrete construction that combined a new aesthetic with a clearer understanding of the structural potential of the 'new' material. Many of his ideas were in

advance of the mathematical theories that would later provide a full numerical analysis of structural behaviour and the subject of some controversy among professionals and the public alike. The overall geometry was usually shaped using graphic statics. His teacher, Wilhelm Ritter, himself a protégé of Culmann, assisted him greatly in obtaining approvals.

Most of the bridges Maillart designed are still in use. His designs express the fluidity of the material shaped by structural intuition; the dimensions of the structure are pared to the minimum. For example, the concrete arch of the Valtschielbach Bridge (1925) in Donath, Switzerland, with a span of 43 metres (141 feet), has a thickness that varies from 23 to 29 centimetres (9 to 11.4 inches) from the crown to the abutments. The variation in thickness follows the compressive forces in the arch, as they increase towards the support. However, the most noted of Maillart's bridges is the Salginatobel Bridge (1930) near Schiers, Switzerland. A three-hinged arch, the form is manipulated to control the stiffness of the cross-section at the crown and each support to allow the bridge to rotate without cracking when subjected to thermal stresses. The bridge was declared a 'world monument' by the American Society of Civil Engineers in 1991.

Robert Maillart, Salginatobel Bridge, near Schiers, Switzerland, 1930
The overall geometry of the arch was developed using graphic statics in response to the self-weight of the bridge. The thickness of the arch increases towards the quarter span and tapers towards the crown and supports to control asymmetrical moments due to vehicle movements.

A product of structural form and material possibility.

Shortly before his death, Maillart produced a splendid exposition of structural form and materials in the Cement Hall for the Swiss Expo in 1939. At 11.7 metres (38.4 feet) in height, yet only 6 centimetres (2.4 inches) thick, this was made possible by controlling the forces through a catenary cross-section. The very thin-edge stiffened shell is supported on a pair of central concrete ribs. The architectural space is created by the demands of the structural form. The building was demolished after the exhibition, in 1940.

Pier Luigi Nervi, Hangar for the Italian air force, Orvieto, Italy, 1935
The ribs and shell of the hangar were constructed *in situ*. In subsequent projects the ribs were prefabricated, which simplified the construction process considerably.

Robert Maillart, Cement Hall, Swiss Expo, Zurich, 1939
The shell of this temporary structure built for the Swiss Expo is only 6 centimetres (2.4 inches) in thickness.

Pier Luigi Nervi

Similar to Maillart, Nervi was both a designer and builder, and formed his own construction company, Nervi and Bartoli, in 1932. He believed in 'building correctly', which implies 'the simultaneous satisfaction of all fundamental requirements; function, economics and aesthetics'.[14]

Nervi had a deep understanding of the nature of concrete; that although it appears to be homogenous, its actual physical properties are controlled by many factors beyond the control of the builder. In a large construction, the mechanical properties of concrete will vary, even if the mix proportions are consistent, according to the temperature and time of pouring among other factors. Simplicity in structural principles and geometry is essential.

The aircraft hangars Nervi constructed for the Italian air force between 1935 and 1936 show a marked progression in 'building correctly'. The formwork for the earlier hangars was constructed entirely *in situ*, requiring extensive scaffolding. In the later projects construction was simplified, consisting of a hybrid of prefabricated elements and *in situ* concrete. The cross-ribbing consists of repetitive prefabricated trusses connected and propped on site, reducing the need for temporary structures. The ribs in turn provide the permanent support for the *in situ* concrete roofs.

His Exhibition Hall in Turin (1949) also used prefabricated elements. However, rather than the ribs being precast, the coffers between them were prefabricated using ferro-cement panels.[15] The panels were designed and arranged to create a criss-crossing series of voids that were subsequently reinforced and filled with *in situ* concrete. The complex curvature of the vault was articulated at the joints and the panels. Thus the apparent intricacy of the soffit is the product of construction simplification. In terms of the construction process, this was an improvement on the hangars, as the continuous ribs provide more effective continuity of structure, no additional formwork is needed once the panels are in place, and the finish of the soffit is more carefully controlled.

Pier Luigi Nervi, Exhibition Hall, Turin, Italy, 1949
The long span vaults were constructed using prefabricated ferro-cement panels to reduce on-site formwork.

Eduardo Torroja

Although the Spanish engineer Torroja was a contemporary of Nervi and shared the same ideas of expressive structure, he differed primarily in his approach to construction. His role was that of designer, and he was more concerned with the form and purity of the design than constructive simplicity: 'Economic factors add nothing to the aesthetic values. The best structures do not have to be the cheapest.'[16] For Torroja, the integration of structural and architectural form was essential. 'The functional purpose and the artistic and strength requirements must be regarded integrally from the initial conception of the project.'[17]

His volume of work may not have been as extensive as those of Nervi and Maillart, but it was probably broader, working with steel and masonry as well as concrete.[18] One particularly interesting project was the Fronton Recoletas stadium (1935) in Madrid. Used mainly for the sport of pelota, the needs of the playing court dictated the overall plan form of 55 x 32.5 metres (180.4 x 106.6 feet). The approach to the structure was quite novel, and plays with the idea of the shell as a structural element. The roof appears to be a pair of thin (8 centimetres/3.1-inches in thickness) asymmetric concrete shells, spanning across the 32.5-metres (106.5-foot) width of the plan. However, the structure actually spans the longer dimension between the two solid sidewalls. The structural action is not that of the shell, predominately in compression, but that of the barrel vault, predominately in bending. While this may appear counterintuitive in terms of structural logic, the action of the vault also eliminates the thrusts from the shell and in doing so allows continuous glazing along the two sides. The structural condition is identical to the rafters in a simple pitched roof supported on a ridge beam spanning between gables; no thrust is generated on the sidewalls. The asymmetry of the vaults is also interesting as it did not conform completely to the existing methods of analysis that assumed that the edges of the vaults were supported by stiff beams and the junction between the two sections should therefore be supported by a beam. Such an inclusion would have destroyed the purity of the surface. The structural behaviour was studied using a 1:10 scale model from which the detailed design was completed. The roof of Fronton Recoletas therefore has the expression of a shell, but the structure of the vault.

Felix Candela

Candela, a Spanish architect, was greatly influenced by Maillart: 'If a rebel was able to produce such beautiful and sound structures there could not be anything wrong with becoming a rebel.'[19] Candela was fascinated by the possibilities of geometry and form in architecture and was awarded a scholarship to study the design of shells in Germany. Unfortunately, he became embroiled in the Spanish Civil War and consequently found himself in Mexico. He later formed the construction company Cubiertas ALA SA.

Like Nervi, Candela distrusted complex theories and their prescriptive application to such a complex material as

Eduardo Torroja, Fronton Recoletas stadium, Madrid, Spain, 1935
The roof of this pelota stadium is constructed as two asymmetrical cylindrical vaults. Although the appearance of the roof is largely that of a vault, the predominant structural action is that of a beam.

concrete. As a builder he also sought simplicity in construction. To this end he became the foremost proponent of the hyperbolic paraboloid[20] as a generator of structural form. A simple way of producing a hyperbolic parabolic surface is to imagine a rectangle or rhombus in plan. Imagine a series of parallel lines drawn between each of the two opposite sides. The surface defined by the lines is flat. If one of the corners is raised relative to the other three, a series of lines can still be drawn across the opposite sides; however, the resulting surface will now be doubly curved. This double curvature provides great stiffness and stability to the form, but equally important the curved surface is produced by straight lines. Candela had the means to produce curved concrete surfaces of great strength and therefore used minimal concrete while simultaneously solving the practical problem of producing curved formwork with straight timbers. His experience led to more complex forms using multiple hyperbolic surfaces or arrangements of surfaces rotated and displaced from each other to create glazing or entrances. His Lomas de Cuernavaca Church (1959) in Mexico shows the hyperbolic surface pulled and stretched to the extreme. The height of the opening above the altar is nearly 22 metres (72 feet).

Felix Candela, Hyperbolic paraboloid roof surface, Mexico, under construction
The warped, double-curved surface is constructed by a series of straight lines that allow the use of straight timber planks as formwork.

Felix Candela, Lomas de Cuernavaca Church, Mexico, 1959
A double-curved saddle roof developed from a hyperbolic surface to create an opening nearly 22 metres (72 feet) in height.

Arguably Candela's most famous building is the Los Manatiales restaurant in Xochimilco, also in Mexico, of 1958. The form is generated from eight separated hyperbolic forms connected to each other along the shared valley joint. The shell is more than 45 metres (147.6 feet) across, but only 4 centimetres (1.57 inches) in thickness.

fabric suspended at each corner. The fabric will sag into a curved surface and creases may form near the sides; however, the fabric can be trimmed to eliminate the creases. The resulting form will be in tension and following the principle of the catenary; the inverted geometry will provide the equivalent compressive structural form. New forms can be developed by displacing the positions of the supports or adding and removing supports. The creative possibilities are almost limitless. Isler calls these 'freeform shells', and the design process he describes as 'creative play'.

Isler's office is part studio, part laboratory, where he works with carefully constructed models.[22] Although not a builder, he developed a close working partnership with the construction company W Boisger AG, and together they completed many projects. The formwork costs were kept to a minimum by using timber profiles, which are often reused. Filling the spaces between ribs was the same problem Nervi faced with his hangars. Isler used wood-wool slabs, cut and fitted to the ribs, that remain after the concrete has set as a permanent layer of insulation. Like Candela, Isler has an extensive portfolio of completed projects. Though he worked in a completely different environment – one of high income and a severe winter climate – his designs were still economic.

Felix Candela, Los Manatiales restaurant, Xochimilco, Mexico, 1958
The geometry here developed from a series of interconnected hyperbolic surfaces. The thinness of the concrete shell is expressed in the elevations.

Heinz Isler, Service station, Deitingen Süd, Switzerland, 1968
The building consists of two symmetrical freeform concrete shells.

Heinz Isler

Heinz Isler continues the tradition of the maverick engineer, interested more in form than the mathematical treatment of structure. A graduate of the ETH in Zurich, he also directly followed Culmann, Ritter and Maillart as part of the Swiss Legacy,[21] and was also influenced by Candela, particularly his Xochimilco restaurant.

Isler's approach to finding form owes much to graphic statics and the catenary. He further developed the idea of the catenary by using suspended fabric to create three-dimensional tension surfaces. Imagine a rectangular piece of

The Deitingen Süd service station (1968) in Switzerland demonstrates his technique effectively. It consists of two symmetrical shells, triangular in plan, 31 metres (101.7 feet) long and 11.5 metres (37.7 feet) in height, and only 9 centimetres (3.5 inches) in thickness, which appear like two sheets of fabric furled into the air and frozen in space.

The Sicli SA factory in Geneva, of 1969, is one of Isler's most complex forms. It comprises two quite distinct yet interconnected shell forms, each proportioned to deal with the two functional aspects of programme: office and factory. One shell turns towards the other, almost overlapping, and

Heinz Isler, Factory for Sicli SA, Geneva, Switzerland, 1969
Isler's Sicli project demonstrates the unconventional geometries that can be found using fabric models.

Eladio Dieste, Entrance canopy for Refrescos Del Norte, Uruguay, 1977
The floating roof form is constructed from a pair of freestanding barrel vaults, cantilevering from a single central row of columns. The vault is constructed from prestressed brick.

the space in between creates a winter garden. The complete structure touches the ground at only seven points, and is only 10 centimetres (3.9 inches) in thickness.

Eladio Dieste

In some ways the Uruguayan engineer Eladio Dieste is the most interesting of the group considered here. He was also a builder, forming the company Dieste Y Montañez in 1955, and shared the same concerns for structure and form made economic by efficient construction processes: 'The resistant virtues of the structures that we seek depend on their form ... There is nothing more noble and elegant from an intellectual viewpoint than this, to resist through form.'[23] However, for Dieste the challenge was to create a language of building that was contemporary and modern but not reliant on technology from the developed world, one more appropriate to the conditions of Uruguay. He achieved this by rediscovering a new structural idiom for brick, one of lightness and minimalism. Brick is the indigenous material of Uruguay and is lighter, uses less cement and is faster to build than concrete.[24] The forms he developed were not a poor nation's replacement for concrete, but a new material with new possibilities. His buildings use brick as frugally as possible, squeezing the maximum out of the structural performance to quite surprising effect; for example, freestanding barrel vaults, acting in double cantilever with spans of more than 12 metres (37.7 feet) but only ever one brick in thickness.

In these structures, the form does everything. There are no stiffening ribs or beams, simply a folded surface. The cross-section of the vault is obtained from the catenary. The vertical concrete support structure consists of the minimum structure necessary for stability. Dieste developed the use the catenary to produce more complex double-curved forms, which he called Gaussian vaults.[25] Simple static analysis of a catenary vault indicates that the compressive forces are low even for long, slender vaults; however, such vaults are liable to buckle under their own weight. The Gaussian vault uses form to resist buckling. The geometry is defined by a series of catenary curves of varying height, each sharing the same springing point. Moving along the springing points, the catenary rises and falls. The resulting surface is double curved, stiffening the vault and preventing buckling. It resists through form.

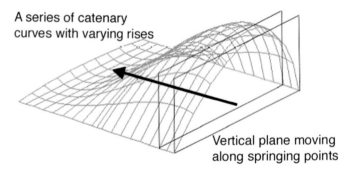

A series of catenary curves with varying rises

Vertical plane moving along springing points

Remo Pedreschi, Geometry of a Gaussian vault, 2000
The double-curved surface of the vault is developed using a series of catenary arches of constant span between springing but variable rises.

The mathematical theory to predict the structural behaviour of the Gaussian vault is rather complex. Unlike others, Dieste eventually developed the theory to verify his structures, although this mathematical resolution postdated his actual constructions by many years.[26] The most well known of his works also includes a particular application of surface and form entirely more appropriate, using masonry rather than concrete: the double-curved wall. The Church of Jesus Christ the Worker in Atlántida, Uruguay, of 1960, uses double-curved walls combined with Gaussian vaults. The walls provide stability and are much simpler to build than concrete.

Eladio Dieste, Gaussian vault under construction, Uruguay, c early 1960s
The vault is subject to an ad hoc load test with a distributed load generated by the workforce. Dieste is the figure standing at the crown.

Eladio Dieste, The Church of Jesus Christ the Worker, Atlántida, Uruguay, 1960
Both the walls and the roof are double-curved surfaces, and the intersection of these shows Dieste's mastery of construction techniques.

Conclusion

While the beginning of the 20th century saw the introduction of reinforced concrete, the end of the century experienced another major new innovation: the use of computers to describe structure and form. This offered new possibilities – 'an explosion of design and production options'.[27]

The critical difference between the use of IT and structure-based form-finding is the possibility to create form without predefinition, without an underlying geometric condition, translating the surfaces of an abstracted volume directly to a digital mapping of the surface. The hyper-rapid numerical processing of the computer makes such projects as the Guggenheim Museum in Bilbao viable, although not necessarily efficient in purely structural or economic terms. The structure is no longer an issue, no longer a determinant of form, instead becoming a subservient facilitator. The technology can now resolve what had always been a point of contention between that which is pragmatic and that which is simply possible. It is important to keep in mind the work of these innovative designers and not lose the idea of structure and form based on natural laws. ∆

Notes

1. The first patent for reinforced concrete is attributed to Joseph Monier (1823–1906) in 1867.
2. D Billington, *The Tower and the Bridge*, Basic Books (New York), 1983.
3. Ibid.
4. C Vallhonrat, 'The invisibility of tectonics, gravity and the tectonic compacts', *Perspecta*, Vol 31 *Reading Structures*, 2000, pp 22–35.
5. F Angerer, *Surface Structures in Building*, Alec Tiranti (London), 1961.
6. Ibid.
7. R Mainstone, 'Intuition and the springs of structural invention', 1973, republished in R Mainstone, *Structure in Architecture*, Ashgate Publishing (London), 1999, pp 1–48.
8. A Becchi, 'Eggs, turnips and chains: Rhetoric and rhetoricians of architecture', in H Schlimme (ed), *Practice and Science in Early Modern Italian Building*, Electa (Milan), 2006.
9. Ibid.
10. K Die Culmann, *Graphische Statik*, Zurich, 1865.
11. W Addis, *Building: 3000 Years of Design Experience and Construction*, Phaidon (London), 2007.
12. For a contemporary text on graphic statics readers are referred to W Zaleweski and E Allen, *Shaping Structures*, John Wiley (New York), 1997.
13. HU Jost, 'The introduction of reinforced concrete in Switzerland (1890–1914): Social and cultural aspects', in M Dunkeld et al (eds), *The Second International Congress on Construction History*, Routledge (London), 2006, pp 1741–53.
14. PL Nervi, PL, *Structures*, FW Dodge (New York), 1956, a translation of *Costruire Correttamente*, Ulrico Hoepli (Milan), 1954.
15. Ferro-cement was developed by Nervi as a means of controlling the wayward elastic properties of concrete. Fine steel wires were distributed about a matrix of the cement and aggregates. The even distribution of steel wires imparts great homogeneity to the concrete. Thin concrete elements of 25 millimetres (0.98 inches) were often manufactured.
16. J Navarro Vera and J Ordonez Fernandez, *Eduardo Torroja: Engineer*, Ediciones Pronaos (Madrid), 1999, p 35.
17. Eduardo Torroja, *Philosophy of Structures*, University of California Press (Berkeley and Los Angeles), 1958, p 327.
18. Navarro Vera and Ordonez Fernandez, op cit.
19. Candela on Maillart. See C Faber, *Candela: The Shell Builder*, Reinhold Publishing (New York), 1962.
20. A hyperbolic paraboloid surface is produced by translating one parabolic curve along another parabolic curve.
21. P Billington, *The Art of Structural Design: A Swiss Legacy*, Princeton Architectural Press (Princeton, NJ), 2003.
22. J Chilton, *Heinz Isler: The Engineer's Contribution to Contemporary Architecture*, Thomas Telford (London), 2000.
23. R Pedreschi, *Eladio Dieste: The Engineer's Contribution to Contemporary Architecture*, Thomas Telford Ltd (London), 2000.
24. Ibid.
25. After the mathematician Gauss, who developed the geometry of the curved surface.
26. R Pedreschi and D Thedossopolis, 'The double curvature masonry vaults of Eladio Dieste', *Structures and Buildings, Proceedings of the Institute of Civil Engineers*, Vol 160, issue SB1, 2007, pp 3–11.
27. K Vollers, *Twist and Build: Creating Non-Orthogonal Architecture*, 010 Publishers (Rotterdam), 2001.

Form, Force, Performance
Multi-Parametric Structural Design

In the 20th century, the classification of structures according to defined building typologies was central to engineering design. Here **Professor Klaus Bollinger**, **Professor Manfred Grohmann** and **Oliver Tessmann** of design engineers Bollinger + Grohmann challenge this preconception. By considering each structure as an individual case in point with inherently complex behaviour, they move away from the notion of a building being a variant of an established type. They further discuss this mode of working, in relation to their own recent projects, in terms of relevant methods and generative techniques, as well as the respective consequences that it has had on the relationship between force, form and structural performance.

Bollinger + Grohmann conceive of structure as an integral part of architecture. The overall performance of an architectural project results from negotiating and balancing a complex network of multifaceted, interrelated requirements. As the design of structure is just one aspect within such a network of manifold relations, the appropriate structural systems cannot be found through single-parameter optimisation. The specific forms derived through such a multi-parametric design process need to be analysed in order to identify zones of favourable structural performance. The related structures adapt their load-bearing capacities to the form and its particular local forces. Thus the resultant structures are highly specific, differentiated systems rather than variations of a defined typology.

The distribution of forces within a massive beam is hidden from the observer's eye as the mass-active system does not indicate its specific load transfer. However, if one visualises the isostatic force trajectories, a number of system-inherent structural types can be recognised; for example arch, truss, lenticular girder and suspension system. The predominance of such vector-active lattice systems can be traced back to a technical innovation in 1866 when Karl Culmann, a professor of engineering science at the Eidgenössischen Polytechnikum in Zurich, published his *Graphic Statics*, including his development of the most important graphic methods for calculating structural behaviour.

Based on Jean Victor Poncelet's scientific work on projective geometry, these versatile graphic methods were also a response to the increasing use of cast-iron structures in the field of construction. With these novel methods being particularly suited for the calculation of lattice girders, no other structural typology signifies better the succinct impact of new calculation methods on the changing understanding and employment of structures.[1]

In the following years, scientific calculation methods and theories gained increasing importance with the simultaneous decline of traditional approaches founded on experience and observation of built examples. In the 1920s the teaching of structures was no longer based on precedent buildings and examples, but general theories and analytical methods.[2] Only in the second half of the 20th century were Culmann's methods of graphic statics superseded by computer numeric procedures. However, the preconceived generic structural typologies defined in the early 20th century and the related scientific methods that prioritise partial analyses and understanding over increasing integration continue to predominate in structural design.

Science works always to achieve general theories that unify knowledge. Every specific natural event, to be scientifically satisfying, must ultimately be related to a general formulation. Engineering, in contrast, works always to create specific objects within a category of type. Each design, to be technologically satisfying, must be unique and relate only to the special theory appropriate to its category.

David P Billington, *The Tower and the Bridge: The New Art of Structural Engineering*, 1985[3]

Bollinger + Grohmann agree with Billington's understanding that structural design provides a unique response to the specific requirements and situation of each project. Moreover, we do not think that structures need to be conceptualised through predefined typologies or conceived of as variations of a particular type.

In our collaborations with architects, form never constitutes the optimum shape derived through a form-finding process driven only by structural optimisation, but rather embodies and integrates a multitude of parameters. Within an overall system we analyse regions with structural capacity and identify morphological zones that can be altered without affecting the architect's spatial and programmatic concept. The structure then unfolds from these regions and adapts its capacity to local requirements. This opportunistic approach erodes predefined typologies in favour of emergent hybrid systems, such as flat space trusses showing shell behaviour or concrete shells turning into landscape.

In this process, external force is just one design aspect among many and thus not the only shape-defining parameter.

Architectural design needs to incorporate complex organisational and functional requirements, and therefore constitutes a recurrent negotiation of analysing existing and requisite conditions as well as generating and evaluating possible responses. Additional knowledge gained through such iterative processes may require further analysis of the specific context or even the adjustment of previously defined design objectives.[4] A project's diverse design criteria can be understood as a network of interdependent nodes. Once this network settles into a state of equilibrium of various influences a high level of integral performance of the building and its structure has been attained. This capacity cannot be achieved through single-parameter optimisation of the overall system, as the linearity of such processes cannot account for the complexity of architectural projects. Thus one of the key aspects of our practice and research work at Bollinger + Grohmann is the integration of optimisation strategies within the complex network of design criteria.

In the following paragraphs we will present strategies for the generation and integration of structure in a number of our recent projects.

Coop Himmelb(l)au, BMW Welt, Munich, Germany, 2008
The shell-like behaviour of the double-cone steel structure gradually transforms into the roof with bending behaviour.

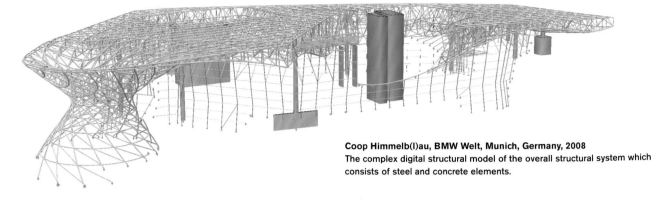

Coop Himmelb(l)au, BMW Welt, Munich, Germany, 2008
The complex digital structural model of the overall structural system which consists of steel and concrete elements.

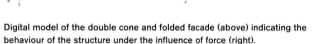

Digital model of the double cone and folded facade (above) indicating the behaviour of the structure under the influence of force (right).

BMW Welt, Munich

The structures we develop do not need to adhere to idealised typologies, which are usually in conflict with the architect's concepts anyway. Rather they result from a multiparty design process. In the BMW Welt project by Coop Himmelb(l)au, which is located right next to the Olympic quarter and adjacent to the BMW head office and plants in Munich, the complex roof structure was designed in a collaborative process.

During the competition we developed a double-layered girder grid which demarcates the upper and lower boundaries of the roof-space phase in alignment with the architectural concept of a floating cloud. Driven by the simulation of anticipated loading scenarios, the initially planar girder grid was deformed so that the upper layer assumed a cushion-like bulge. The lower layer also reacts to a number of spatial and structural criteria; for example, the roof integrates the customer lounge, a large incision that opens the views towards the famous BMW headquarters tower and channels the forces to the defined bearing points. The combined capacity of both girder grid layers to act as one spatial structure with locally differentiated behaviour is achieved through the insertion of diagonal struts within the interstitial space. In response to local stress concentrations, the structural depth of the system varies between a maximum of 12 metres (39.4 feet) and just 2 metres (6.6 feet) in areas of less force. In the northern part of the building the roof merges with a double cone, typical of Coop Himmelb(l)au's work, to form a hybrid shape. Similarly, the related bending behaviour of the roof structure gradually transforms into the shell-like behaviour of the double cone.[5]

From a structural engineering perspective one particular challenge proved to be the geometric complexity of building elements and their interaction, as each local change had consequences on the global scale of the system. This high level of interdependency needed to be integrated in the analytical models of the structure, which required, for example, the set up of an extensive model of the complete roof structure including all load-bearing elements. Any significant change to the stiffness of one of the cores, for instance, had considerable repercussions for the overall behaviour of the structure necessitating the re-evaluation and recalculation of the overall system. Consequently, this elaborate, iterative design process depended entirely on intense collaboration with the architects and related, clearly defined protocols of data exchange.

School of Management and Design, Essen

In 2006, the School of Management and Design was completed in the former coal-mining area of Zeche Zollverein in Essen, which has been a World Heritage Site since 2001. In response to the industrial scale of the surroundings, Japanese architects Kazuyo Sejima and Ryue Nishizawa (SANAA) proposed a cubic building. The monolithic character of the concrete block is perforated by a large number of rectangular openings.

The structure consists of flat slabs supported by two steel composite columns, three cores and the external walls. With clear spans of up to 16 metres (52.5 feet), the weight of the 50-centimetre (19.7-inch) thick flat slabs needed to be reduced through void formers. The distribution of these hollow plastic spheres needed to be negotiated with the placement of the reinforcement, the thermal activation pipework and the lighting inserts. This required close collaboration between the HVAC and light and structural designers in order to find specific local solutions for each sublocation within the overall structure. For instance, the high degree of reinforcement required by crack limitation in the lower layer of the ceilings and necessitated by substantial shear load concentration close to cores and columns needed to be coordinated with the placement of void formers and the installation of thermal activation systems.

To reduce wall thickness to conform with the architectural concept, the structural external walls are at the same time an active thermal insulation integrating hot-water pipes cast into the concrete and fed by the 30°C (86°F) waste water of the former coal mine, which used to be channelled straight into the river Emscher. This formerly untapped resource of energy now warms up the external walls, constituting not a heating system, but rather an integral active insulation in place of common passive thermal insulation packages.

SANAA, School of Management and Design, Essen, Germany, 2006
The void formers and thermal activation pipework in the concrete slabs, as well as the active thermal insulation of hot-water pipes cast into the concrete of the external walls, are still visible during the construction process.

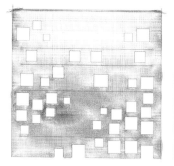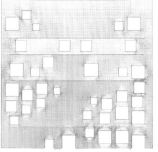

Digital structural analysis showing the main moments (left) and membrane forces (right) within one of the external walls perforated by a large number of rectangular openings.

This integration of insulation, structure, cladding and drainage in one element allowed for a considerable reduction of wall thickness.

Such compactness cannot be conceived of as a reduction of each single element as, for example, the dimensions of the reinforcement in this case rather increase and the insulation pipework's diameters are predefined. Thus all necessary elements and related functions need to be integral systems within the walls' highly confined internal space, which contrasts with their archaic external simplicity. In order to achieve such high-level integration, the design process recurrently negotiated the positioning of openings, the layout of active insulation and drainage pipework, the distribution of reinforcement and the anticipated formwork. This entailed intense collaboration with all the engineers and construction companies developing the specific systems and construction sequences, which were tested on a full-scale prototype on site.

Reducing a building to its essential solid and transparent qualities requires an integral approach to all functional aspects so as to overcome the common separation of technical and structural systems. Thus the design development of the School of Management and Design results from the collaborative planning process incorporating the users, architects and engineers. Based on the initial architectural concept, the overall performance of the project evolved through the increasing integration of design, technological, economic and ecological aspects. Such an approach does not foreground the optimisation of single elements or systems. Rather it is based on the continual integration of design criteria of all involved disciplines and parties.

Lakehouse Patagonia, Argentina

Bollinger + Grohmann focus on integrating material capacities and anticipated forces within the digital design setup, replacing merely geometric description with models that represent the dynamic equilibrium of a network of building services, and structural and architectural parameters.

The Lakehouse Patagonia project by architects ArchiGlobe is an extension of an existing house in Argentina. The design process focused on developing spatial articulation through a roof structure that intrgrated functional and load-bearing characteristics. Based on Lindenmayer systems, a script-driven procedure generates a tree structure in response to the specific design context. The growth of the structure reacts to architectural criteria such as spatial volumes and views, and to structural aspects. The structure's gradual change in density interacts with the open space to create varied spatial qualities and atmospheres. The algorithmic process is implemented in the architect's design environment as a generative tool capable of deriving a large number of design iterations. Variation is driven by random modifications to parameters that influence the branching angle and branch length.

For subsequent structural analysis, the script also generates each individual's data set containing all relevant

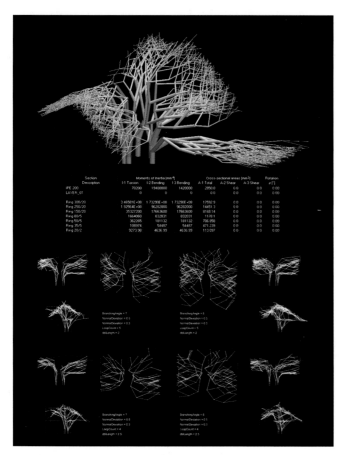

Section Description	Moments of Inertia [mm⁴]			Cross-sectional areas [mm²]			Rotation
	I-1 Torsion	I-2 Bending	I-3 Bending	A-1 Total	A-2 Shear	A-3 Shear	α [°]
IPE 200	70200	19400000	1420000	2850.0	0.0	0.0	0.00
LAYER_01	0	0	0	0.0	0.0	0.0	0.00
Ring 300/20	3.46581E+08	1.73290E+08	1.73290E+08	17592.9	0.0	0.0	0.00
Ring 250/20	1.92564E+08	96262000	96262000	14451.3	0.0	0.0	0.00
Ring 150/20	35327200	17663600	17663600	8168.14	0.0	0.0	0.00
Ring 80/5	1664060	832031	832031	1178.1	0.0	0.0	0.00
Ring 50/5	362265	181132	181132	706.858	0.0	0.0	0.00
Ring 35/5	108974	54487	54487	471.239	0.0	0.0	0.00
Ring 20/2	9273.98	4636.99	4636.99	113.097	0.0	0.0	0.00

ArchiGlobe, Lakehouse Patagonia, Argentina, 2007
Different versions of the Lakehouse structure are derived by a generative
digital process driven by stochastic as well as arithmetic parameters.

z-coordinate within defined thresholds. A tube-like column
folded out of the roof reaches the ground and acts as a
support structure. To achieve cantilevering capacity and a
minimum of node displacement just by folding the
triangulated plane, the behaviour of the entire structure was
simulated in RStab software. By encoding the z-coordinates of
all nodes into a genome and using a genetic algorithm that
allowed for crossover and mutation, the performance of the
structure could be significantly improved over the run of 200
generations with 40 individuals each. As a fitness criteria, the
displacement of the nodes under self-weight was calculated by
the analysis software, the worst node defining the inverse
fitness for each individual.

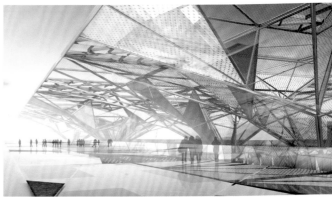

**Dominique Perrault, Undergound station roof, Piazza Garibaldi,
Naples, Italy, 2007**
Competiton proposal for the differentiated branching structure.

digital information including coordinates, nodes and
elements, and the related centre-line models. The evaluation
of each iteration included both architectural as well as
structural aspects, considering not only topological relations
but also the related dimensioning of elements, as this has a
substantial impact on the incidence of light and the views
towards the surrounding landscape.

Undergound Station Roof, Piazza Garibaldi, Naples

Computational processes enable us to generate and evaluate a
large number of possible structural articulations. During the
design study for an underground station roof at Piazza
Garibaldi in Naples by Dominique Perrault, entire populations
of structures were evolved and individuals were selected
through predefined architectural and structural fitness criteria.
These processes evolved articulations in response to specific
criteria without relapsing into *a priori* defined typologies.

In collaboration with Fabian Scheurer of the ETH Zurich,
we conducted a design study on improving the performance
of the folded roof structure through genetic algorithms.
Topologically the roof structure can be described as a two-
dimensional plane based on a system of self-similar triangles
folded in the third dimension. Each node is assigned a random

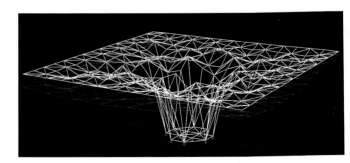

Analysis of the specific load-bearing behaviour of each individual branching
structure derived through the evolutionary process.

Learning Centre, EPFL, Lausanne

We admire the elegance of Felix Candela's shells, the
virtuosity with which he constructed these hyperparabolic
structures and the breadth of his design repertoire. Ove Arup
assumed the reason for the excellence of Candela's works was
due to him combining architect, engineer and contractor in
one person, with a clear dominance of engineering over
architecture. He believed that the creative process needs to be
synthesised in one mind that is aware of all aspects relevant
to the success of a project.[6]

SANAA, Learning Centre, EPFL, Lausanne, Switzerland, 2008–
The artificial landscape of the new Learning Centre includes patios, openings and shell-like regions.

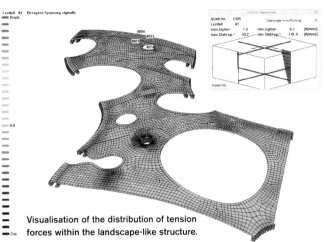

Visualisation of the distribution of tension forces within the landscape-like structure.

As this situation is extraordinarily rare, architecture is usually the product of a collaborative effort. Thus even a shell can integrate a wide range of design criteria far beyond just structural aspects. SANAA's Learning Centre project for the campus of the École Polytechnique Fédérale Lausanne (EPFL) provides different spatial situations through the undulations of the single-storey building. Containing the central library, service and study rooms, exhibition spaces, concert halls, cafés and a restaurant, the building will be the functional and visual centre of the campus.

From an engineering perspective, homogenous, idealised shells are elegant as they transfer forces without incurring bending forces and thus can be constructed with minimal material thickness. However, any incision in such an ideal shape as, for instance, a door, leads to fundamental, problematic changes in the structural behaviour. SANAA,s undulating landscape building includes patios, openings and various spatial qualities and thus results from a design process in which structural aspects were just one set of design criteria among many.

Rather than prioritising the idealised geometries of Candela's projects, here the work focused on analysing and identifying local areas of shell or arch behaviour, which were subsequently further developed and modified in an ongoing dialogue with the architects. Classic form-finding is superseded by processes of tracing performative capacities in the specific morphology. As the load-bearing characteristics vary across the landscape like articulation, no region represents a pure structural typology. The analysis also reveals problematic areas that would necessitate a disproportionate thickness of the concrete shell. Wavy tensile force progression, high bending movements and redirected forces combined with the lack of support points in the patio areas were addressed by redirecting the force flow between the shell perimeters through modification to geometry, size and location of the patios. Such an iterative process of tracking performance in collaboration with the architects entails ongoing design and evaluation cycles.

Conclusion

These evolutionary strategies depend on the fitness ranking, as selection constitutes the only control mechanism to direct the development. In nature individual fitness is evaluated on the phenotypic level as the likeliness for further reproduction.[7] Likewise, in digital processes each individual structure needs to be fully defined and modelled in order to be evaluated. Each evolved structure is based on the genetic information of a previous generation and has undergone further adaptation.

Thus the definition of the fitness criteria is critical for the quality of the building and its structure in that they control the direction of the evolving process. Our goal is the integration of such criteria for many different nodes within the complex network of requirements, to achieve performative and differentiated buildings and structures.

We assume there is similarity between these processes and the design methods of the aforementioned masters, who developed their structures through experience and observation of constructed buildings. This can also be understood as an evolutionary method, one that is not limited by the availability of calculation and analyses methods. Contemporary digital methods make possible the simulation of such processes, and thus enable us to refer back to the empirical methods of previous generations. △

Notes
1. Hans Straub, Die Geschichte der Bauingenieurskunst, *Überblick von der Antike bis in die Neuzeit*, Birkhäuser Verlag (Basle), 1992.
2. David P Billington, *The Tower and the Bridge: The New Art of Structural Engineering*, Princeton University Press (New York), 1985.
3. Ibid
4. Bryan Lawson, *How Designers Think: The Design Process Demystified*, Elsevier (Oxford), 4th edn, 2006.
5. Klaus Bollinger, Manfred Grohmann, Daneil Pfanner and Jörg Schneider, Tragkonstruktionen der BMW-Welt in München, *Stahlbau* , Vol 7, 2005, pp 483-91.
6. Ove Arup, *Candela: The Shell Builder*, Reinhold Publishing Corporation (New York), 1963.
7. Ernst Mayr, *What Evolution Is*, Basic Books (New York), 2001.

Metabolism and Morphology

Architecture is on the cusp of systemic change, driven by the dynamics of climate and economy, of new technologies and new means of production. There is a growing interest in the dynamics of fluidity, in networks and in the new topologies of surfaces and soft boundaries. This is part of a general cultural response to the contemporary reconfiguration of the concept of 'nature' within the discourse of architecture; a change from metaphor to model, from 'nature' as a source of formal inspiration to 'nature' as a mine of interrelated dynamic processes that are available for analysis and digital simulation. **Michael Weinstock** presents an account of the dynamics of natural metabolisms, and suggests an agenda for the development of metabolic morphologies of buildings and cities.

Form has been a central focus in the theories and practice of architecture throughout history, and over time has been aligned with many different ideologies and methods of generating the shape of buildings. The design of surfaces that capture or modify light, the design of heat-generation and transportation systems, and of systems for the movement of air are applied to forms that have been designed according to other criteria. In built architecture, morphology is prior to and separate from metabolism. In city morphologies, the designation of parks and other spaces as the 'lungs' of cities is an inexact metaphor – and a metaphor chosen from the wrong metabolism.

In the natural world, form and metabolism have a very different relationship. There is an intricate choreography of energy and material that determines the morphology of living forms, their relations to each other, and which drives the self-organisation of populations and ecological systems.

Theoretical optimal ratios of branch lengths produce the most equitable distribution of leaf clusters in computed branch systems, and are similar to the observed ratios in real trees.

In the natural world, form and metabolism have a very different relationship. There is an intricate choreography of energy and material that determines the morphology of living forms, their relations to each other, and which drives the self-organisation of populations and ecological systems.

All living forms must acquire energy and materials from their environment, and transform this matter and energy within their bodies to construct their tissues, to grow, to reproduce and to survive. D'Arcy Wentworth Thompson argued in *On Growth and Form* that the morphology of living forms has a 'dynamical aspect, under which we deal with the interpretation, in terms of force, of the operations of Energy.[1] Living forms are able to construct and dynamically maintain themselves by the exchange of energy and material through their surfaces, and in doing so excrete changed materials and energy back into the environment. Morphology and metabolism are intricately linked through the processing of energy and materials. Metabolism is the fire of life,[2] and occurs at all levels from the molecular to the intricate dynamics of ecological

systems. There are common metabolic characteristics for whole forms, in the relations between the geometry and overall size of the body plan, the internal operating temperature and the mode of existence in the environment.

Performance has been a central concern of discourses on contemporary architecture, and it is clear that architects today are increasingly becoming engaged with the natural world. There is a new sensitivity to the 'life' of buildings, and an understanding that performance and behaviour can be inputs to the process of design rather than functions applied later to a form. The study of natural metabolisms is a significant resource for design as it reveals that shape or morphology is deeply integrated within the means of capturing and transmitting energy. The organisation and morphology of energy systems of the natural world provide a set of models for what will become the new 'metabolic morphologies' of future buildings, and ultimately of cities.

Metabolism determines the relations of individuals and populations of natural forms with their local environment. Higher levels of biological organisation emerge from metabolic processes, in the relations between species, and in the density and patterns of distribution of species across the surface of the earth. All metabolic processes stem from the sunlight that falls on the surface of the earth. A very small percentage, perhaps less than 2 per cent, of that light energy

Branching system, leafless tree in winter. In the anatomical organisation of trees, the transportation network for fluids and the structural support for the leaf array have evolved as a fully integrated morphology. Branch angles and the ratios of length in sequential 'mother to daughter' branches determine the effective leaf area and constrain the overall morphology of a tree. They are also intrinsic characteristics of a species, so that different angles and ratios appear in different species.

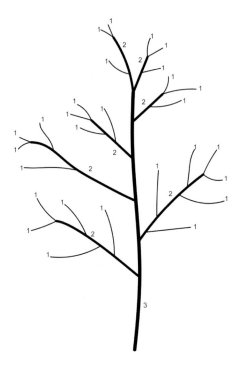

Horton's general hydrological classification of the hierarchy of stream networks. 'Horton's ratios' are morphometrics, constant ratios of bifurcation and the relative length of each segment.

enters ecological systems through the photosynthesis of plants. Light energy is transformed into chemical energy, bound in organic molecules, and used to construct the tissues of plants. The flow of energy through all living forms is often thought of as a food chain, and although this description is topologically inaccurate (web is a more accurate description than chain), it is a useful description of the general direction of energy flow. Plants produce biological materials that can be reprocessed to release energy, and all other forms of life consume them in sequence; herbivores feed on the plants, converting them into heat energy, and in turn carnivores feed on the herbivores or other carnivores, and humans consume all other forms of life. Dead organic matter is broken down by microbes and fungi into prebiotic molecules. At each level, energy is used up so that only a small percentage of the energy available at one level is transferred to the next level. Matter is recycled, but energy is dissipated, used up and lost to the system. All metabolic processes cease without a constant source of energy, although most living forms are capable of storing some energy in chemicals to survive temporary fluctuations in energy supply.

There are common features in all natural energy systems. All organisms must not only capture and produce energy, they must also transport it; and the morphology of branching networks is found in all forms of life. There is also a relationship between energy, lifespan and body mass; small organisms are typically more metabolically active than larger organisms, and the larger the organism, the slower the metabolism. Bigger organisms live longer than small

organisms. Metabolic relationships to mass and lifespan are complex, but a gram of living tissue consumes approximately the same amount of energy during its whole lifespan independently of the form or species of which it is part. Within any specific taxa, such as mammals or plants, the metabolic rate of activity will vary from species to species, but it is generally observed that the rate of energy consumption per unit of body mass declines as the body size increases. A gram of tissue in a mouse uses up 25 times more energy in any unit of time than a gram of tissue in an elephant, so that the mouse must eat much more frequently, and much larger quantities in relation to its body mass, than the elephant. But when unrelated taxa that differ greatly in size are compared, such as a comparison between bacteria and mammals, the metabolic activity per unit body mass is approximately the same. What varies is the lifespan, by many orders of magnitude. Bacteria may live for a few hours, a mouse two to three years, an elephant up to 60 years.

There are no comparable studies in the history of architecture, yet it is clear that the metabolic 'rate' of a building, and the relationship of that rate to the mass and form of the building will not only form a stable set of criteria for the evaluation of all buildings, but can also be inputs in the generative phase of design. Culture, climate and the economy of energy are today undergoing radical revision, and new instruments and precepts for future buildings and cities are essential. The study of natural metabolisms commences with their architecture; the spatial and material organisation of a system for capturing, transforming and transporting energy.

Photosynthetic Metabolism and Plant Morphologies
Plants are 'autothrophs', or self-feeders, constructing their own materials, molecule by molecule from sunlight, water and carbon dioxide, and a few trace minerals in tiny proportions from the soil. The process is a sequence of chemical reactions known as photosynthesis, and drives the metabolism of marine unicellular organisms including cyanobacteria and algae, and all the larger plants on the surface of the earth. Oxygen is the by product.[3] Carbon dioxide enters the plant, and oxygen is excreted along with water vapour, through the stomata, the pores in leaves and stems.[4]

Plants that are adapted to hotter regimes, including many of the summer 'annual' plants, have evolved a faster-acting modified photosynthetic chemistry.[5] The stomata stay open for shorter periods during the day to absorb carbon dioxide, and so less water is lost by transpiration. A third modification of photosynthetic metabolism[6] is found in Crassulaceae and other cacti, succulents and bromeliads. The stomata open at night, minimising evaporation, and close during the day. In these plants metabolic activity may be internalised altogether in extremely arid conditions, and stomata are closed night and day. This enables the plant to survive dry spells, and when water is available again there is a rapid uptake of it and recovery occurs. The body of the plant includes specialised water-storage tissues, and some root systems are similarly adapted.

Leaf Arrays

The characteristic silhouette of trees, the outer boundary of the volume of leaves, is constrained by the shape and size of the individual leaf geometry specific to the species and the extent to which leaves shade each other from the light.[7] In environments with high levels of light, several layers of leaves may be arrayed before the lowest leaf is so shaded that it cannot capture sufficient light for photosynthesis. It has been argued that 'pioneer' trees, the early species in developing forests, tended to have leaf arrays organised in deep multilayered crowns. In consequence, later 'climax' species adapting to the lower light environment between established species, reduce their self-shading by developing flatter, shallow monolayered crowns with a single layer of leaves on the boundary of the leaf volume.[8] However, many trees appear to have stacked monolayers, one above the other, and other varied morphologies do not strictly conform to either organisation.

The arrangement of leaves on a twig or stem, phyllotaxis or leaf ordering, is significantly related to the avoidance of self-shading. Leaves spring from a twig or stem at more or less the same angle, but in sequence are rotated so that they are offset from each other. Elm trees, for example, have successive leaves on opposite sides of the twig, which is also expressed as an angle of offset, in this case 180°. On beech and hazel trees the leaves are rotated 1/3 of the circumference of the twig, or 120°, on oak trees the rotation is 2/5, or 144°, on poplar and pear trees it is 3/8, or 135°, and on willow and almond trees it is 5/13, or 130.46°. The fractional numbers are recognisable as quotients of alternative Fibonacci numbers,[9] and are commonly found across many scales and in many different modular components, including petals and cones. Changes in leaf shape and orientation and in stem length can compensate for the negative effects of leaf overlap produced by phyllotactic patterns. The effectiveness of phyllotaxy in limiting self-shading is not absolute, and is modified by the shape and orientation of the leaves, and distance along the stem between leafs.[10]

All transpiration takes place through the stomata, and they typically slow down diffusion of water vapour into the atmosphere; the resistance to the flow of liquids is typically hundreds of times greater in leaves than it is in the roots, stem and branches.[11] The pattern of veins for the movement of fluids within the leaf varies across the species, but the rate of flow of water through the tree is slowed and controlled by the leaf array. Both gases and water vapour are controlled by the stomata, so the rate of transpiration is closely coupled to the rate of exchange of gases. Both gas and fluid flow are highly dynamic, varying between night and day, between young leaves and old leaves, and generally in response to changes in temperature and in the water supply from the roots. It follows that the photosynthetic metabolism of a tree is a product of the total surface area and mass of leaves in the array, and the lifespan of the leaves, and that these have an intricate mathematical relationship with the fluid distribution network of the whole tree and its overall morphology.[12]

Branching Networks

Branching patterns have been studied intensively in many disciplinary fields. Two of the most cited works in geomorphology are studies of the geometrical properties of hydraulic branching networks of streams and river systems.[13] In the anatomical organisation of trees, the transportation network for fluids and the structural support for the leaf array have evolved as a fully integrated morphology.[14] Branch angles and the ratios of length in sequential 'mother to daughter' branches determine the effective leaf area[15] and constrain the overall morphology of a tree. They are also intrinsic characteristics of a species, so that different angles and ratios appear in different species. The number and the position of a branch in the hierarchy of branches from the outermost twig to the trunk, and the length of each branch, are said to have a logarithmic relation.[16]

There are two elaborate branching networks of vessels that extend throughout the plant, from the roots to the stomata of the smallest leaf. One system, the 'xylem', consists of many bundles of narrow tubes, and water that is absorbed from the soil into the roots is drawn up through the plant to the leaves, where it evaporates through the stomata. The evaporation creates a negative water pressure in the column of water in

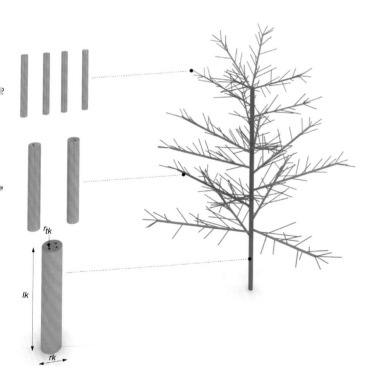

A script to generate a branching pattern was developed (in Maxscript 3D Studio Scripting Language) for a simple tree-like branching structure, using the West Brown Enquist theoretical model combined with the phylotactical pattern of a pine tree, as defined by Turing. The base of the script is a Fibonacci sequence that has a random factor and a divergence angle of 137.51°. A radius differentiation of 1/4r was introduced to the branching hierarchies. Finally three additional parameters were defined: to control the total height, the amount of medium-scale branches, and the quantity of small branchings.

the xylem tubes. The other system, the 'phloem', moves the carbohydrates that are assembled in the leaves to other metabolically active parts of the plant. Water is needed to maintain the pressure inside the living cells, and most of the metabolic processes of the cells require water molecules. However, almost all of the water that enters the plant system is 'transpired', or evaporated from the leaves, and this movement of cool water up from the soil regulates the internal temperature of the plant. The humidity and temperature of the air around the plant will affect the rate of transpiration. Low temperatures or high humidity slow transpiration, and high temperatures or low humidity accelerate transpiration. Very little of the energy that falls on a plant is used for the metabolic assembly of complex molecules; some light energy is reflected, but most, up to 75 per cent, is dissipated as latent heat in the water vapour that evaporates from the stomata.

There is relationship between the total mass[17] of a plant form and its lifespan.[18] Big plants live longer than small ones, and this appears to be true for all plants, from phytoplankton that live for one day to giant sequoia which may live for up to three thousand years.[19] Size is a critical factor in the rate of metabolism, and the geometry of the vascular network scales with the size, volume and mass of the plant form.[20] There are invariant ratios across the diversity of plant morphologies, relationships between the surface area of leaves, the total volume the plant occupies, the geometry of its branching networks, and the metabolic rate and lifespan. Variations of these characteristics are all dependent on the size, or rather the total mass, of the plant form. The relationship of any morphological or metabolic characteristic to mass is known as allometry.[21] For example, the number and mass of leaves in a plant, the rate of fluid flow in the vascular network, and the total carbon assimilation or gross photosynthesis scale proportionally to each other. They all scale at the quarter power of the mass.

It is clear that a metabolic system for buildings and cities can begin with the development of systems that are conceptually and mathematically related to the metabolic morphologies of plants. The metabolic imperative is identical in plants and buildings: the spatial organisation of large surface areas to capture light and for the exchange of gases, the structural system for the deployment of those surfaces, and an internal transportation system for moving water (and heat) or metabolic products. In plants and buildings, the need to deploy the maximum surface area for photosynthesis or light is constrained by the necessity for a stable structural configuration that will be strong enough to resist buckling under its own weight, and to resist additional imposed loads such as snow and wind pressure from all directions. The structural properties and the morphology of trees emerge from the interaction of the volumetric array of leaves and the patterns of branching networks that support them and enable their metabolisms. Developing comparable metabolic morphological systems for buildings will necessarily include

other interactions, with differing volumetric and material constraints, but the metabolic imperatives are consistent across the different domains.

Thermal Metabolisms and Animal Morphologies

Animal metabolisms process the chemical energy stored in plants, or in the flesh of other animals. They are thermal or heat-producing metabolisms, and are characterised by the relationship of their internal body temperature to the temperature of their immediate environment. It was once common to refer to 'hot blooded' or 'cold blooded' animals, but this is inaccurate. For example, the body temperature of 'cold blooded' reptiles can be extremely high when they are in sunlight for any length of time. Animal metabolisms may either maintain a constant internal temperature regardless of the ambient temperatures, or they may allow their internal temperature to vary according to the rise and fall of the temperature of their environment. Most animal metabolisms are predominately one or the other regime, but combine some behavioural aspects of both regimes.

Endotherms generate heat internally to maintain their body temperature. Maintaining a constant body temperature is a demanding energy regime for a living form. The rate of metabolic activity is high and the majority of food must be used as fuel for body temperature, with little left over to be converted into body tissues or mass. Food consumption is up to ten times more than a comparable-size animal with a variable temperature metabolism, and elaborate morphological and system adaptations are necessary. This in turn presents difficulties when the external temperature rises and falls through seasonal variation. Constant temperature metabolisms have the advantage of remaining active in very cold climates, by increasing the rate of metabolism, but of course they do need to do so in order to acquire food to maintain their energy regime. The development of enhanced insulation in layers of fat, fur and feathers increases the retention of heat, but there are far fewer adaptations that enhance the shedding of heat. Few animals with constant body temperature metabolisms can survive in very hot environments.

Ectotherms absorb heat from their environment to raise their body temperatures. Variable temperature regimes, such as the metabolisms of most amphibians and reptiles, are less energy demanding. Metabolic activity is more chemically complex, but the rate of activity is slower, and heat production is so low that the external environment effectively regulates the body temperature a little below the environmental temperature. High body temperatures are achieved by basking in the sun, for example lizards or snakes resting on warm rocks in the hot sun. Much more of their food intake can be converted into body mass. They are less active as the temperature drops, but do not need to be so active to acquire food. In fact they can survive long periods without food, and some can reduce their metabolic rate when food is scarce. They cannot survive in very cold environments.

X-ray of *Coleus* leaf, showing branching system of venation. The pattern of veins for the movement of fluids within the leaf varies across the species, but the rate of flow of water through the tree is slowed and controlled by the leaves. The photosynthetic metabolism of a tree is a product of the total surface area and mass of leaves, and the lifespan of the leaves. They have an intricate mathematical relationship with the fluid distribution network of the whole tree and its overall morphology.

The energy requirements of amphibian and reptilian metabolisms are lower than those of birds and mammals by a whole order of magnitude.

The difference in energy production capacity between the two regimes is apparent in the organisation of body organs and tissues. The endothermic of mammalian and bird forms have larger internal organs than amphibian and reptilian forms, the organs have a far greater density of mitochondria, and the mitochondria themselves have a greater surface area.[22] It is clear that the constant temperature metabolisms of mammals and birds are energetically very demanding, and that the ectothermic metabolisms, with their fluctuating internal temperatures, provide an interesting model for architecture that is not constrained by very low temperatures.

Body Size, Surfaces and Metabolic Rate

Metabolic processes have a relation to body mass; fluid energy transportation in particular is an essential determinant of body plan and overall morphology, and the size of elements within the transportation network, such as aortas, lung branches and tree trunks scale at the quarter power of body mass. Size is critical[23] in so far as it changes the ratio of the surface area to the volume enclosed by that surface. Heat loss is directly related to surface area, so the larger the surface

area the greater the heat loss. It follows that overall morphology is a significant strategy; conserving heat in cold climates is best done by large rounded forms, as proportionally they have a greater enclosed volume for their surface area. In hot climates, smaller and narrow morphologies shed heat more easily, as proportionally they have more surface area for enclosed volumes.

The body plan of living forms and the organisation of surfaces for metabolic exchange change as size increases. Thermal metabolisms evolve their long intestinal tube with its large number of convolutions to increase the surface area, and use muscles to accelerate the passage of food. The evolution of greater surface areas for respiration is a similar strategy, with the branching networks of lungs enabling very large surface areas. The evolution of body plans has been driven by natural selection acting on metabolisms, and has resulted in the organisation of systems that are simultaneously morphological and metabolic, for the capture of light and heat, for the exchange of gases, for the transportation of energy, and for structural stability.

Metabolic rates, the speed of energy and material transactions scale at the three-quarters power of the body mass. Other anatomical organisations and metabolic processes also scale in relation to mass. These allometric relations have long been studied, but the comprehensive model developed by

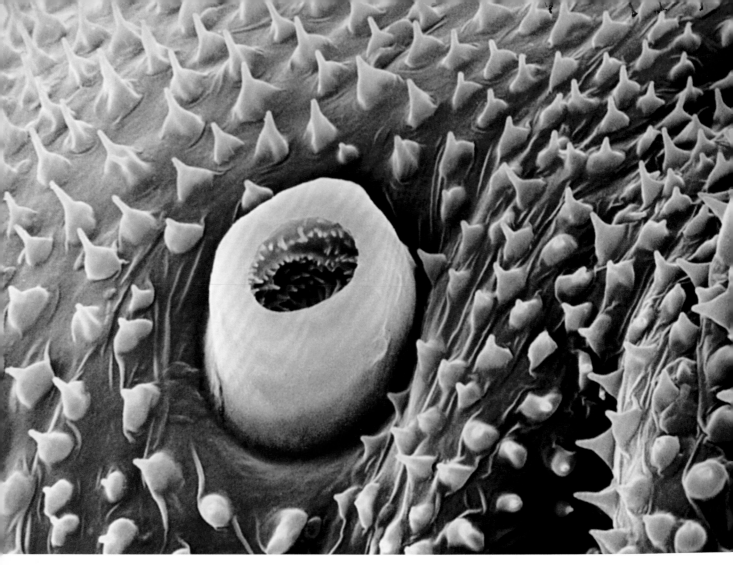

Branching network: insect respiration. Coloured scanning electron micrograph (SEM) of a spiracle of a garden tiger moth caterpillar (*Arctia caja*). Air diffuses into the spiracle and is carried around the body by a network of tubes called tracheae. Oxygen diffuses from the tracheae directly into the tissues, and carbon dioxide exits the tissues by the same system. Spiracles are found in pairs on either side of most body segments. Magnification: x 1130 when printed at 10 centimetres (3.9 inches) wide.

West, Brown and Enquist demonstrates that the geometry of branching networks for transporting energy and materials determines many morphological parameters across all species and taxa. For example, the scaling laws of branching networks occur in both the vascular system of trees and in the cardiovascular and respiratory system of mammals. The model characterises both structure and function, and demonstrates that the scaling of many ecological processes and patterns of distribution[24] occur in relation to the mass or size of an organism, including the patterns of plant populations and communities. The application of this mathematical model to buildings and cities has barely begun, and necessarily crosses the boundaries of many disciplines.

Conclusion

The dynamics of change in the natural world are being accelerated and perturbed by human activities at an unprecedented scale. Global climate change is upon us, and its effects will be local and regional – more energy trapped in the atmosphere produces more intense weather systems, which in turn accelerates desertification in arid regions, increased intensity and frequency of storms in other regions, and the warming of Arctic and cold weather regions. It is axiomatic that the emergent behaviour of the climate 'metasystem' is not entirely predictable. So, too, the emergent behaviour of economies and cultures, now connected and interlinked globally, are in the process of substantial reconfiguration, with uncertain outcomes. The significant recent changes to culture, climate and energy economies have destabilised the equilibrium of the cultural and physical ecology in which architecture lives. The ecological opportunity that has arisen is part of the growing cultural fascination with fluidity and dynamics, with networks and new topologies, and with soft boundaries between private and public domains, and between interior and exterior space. The experience of being in spaces that flow one into one another, where differentiation between spaces is achieved less by rigid walls than by extended thresholds of graduated topographical and phenomenological

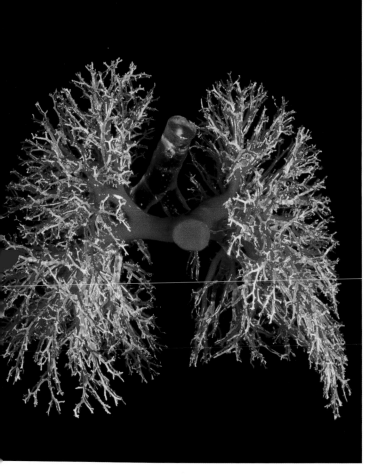

Branching network of pulmonary arteries and bronchi. Resin cast of the system supplying blood and air to the lung, viewed from the front. Clear resin was used to fill the airways, red in the case of the pulmonary arteries. The trachea branches into the left and right principal bronchi: the large pulmonary trunk divides into the right and left pulmonary arteries in front of the left principal bronchus. On the left of the image, the branch of the right pulmonary artery to the upper lobe of the lung is evident.

character, and in which connectivity and integration are enhanced, is central to contemporary existence.

The emerging architecture that relates pattern and process, form and behaviour, with spatial and cultural parameters, has a symbiotic relationship with the natural world. The study of metabolisms suggests the means of developing an architecture that is strongly correlated to the organisations and systems of the natural world. The logic of photosynthetic and ectothermic metabolisms can be extended to develop metabolic morphologies and material systems for buildings and cities. New concepts and geometries of building surface arrays, of metabolic networks for individual, and groups of, environmentally intelligent buildings can be explored through the development of 'process' models and simulations, in design explorations that begin within the relationships of metabolism and morphology. The proliferation of 'metabolic morphologies', of a symbiotic architecture that will invade and colonise towns and cities, has barely begun. Yet it is clear that the intellectual history of these ideas is very long, and that the climatic, cultural and economic pressures that are changing the world are very great. Architecture is within the horizon of a systemic change. ⌂

Notes

1. D'Arcy WentworthThompson, Prologue to *On Growth and Form*, first published 1917, Cambridge University Press (Cambridge), 1961.
2. M Kleiber, 'Body size and metabolism', *Hilgardia* 6, 1932.
3. $6CO_2 + 12 H_2O + light energy = C_6H_{12}O_6 + 6O_2 + 6H_2O$
4. Referred to as C_3 photosynthesis, as the first metabolic product has three carbon atoms.
5. Referred to as C_4 photosynthesis, as the first metabolic product has four carbon atoms.
6. Referred to as CAM photosynthesis, Crassulacean Acid Metabolism, after the plant it was first discovered in.
7. Werger Poorter, 'Light environment, sapling architecture, and leaf display in six rain forest species', *American Journal of Botany* 86,1999, pp 1464–73.
8. HS Horn, *The Adaptive Geometry of Trees*, Princeton University Press (Princeton, NJ), 1971.
9. Fibonacci number series begins: 0, 1, 1, 2, 3, 5, 8, 13, 21, 34, 55 and so on.
10. KJ Niklas, 'The role of phyllotatic pattern as a "developmental constraint" on the interception of light by leaf surfaces', *Evolution* 42, 1988.
11. L Sack and NM Holbrook, 'Leaf hydraulics', *Annual Review of Plant Biology* 57, 2006, pp 361–81.
12. CA Price and BJ Enquist, 'Scaling mass and morphology in leaves: An extension of the WBE Model', *Ecology*, May 2007, pp 1132–41.
13. RE Horton, 'Erosional development of streams and their drainage basins: hydrophysical approach to quantitative morphology', *Geological Society of America Bulletin*, Vol 56, No 3, 1945, pp 275–370; and LB Leopold and T Maddock, 'The hydraulic geometry of stream channels and some physiographic implications', *US Geological Survey Professional Paper 252*, Reston, Virginia, 1953.
14. KJ Niklas, 'Branching patterns and mechanical design in palaeozoic plants: A theoretic assessment', *Annals of Botany* 42, 1978, pp 33–9.
15. H Honda and JB Fisher, 'Tree branch angle: Maximizing effective leaf area', *Science* 199, February 1978. pp 888–90.
16. LB Leopold, 'Trees and streams: The efficiency of branching patterns', *Journal of Theoretical Biology* 31, 1971, pp 339–54.
17. The weight, or mass, of an organism is a function of its size and is directly proportional to the organism's volume. Living forms are composed mainly of water, and as 1 cubic centimetre of water has a mass of one gram, living tissues are a little more than one gram per cubic centimetre.
18. N Marbà, CM Duarte and S Agustí, 'Allometric scaling of plant life history', *Proceedings of the National Academy of Sciences* 104, October 2007, pp 15,777–80.
19. C Loehle, 'Tree life history strategies', *Canadian Journal of Forest Research* 18(2), 1987, pp 209–22.
20. CA Price, BJ Enquist and VM Savage, 'A general model for allometric covariation in botanical form and function', *Proceedings of the National Academy of Sciences* 104, 2007, pp 13,204–09.
21. The term 'allometry' was introduced by English biologist Julian S Huxley in his 1932 book *Problems of Relative Growth*, Methuen (London), 1932.
22. PL Else and AJ Hulbert, 'Comparison of the "mammal machine" and the "reptile machine": Energy production', *American Journal of Physiology* 240, 1981; and PL Else and AJ Hulbert, 'Evolution of mammalian endothermic metabolism: "leaky" membranes as a source of heat', *American Journal of Physiology* 253, 1987.
23. L Demetrius, 'Directionality theory and the evolution of body size', *Proceedings of the Royal Society London B*, December 2000, pp 2385–91.
24. BJ Enquist, 'Allometric scaling of plant energetics and population density', letters to *Nature*, September 1998; and GB West et al, 'A general model for the origin of allometric scaling laws in biology', *Science* 276: 122–6, 1997; and DL Turcotte et al, 'Networks with side branching in biology', *Journal of Theoretical Biology* 193: 577–92, August 1998.

An extended version of this article will be published in *The Architecture of Emergence: The Evolution of Form in Nature and Civilisation*, by Michael Weinstock, to be published by AD Wiley in 2008.

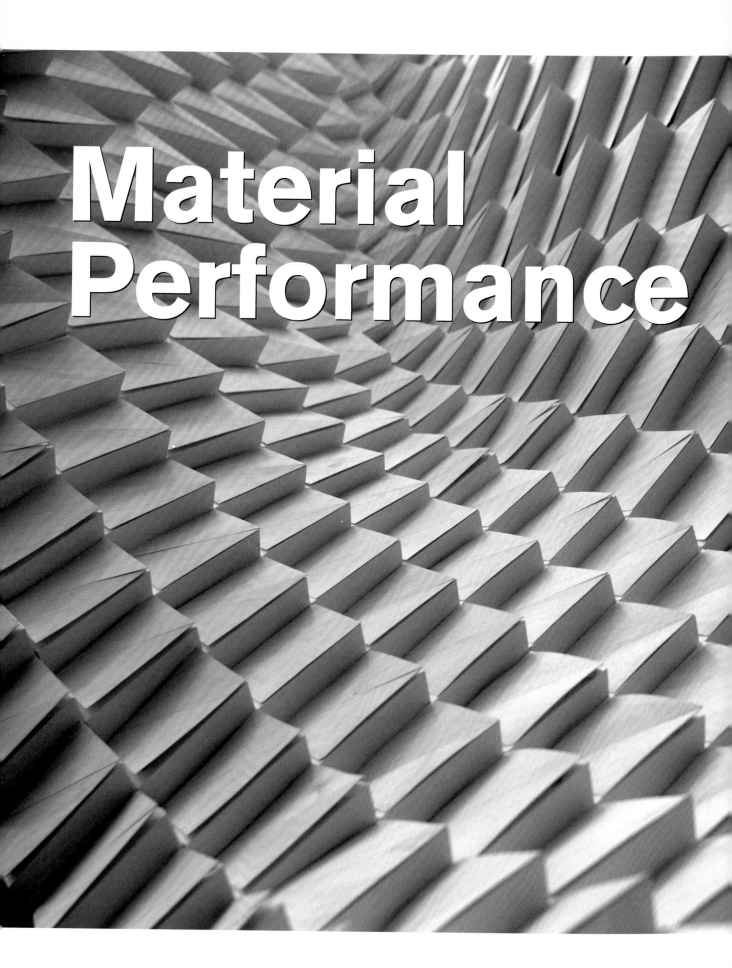

Material
Performance

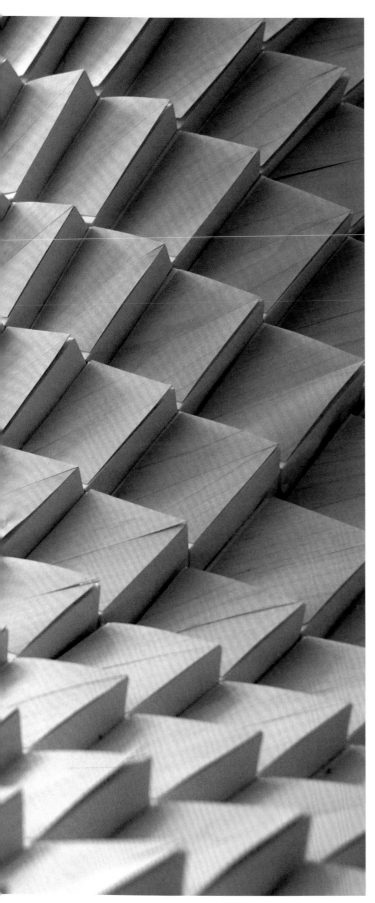

A central concern of architecture as a material practice is the way in which built and natural environments interact to provide exciting and sustainable modes of habitation. Key to this is the way in which material performance is understood and instrumentalised. In the first part of this article, **Michael Hensel** and **Defne Sunguroğlu** research the characteristics of wood in order to explore how a material's variable behaviour and its response to extrinsic stimuli might substantially contribute to performance-oriented design. This leads them to argue for a wider, more inclusive definition for 'smart materials' that puts less emphasis on the new and fully recognises the potential of variable behaviour. In the second part, **Achim Menges** discusses a research project that demonstrates the full impact of this approach to material performance and the integral relationship between formation and materialisation processes.

Towards Material Smartness:
Embedded Responsiveness and Mutability

Today the amount of literature on materials is entirely overwhelming. Publications range from *très chic* catalogues of 'new', 'smart', 'advanced' materials for a broader audience with modest actual content yet luxuriously illustrated with high-resolution colour pictures; popular science books on 'new', 'smart', 'advanced' materials, also for a broader audience, often elaborated at the atomic scale and illustrated with descriptive and explanatory diagrams; material science books that deliver hard facts for specialists, including charts and diagrams on material properties and behaviour; publications on biological materials or materials inspired by such, frequently under the label of biomimetics, often on a microscopic and molecular scale and illustrated with grainy black-and-white microscopic images, digital analysis, charts and diagrams.

So, you may ask yourself, what should I read then? And this is indeed a pretty good question. If you require only quantitative information on material characteristics, things may well be easy enough, but as soon as you venture further you may begin to sense a rift among arguments that

Steffen Reichert, Responsive Surface Structures, Department for Form Generation and Materialisation (Achim Menges), Hochschule für Gestaltung (HfG), Offenbach, Germany, 2006/07
Responsive surface structure of veneer composite components with the capacity to adapt surface porosity in response to changes in relative humidity.

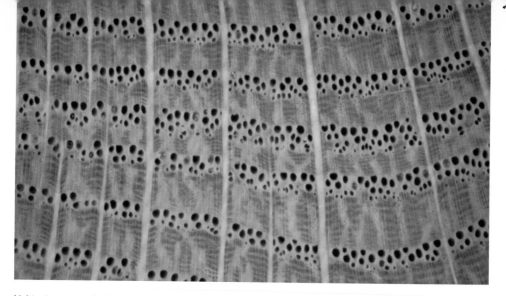

Light micrograph of a transverse section through the wood (secondary xylem) of an oak tree (*Quercus robur*). The section shows annual growth rings, the horizontal bands, prominent rays, and the pale, vertical stripes. Xylem tissue is composed of tracheary vessels that carry water and nutrients from the roots to the leaves. The porous horizontal bands are layers of large-vesselled spring wood, while the bands of dense, compact wood were laid down in the summer, at the end of the growing season. The change from spring to summer wood occurs suddenly in oaks, whereas the transition is often much more gradual in other trees.

celebrate the realm of 'new' materials and those that search for untapped potentials of 'old' materials, the ones that we have had at our disposal for quite some time. The labels and claims of one seem often not to befit the other; difference is declared vigorously and superiority claimed emphatically, with dogmas abundant left, right and centre. We will begin this inquiry into material performance by probing the rift between the entrenched positions by asking why some materials are called 'smart' and others not. We will then proceed to test this label for materials it was not intended for, and look at the ensuing consequences to attempt a revised notion of material performance.

Architecture is a material practice. Materials make up our built environment, and their interaction with the dynamics of the environment they are embedded within results in the specific conditions we live in.

Moreover, culture and the way materiality and materials are understood and instrumentalised mutually condition one another. Herein lies the great challenge for architecture as material practice. Materiality and material performance is thus by no means a subordinate question of detailing, but, instead, one of key significance.

Materials enter production and manufacturing processes as raw substances. They are processed to become semi-finished materials and at a later stage of fabrication finished materials. These stages are defined by the way in which the desired performance of a material is becoming increasingly specific through particular treatment that affects material characteristics and behaviour. Material is thus processed towards its desired performative capacity, often already anticipated as components within a projected material assembly.

'Smart' materials have one or several properties that can be significantly changed in a controlled way by external stimuli, such as stress, temperature, relative humidity and so on. They include, for instance, thermo-responsive materials such as shape memory alloys and polymers that can assume different shapes

at different temperatures, or chromogenic systems that change colour in response to electrical, luminous and thermal stimuli.

Given this definition one may ask why are all materials not considered smart, as none are entirely inert in a dynamic environment. This is a question with powerful consequences. Why have materials not been understood and utilised with regard to their inherent capacity towards responsiveness?

Throughout architectural history, materialisation was predominantly to do with reducing change and neutralising its effect through some way of stabilisation or compensation. Think, for instance, of the dimensional changes of materials due to changes in environmental conditions, such as thermal expansion. This was seen as undesirable, problematic and to be avoided at all costs. Does this amount to the biggest missed opportunity in the history of architecture as material practice? Yes, actually.

The definition of smart materials could contribute most significantly to our sensibility and understanding by positing the notion of change of material properties and dimensions fundamentally as a positive project. Look, for instance, at thermo-responsive materials, a key group of smart materials that change shape in relation to thermal stimuli. Why would a crafted material be declared smart due to its embedded capacity for responsiveness, and a piece of wood that can perform in pretty much the same way not? According to Philip Ball: 'Today we still do not have a material that rivals wood in its subtlety of structure and property.'[1] This is a crucial realisation in two ways: first, and more obviously, we do not have any other such material; and second, and more implicitly, we may not have understood and deployed its full capacity given that we have largely subdued or eliminated the capacity of wood with regard to its mutability in response to extrinsic influences. It also is important to understand that biological systems display an integral material articulation across many scales of magnitude, ranging from the molecular to the macro-structure; that is, from polymer chains to the

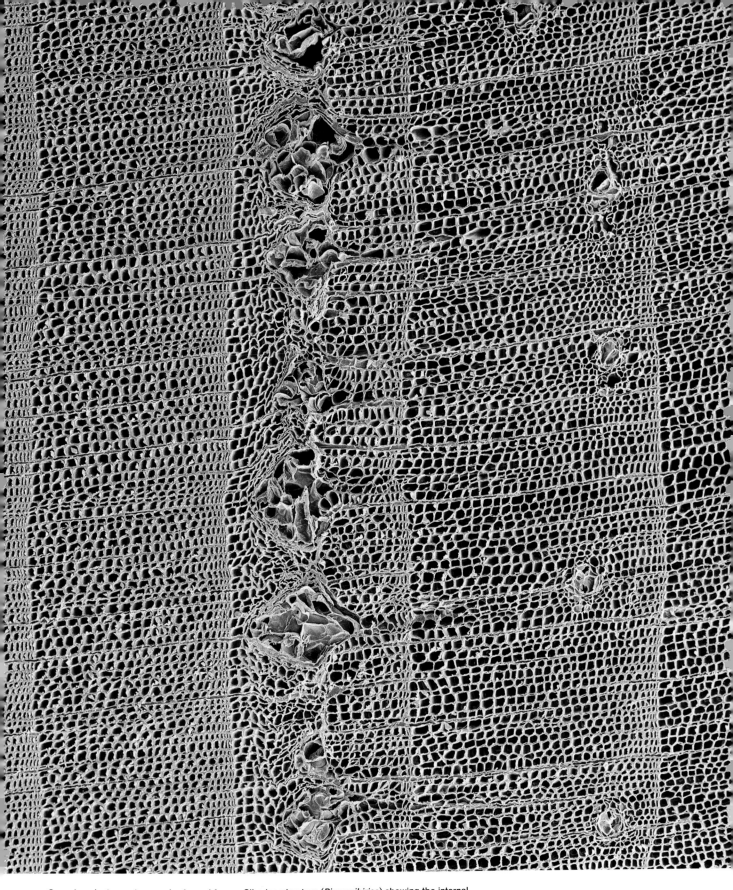

Scanning electron micrograph of wood from a Siberian pine tree (*Pinus sibirica*) showing the internal differentiation of wood. The vertical sections are the growth rings, one for each year in the life of the tree. This specific part of the tree dates from AD 534 (left) to AD 539 (right). In AD 536 the northern hemisphere underwent severe cooling, which caused deformations in the structure of the wood due to water freezing within the cells. The following year was cooler than average, too, yielding a decrease in growth.

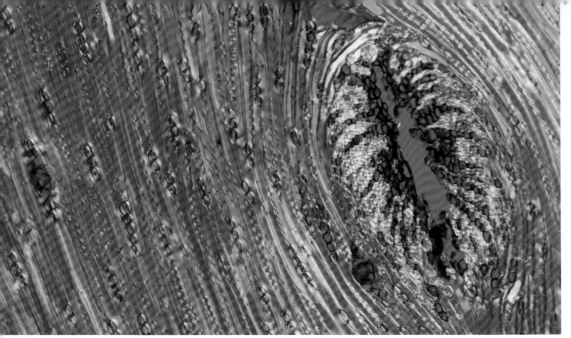

Polarised light micrograph of a vertical section through the secondary xylem of a pine tree, (*Pinus* sp.). The section shows the structure of the wood around a knot seen as a blue oval to the right. Knots are formed where branches converge on the trunk of the tree. The image also shows sap-conducting tracheids, elongated cells in the xylem of vascular plants, shown here in pink. The tracheids have thick walls studded with small pores, so-called pits that allow the sap to flow from one cell to another. All tracheary elements will develop a thick lignified cell wall and affect the mechanical behaviour of the wood.

global form of an organism, such as a tree. The integral character of the material articulation implies that changes on the molecular scale or other scales of the tissue articulation will have tremendous effects on the performance capacity and appearance of the overall system. If variability and responsiveness could become a desired characteristic, then differentiation of material make-up across several scales of magnitude would be the means.

Biological tissues, such as wood, display inherent directionality in their material make-up: they are anisotropic. They display different characteristics in different directions, resulting also in differentiated behaviour in different directions. Such materials are made from fibres and a binding matrix. Fibres are continuous filaments or discrete elongated elements bound by a matrix material to form biological tissue or fibre-reinforced composite materials. It is its specific anisotropic make-up that enables wood to change dimensions due to fluctuations in extrinsic conditions. Wood is hygroscopic; that is, due to its complex capillary structure it absorbs moisture from its environment and yields it back so as to reach equilibrium between moisture content and the relative humidity of the environment. Fluctuations in moisture content yield dimensional changes at different rates along different axes; for example, through shrinkage upon reduction of moisture content. Take pine cones, for instance: after detachment from the tree, they can open and close, time and again, due to changes in the moisture content of the material and in reaction to the relative humidity of the environment, in order to release seeds when relatively high environmental humidity grants favourable conditions for proliferation. A lot of such behaviour is determined by intrinsic differences in material make-up, which are often seen to be disadvantageous, with many an expert positing that variability in the make-up and thus performance of wood is one of its inherent deficiencies.

Included in these deemed undesirable properties are low compressive strength or high shrinkage, which occur in juvenile wood. However, Frei Otto and others have successfully demonstrated the use of young low-compressive strength timber in tension instead; for example, in the refectory and workshop in Hooke Park, Dorset. With England importing 90 per cent of its construction timber, the utilisation of its home-grown wood from reforested areas would be very useful indeed, were it not deemed inferior with regards to its low-compressive strength.

Is variability in material make-up and behaviour bad, and mutability in contradiction to stability? Not if multiple stable states can be achieved. The pine cone shows the way and does so with great beauty. In reappropriating the saying that there is no bad weather, but only inappropriate dressing, we may posit that there are no inferior materials, but only inappropriate and unimaginative use and an insufficient understanding of how properties deemed inferior can be looked at and utilised in a more opportunistic manner.

Some architects declare that since the avant-garde, within which they count themselves, managed in recent history to divorce form from structural logic, so should form now be divorced from material logic to usher in an era of hitherto unimaginable formal freedom of expression wholly liberated from all constraints (and later to be milled from solid stone). How hilarious is this: to declare the relationship between form and material exhausted vis-à-vis today's limited understanding of material performance and the potential repertoire of formal experimentation enabled by material responsiveness and mutability, together with the scope of architectural effects made possible by this? Whether the avant-guardians like it or not, the integral relationship between formalisation and materialisation processes based on the interaction between material and environment will have the most profound impact on the discipline of architecture and our human environment by providing exciting, performative and beautiful settings for human inhabitation.

Michael Hensel and Defne Sunguroğlu

Responsive Surface Structures: Instrumentalising Moisture-Content Activated Dimensional Changes of Timber Components

Steffen Reichert, Responsive Surface Structures, Department for Form Generation and Materialization (Achim Menges), HfG, Offenbach, Germany, 2006/07
Nine veneer composite components indicate the change of surface shape and related surface porosity in response to an increasing level of relative humidity. Key design parameters, such as fibre orientation or the ratio of thickness, length and width, can be related to the element's specific response to changes in moisture content and resultant shape change.

The response of a given material to changes in environmental conditions presents interesting opportunities for performance-oriented design. This research, conducted by Steffen Reichert of the Department for Form Generation and Materialisation at the Hochschule für Gestaltung (HfG) in Offenbach, Germany, in 2006/07, explores the possibility of utilising the dimensional changes of wood induced by changes in relative humidity in the environment. The project was aimed at developing a surface structure that adapts the porosity of its skin, and related cross-ventilation, in response to relative humidity without the need for any mechanical control devices. Here the response is triggered by the changes in moisture content of the material and actuated through related shape changes in a material element, which affects the structure's degree of porosity. These complex dynamics of the mutual modulation of environmental

influences, material responses and the system's behaviour need to be taken into account during the design process.

Initial experiments focused on the behaviour of simple veneer elements. Key design parameters, such as fibre orientation or the ratio of thickness, length and width, were tested in relation to the element's response time to changes in moisture content and resultant shape change. These basic tests resulted in the definition of a component based on material performance and anticipating the assembly of a larger system. The component consists of two critical parts: a load-bearing substructure and two moisture-sensitive veneer composite elements. In order to facilitate both, the connection to adjacent components and the attachment of the veneer elements, the substructure is parametrically defined as a folded system with planar faces that can be manufactured from sheet material. As a result the underlying constraints of the fabrication and assembly process are embedded in the set-up of the related computational model. The second critical component elements are two triangular veneer patches. The cutting pattern of these elements is related to the veneer

In order to release seeds when relatively high environmental humidity grants favourable conditions, pine cones can open and close, time and again, due to changes in the moisture content of the material and in reaction to the relative humidity of the environment.

grain in such a way that the main fibre direction is always parallel to the long edge of each triangle, which is then firmly attached to the substructure. An increase in relative humidity and related moisture content of the material causes the veneer elements to swell. As a result, and due to the fibrous restrictions, the surface expands mainly orthogonally to the main fibre direction. The ensuing gradual shape change opens a gap between the curving element and the substructure and thus increases the component's degree of opening. The material's hygroscopic capacity of absorbing and retaining moisture is fully reversible and, given an extreme change in relative humidity, pretty rapid with the shift from a closed to a fully open state taking less than 20 seconds. The innate material capacity of the developed component integrates a humidity sensor, change actuator and porosity control element. The component's direct responses to environmental changes suggest a locally controlled system in which each sub-location senses and reacts independently as part of an emergent overall environmental modulation.

The global articulation of the component assembly also plays a critical role in the intricate interaction of system and environment. For example, the overall curvature of the system not only contributes to its structural capacity, but also provides for different orientation and exposure of each responsive element to relevant environmental influences. In order to account for the relationship between individual components, their location within a larger system and the resultant micro- and macro-thermodynamic modulations, the development of the global surface is based on a mathematical definition. This enables a computational, hygromorphic evolution in which manipulations to the local element setup, regional component assemblies or the overall system are directly related to environmental modulations and vice versa. This feedback provides the relevant data for continuous parametric alterations of the computational model. In the resultant system morphology, the double curvature of the load-bearing structure orients the veneer elements towards or away from specific environmental input. In this way the elements can either be exposed to or removed from the impact of critical influence of humid airstreams such as sunlight, thermal energy and global airflow. The fine calibration of local dimensional changes, resulting shape change, overall curvature and orientation enables an equally specific calibration of environmental response and modulation. The parametric setup of this computational differentiation process also incorporates the constraints of manufacturing and construction and derives the necessary cutting patterns and assembly protocols at the same time.

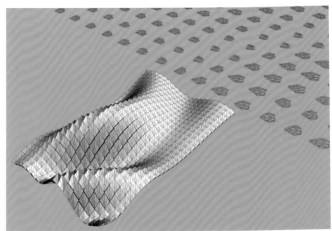

In order to construct a functional, self-supporting prototype, the substructure is defined as a folded component system developed through paper models. The folded components are parametrically proliferated on a mathematically defined surface and the related cutting patterns are automatically derived. This cut geometry can be directly used on a cutting plotter to fabricate the components from heavy-duty propylene sheets, which are subsequently folded and assembled into a full-scale prototype.

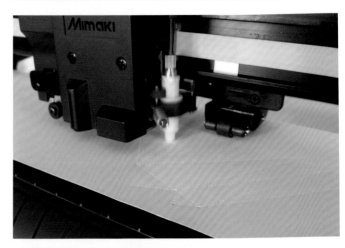

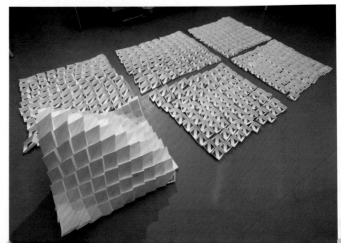

The functional full-scale prototype of the Responsive Surface Structures research project.

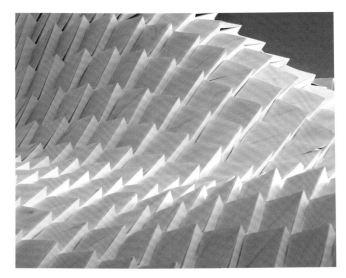

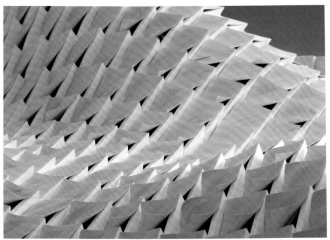

The functional full-scale prototype demonstrates the performance capacity of the system resulting from different and changing degrees of porosity across the surface. In response to changes in relative humidity and related moisture content absorbed by the veneer composite, the swelling of the veneer surfaces and the related shape change facilitate the opening and closure of each local component.

Assembled from more than 600 geometrically different veneer composite components, the full-scale prototype is both structure and responsive skin.

A functional, full-scale prototype consisting of more than 600 geometrically variant components was constructed and tested. Once exposed to changes in relative humidity, the veneer composite patches swell or shrink and thus facilitate the opening and closure of each local component resulting in different degrees of porosity across the surface, which is both a structure and responsive skin. This high level of integration of form, structure and material performance enables a direct response to environmental influences without the need for additional electronic or mechanical control. ∆

Achim Menges

Note

1. Philip Ball, *Made to Measure: New Materials for the 21st Century*, Princeton University Press (Princeton, NJ), 1997.

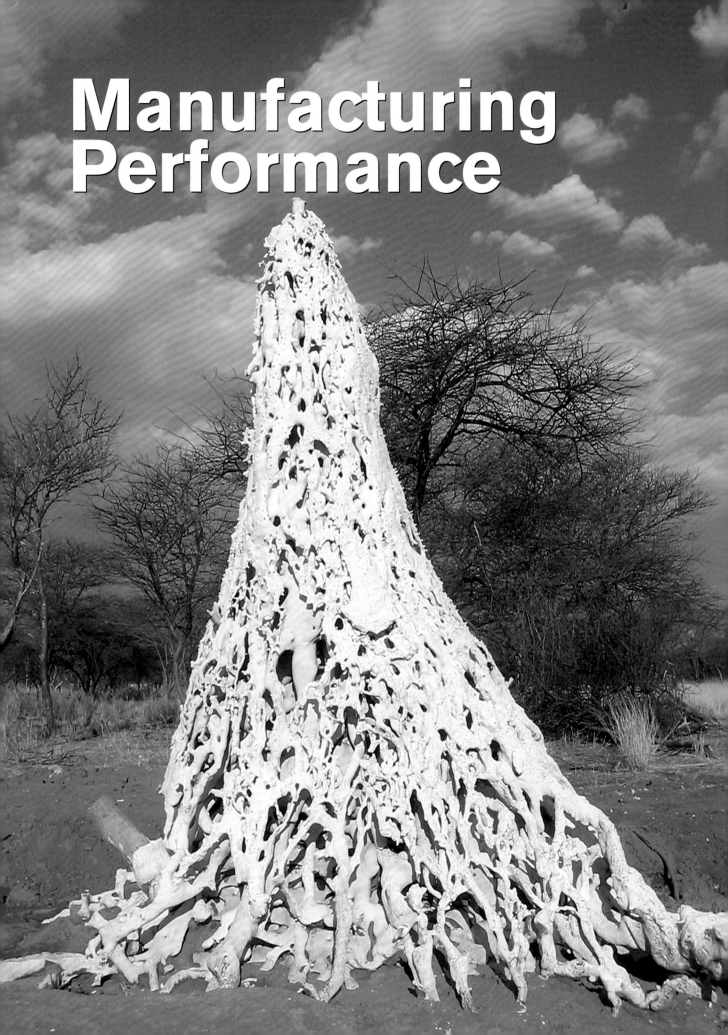

Manufacturing Performance

The use of rapid prototyping to produce scale models has in recent years become commonplace in architectural practices and universities. Employing such layer manufacturing processes at the scale of construction opens up entirely new possibilities for articulating and manufacturing a performative built environment. **Achim Menges** discusses Freeform Construction, a collaborative effort between Loughborough University's Civil & Building Engineering Department and Loughborough's Wolfson School of Manufacturing and Mechanical Engineering to develop construction-scale rapid manufacturing processes. Crossing conventional boundaries of the manufacturing domain, the research is not only concerned with developing new modes of production, but also contributes to establishing an alternative approach for designing performative architecture where form, material, structure and performance are understood as inherently related and integral aspects of the manufacturing and construction process.

In the construction industry, novel manufacturing technologies are predominantly developed to overcome a defined manufacturing problem or shortcoming. In this way, computer-aided manufacturing in architecture has been mainly conceived as a more precise, rapid and versatile evolution of established fabrication processes that satisfies both the demand for increased production efficiency and the desire for more economic construction of geometrically complicated buildings. Thus in most applications advanced manufacturing technologies are the facilitative means of constructing projects conceived through established and well-rehearsed design processes.

At the other end of the spectrum, a new kind of computer-controlled manufacturing technology is emerging, one that fundamentally challenges not only the way we build, but also the way we envisage architectural design. From a rapid manufacturing perspective, Loughborough University has been at the forefront of developing computer-controlled layer, or additive, manufacturing processes and related rapid prototyping technologies, and has ventured into rapid tooling and defined rapid manufacturing for a wide range of different fields including aerospace, automotive, sports, medical, pharmaceutical and the aforementioned construction applications. As a derivative technique of rapid prototyping, rapid manufacturing is currently characterised by the same key process sequence of material preparation, material delivery, layer-by-layer fabrication on a support system, phase change of a build or bonding medium and subsequent post-processing. The Freeform Construction group defines rapid manufacturing as the use of a computer-aided design (CAD)-based automated additive manufacturing process to construct parts that are used directly as finished products or components. The term 'additive' manufacturing is used in preference to 'layer' manufacturing as it is likely that some future rapid manufacturing systems will operate in a multi-axis fashion as opposed to the current layer-wise manufacturing encountered in todays rapid prototyping.[1]

In recent years Freeform Construction has focused on investigating how the technological transfer of additive manufacturing processes could be applied to construction practice and the architectural design process. Very soon the group came to realise that in this context the shift from rapid prototyping to rapid manufacturing is not just a case of producing stronger parts with better materials. Rather than just providing a greater degree of geometric freedom in the design of parts and assemblies, additive manufacturing technologies allow for higher-level functional integration. Here the consideration of performance capacities and related morphological differentiation enabled by the manufacturing

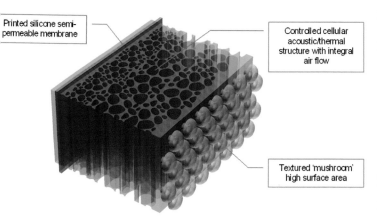

Printed silicone semi-permeable membrane

Controlled cellular acoustic/thermal structure with integral air flow

Textured 'mushroom' high surface area

Model generation of a spatially folded, single-material structure demonstrating both form and function, with texturing to interact with wind and control of macro-permeability of structure, and 2-D cellular structure to channel energy gradients down vectors for matter minimisation. The orange plane denotes simultaneous printing of semi-permeable fluid.

Freeform Construction, Civil & Building Engineering Department and the Wolfson School of Manufacturing and Mechanical Engineering, Loughborough University, Leicestershire, UK, ongoing
As part of the Freeform Construction research project, the morphology of a complete internal plaster cast of main ventilation channels in a *Macrotermes michaelseni* termite mound has been scanned and analysed in order to be instrumentalised for additive manufacturing.

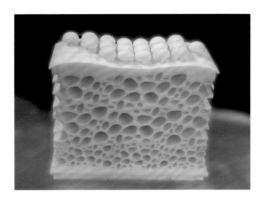

Single-material structure printed by selective laser sintering (SLS) and showing the freeform curvature of the surface.

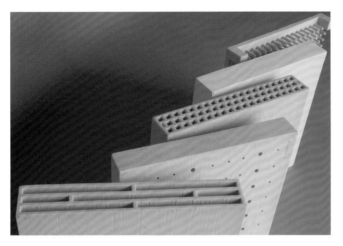

Test panels generated on a Z-Corp 800 series 3-D printer. The panels were used to test the integrated thermal and acoustic structures. The large panel at the rear features arrays of Helmholtz resonations for broadband frequency absorption. The remaining panels explore the control of conductive over convective behaviour.

technology needs to inform and drive the design process from the start. The aim of this article is to gain an insight into the group's research on related technological advances, manufacturing processes, integral design techniques and their potential repercussions on performance-based architecture.

Large-scale automated layer manufacturing systems are not entirely new to the field of construction. In fact, the term layer manufacturing was coined by Shimizu Corporation, one of a number of Japanese companies exploring alternative ways of constructing skyscrapers in the late 1980s and 1990s. Similar to other approaches in Japan during that time, Shimizu's SMART system is based on a movable automated factory formed by robotic systems that is gradually lifted up in the process of erecting the building. Constructing storey by storey on its way up, the automated system is fed with materials, components and entire modules. While this demonstrates the feasibility of very large-scale layer manufacturing in its broadest sense, it is interesting to note that most of the Japanese approaches were based on automated assembly of prefabricated parts. The preference for

such dry construction methods is common in the construction industry, which increasingly aims at reducing or even eliminating wet construction on site. The Freeform Construction research questions the current tendency towards dry systems. Its approach identifies and argues for the significant potential of additive manufacturing technologies in construction practice based on computer-controlled preparation, delivery and deposition of wet or wetted liquids, powders, binders and aggregate systems. Although the roots of Freeform Construction clearly lie within the field of rapid manufacturing, it is not possible to simply scale up existing processes due to the specific material and context constraints of construction. The considerable size difference between manufacturing mechanical parts and constructing entire buildings poses a number of challenges. One particularly critical aspect is the relationship between the minimum resolution, in this instance the smallest feature that the process can define, and the bead size and correlated deposition rate of additive manufacturing processes. Scaling up existing processes has an inversely proportional impact on the resolution that can be achieved in the subsequent structure. Thus the fast production speed and bulk deposition rates necessary for construction-scale manufacturing and the related increased bead or drop size conflicts with the detail articulation required for embedding performative capacities in the 3-D printed system. In order to meet these opposing requirements, one area of the research focuses on developing new processes capable of depositing material at multiple resolutions simultaneously, which ensures both bulk deposition and detailed, high-resolution features.

The careful mediation of critical parameters such as the resolution to be achieved, the volume of material to be deposited and the deposition speed at different scales leads to an additive manufacturing process of structures that consist of a reduced number of materials or even a single material differentiated on various scales of magnitude. The manufacturing process allows for treating or structuring a single material construction so that it has multiple material characteristics achieved through scalar differentiation and hierarchical build-up as found in natural systems. These intricate modifications of a material's structure enable it to behave like various combined materials. Rupert Soar, the principal investigator of the Freeform Construction research project, refers to this as quasi composite material, which can acquire a wide range of physical and mechanical properties through multiscalar variations in the manufacturing process of a single material.

The capabilities of this approach are apparent in an initial set of experiments with as basic a material as gypsum. Though gypsum is a familiar construction material found, for example, in wall boards, it can exhibit a wide range of properties if its structure is modified in the 3-D printing process. In combination with digital simulations the additive manufacturing process allows for the geometric differentiation of a gypsum element's surface articulation and

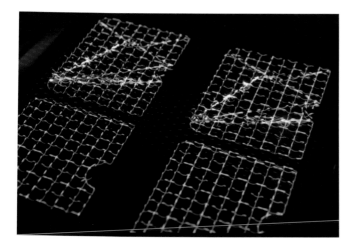

A UV laser trace with an open 10-second shutter. The laser traces the support structure of the main build for the photolithography process.

Complete internal plaster cast of the main ventilation channels in a *Macrotermes michaelseni* termite mound in Namibia. The mound is first filled with gypsum and the soil washed away to reveal this magnificent structure, analogous to an bronchial bifurcation in animals. The capillary system (known as egress channels) is not visible here.

internal make-up in response to structural, thermal, acoustic and ventilation requirements. For example, high-resolution textures provide for variable and passively moisture-driven permeability by increasing the external surface area. At the same time the manufacturing of the element's internal capillary structure can be driven by load-bearing requirements and the provision of ducts and channels. As gypsum can even be processed to have translucent qualities, including a glass-like structure known as selenite, the number of materials required for a building element can be dramatically reduced while at the same time its performance capacity significantly increases. Furthermore, such single-material elements can be directly and easily recycled on site, through grinding, re-calcinations and subsequent reprinting processes. Beyond these considerable advantages in regard to waste reduction and management, a single-material quasi composite approach to manufacturing may have a more fundamental impact on architectural design. The possibility of scalar differentiation and hierarchical articulation within one material system enables a level of functional integration and versatility that is unknown to the construction industry, yet is a familiar feature of many natural structures.

Consequently, rather than just delving into immediate applications, the research group realised that an alternative approach to designing performative architectural systems needed to be developed if the latent potential of additive manufacturing technology was to be fully explored. In order to reveal, comprehend and ultimately instrumentalise processes capable of unfolding high-level integration of system morphology and function, they set out to investigate some of the most sophisticated structures: the termite mounds of *Macrotermes michaelseni* common throughout sub-Saharan Africa.

In contrast to the tall, open, chimney-type mounds frequently referred to as models for passive ventilated architecture, these mounds do not expose an obvious ventilation system. Yet they still protect the colony, which consists of the termites as well as symbiotic fungi, from the hostile outside environment by directly maintaining levels of oxygen, carbon dioxide and water vapour, and indirectly maintaining temperature concentrations within narrow limits. It is important to understand that the termite colony does not reside in the mound, but rather that the mound constitutes a physiological infrastructure continuously (re)constructed by up to one million worker termites inhabiting the subterranean nest. Using minerals found in underground soil, the termites have evolved construction processes that extend the homeostatic regulation systems common to all organisms into the structures they live in.[2] These respiratory and thermo-regulatory systems enable continual adaptation to dynamic external influences and changing internal conditions, and thus provide a climatic equilibrium for the colony, termed structural homeostasis. The ongoing adaptive modifications of the mound architecture are facilitated by the upward and outward movement of soil from underlying strata via individual termites acting as conveyors. This movement is a closed-loop, self-organised process driven by positive feedback phenomena, including pheromone dispersal known as stigmergy, acoustic signalling, response to perturbation and the related interactions between countless termites, and partly directed by differential concentration of respiratory gases in larger fields, or negative feedback, within the mound. The termites' self-organised construction process and soil transport is guided by a map given through the metabolism-generated temporal and transient gradients in carbon-dioxide and moisture concentration. Through local variations in gas transport and related changes in the soil-depositing behaviour of termites emerge the mound's morphological features and related homeostasis of the nest atmosphere.

While termite mounds have been the subject of various studies for over a century, as of yet it remains unclear how these complex functions are achieved through apparently morphological rules.

In order to understand how the mound's intricate architecture integrates structure and homeostatic regulation, its complex geometry needed to be closely examined and digitised for subsequent computer fluid dynamics simulations. This involved designing and constructing a mobile scanning unit measuring 5 x 5 x 6 metres (16.4 x 16.4 x 19.7 feet). In Namibia the research team prepared a mound by casting its extensive network of tunnels and caverns in plaster of Paris, which was then sliced and scanned in 1-millimetre (0.04-inch) increments by the bespoke machine. After more than a month of scanning time an enormous data set captured the morphological complexity of the central closed chimney, a vertically oriented void capped by porous soil, the narrow channels of the surface conduits and the highly reticulated network of lateral connectives. The resultant digital model, combined with data collected through measurements of key material properties such as thermal conductivity, the resistance to airflow, diffusivity of respiratory gases and radiative surface emissivity, a comprehensive computational fluid dynamics model was set up to explore the mound's homeostatic regulation systems.

Contrary to the common conception of buoyancy-driven circulatory flow caused solely by the metabolic heat of the colony, the nest appears to be tidally ventilated through pressure fluctuation resulting from the changes of wind direction and speed in the dynamic outside environment. Three phases of respiratory gas exchange of this tidal ventilation correspond to specific zones within the mound's structure. External wind drives the exchange in the chimney cap and surface conduits through a forced convection regime, whereas the gas exchange in the lower chimney is mainly based on natural convection driven by differences in air density resulting from nest metabolism. A mixed forced-neutral convection system enables the exchange in the middle chimney and the lateral connectives.

Consequently the *Macrotermes* mound is not a means of isolating the inside colony from the outside environment, as

Large-scale digital slice and scanning apparatus as used in Namibia in August 2006 to slice 1 millimetre (0.04 inches) at a time from the mound. The exposed top face is then digitally scanned, generating thousands of scan images of the internal geometry of the actual mound.

Cross-section from the scanned mound showing how the gypsum infill produces the threshold required for the computer to derive and assemble the final 3-D model.

it has often been assumed. On the contrary, a colony-level performance such as ventilation appears to be the synergetic effect of integrating two energy sources: the external wind pressure and the internal metabolism-induced buoyancy. Other factors also come into play that influence ventilation and environmental regulation, such as the response of the material that makes up the mound skin. Localised insulation effects dry the mound skin, inducing greater permeability, whereas moisture, in the form of external rainfall and internal metabolic moisture, reduces permeability to airflow into and out of the mound. The effect is a dynamic interaction of all variables leading to a complex permeability map over the mound skin. Termites will physically open small channels, known as egress channels, through the mound skin when permeability is restricted and ventilation must be sustained. The mound essentially utilises solar power, wind power, evaporative and passive cooling purely

Full 3-D digital model of ventilated termite mound structure.

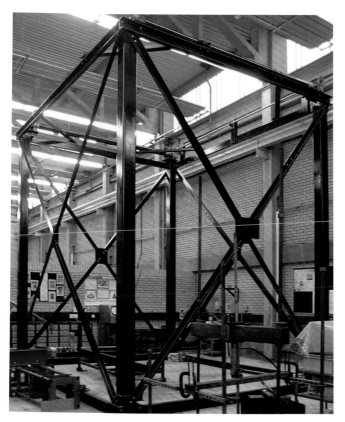

The opposite of the digital scanning machine used in Namibia. A custom-made material deposition head is being made at Loughborough University to add to the gantry system to print complex 3-D structures.

through the construction and maintenance of a permeable surface. Termites will even remodel the structure so that the region of activity or zone of structural homeostasis shrinks to a region around only the nest during the cooler, dryer parts of the year. Interestingly, during the dry season the rest of the mound is almost redundant. As, and even before, the main rains arrive, the zone of mound homeostasis then appears to expand rapidly to fill the mound volume. At Loughborough University, further evaluation of the mound structure's performative morphology is currently under way in parallel to developing and constructing the next generation of a large-scale additive manufacturing machine. While in the built environment we may be a long way from achieving the versatility and adaptability epitomised in termite mounds, the Freeform Construction work renders higher-level performance integration a tangible proposition rather than a mere phantasm.

The group's research not only advances manufacturing technologies for the construction industry, it also provides alternative inroads to performance-based architecture. Sooner than most of us may anticipate, the synthesis of novel design approaches based on emergent systems and physiological processes in sync with emerging manufacturing capabilities will enable architects to embed and integrate manifold performance capacities in the fabric of our habitats. In the

future, once the technology has matured to a point when, as Rupert Soar envisions, thousands of devices collaborate in ongoing swarm construction processes driven by continual adjustments to individually sensed internal and external conditions, the research under way now may be understood as the beginning of the inevitable convergence of inorganic and organic construction. ⬠

Notes

1. N Hopkinson, RJM Hague and PM Dickens, *Rapid Manufacturing: An Industrial Revolution for the Digital Age*, John Wiley & Sons (Chichester), 2006.
2. JS Turner; *The Extended Organism: The Physiology of Animal-Built Structures*, Harvard University Press (Cambridge, MA), 2000.

This article is based on in-depth research into the current possibilities and future perspectives of fully integrated computer-aided design and manufacturing. As part of this exploration, Achim Menges visited the Freeform Construction research facilities at Loughborough University and had long conversations with Dr Rupert Soar who is the principal investigator of the Freeform Construction research project. The article is the third part in a series of two previous articles: Manufacturing Complexity in AD Emergence: Morphogenetic Design Strategies, Vol 74, No 3, May/June 2004; and Manufacturing Diversity in *AD Techniques and Technologies in Morphogenetic Design*, Vol 76, No 2, March/April 2006.

Project credits
Application Research for Freeform Construction Processes
Rupert Soar (principal investigator); Professor Alistair Gibb, Professor Tony Thorpe, Dr Francis Edum-Fotwe (co-investigators); Dr Richard Buswell (post-doctoral research associate); Oliver Godbold, Bertand Ngim (research students)
Funding body: IMCRC
Industrial partners/collaborators: BPB plc, Z-Corporation, Martyn Pendlebury
Freeform Construction: Mega-Scale Rapid Manufacturing for Construction
Dr Rupert Soar (principal investigator); Professor Simon Austin, Dr Richard Buswell, Professor Alistair Gibb, Professor Tony Thorpe (co-investigators); Dr David Swift, Dr Yuanming Zhang (post-doctoral research associates); Craig Davidson (research student); Adam Phillips, John Webster (technicians)
Funding body: IMCRC
Industrial partners/collaborators: HelmX, Putzmeister, Buro Happold Ltd, Foster and Partners, University of Southern California, Shotcrete, BPB/Saint-Gobain, Laser Optic Engineering, Weber Building Solutions
Integration of Structural Homeostasis with Mega-Scale Rapid Manufacturing
Dr Rupert Soar (principal investigator); Dr W Malalasekera, HK Versteeg, Professor Dennis Loveday, Dr J Scott Turner (co-investigators); Dr Srikar Vulli (research associate); Haitham Abou-Houly (research assistant)
Funding body: EPSRC

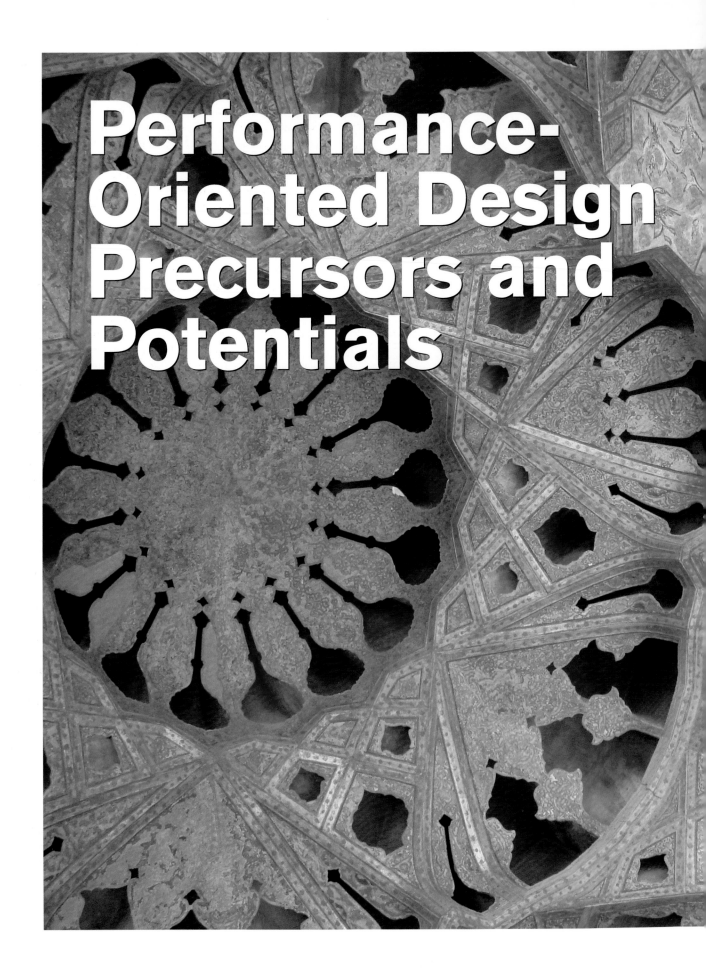

Performance-Oriented Design Precursors and Potentials

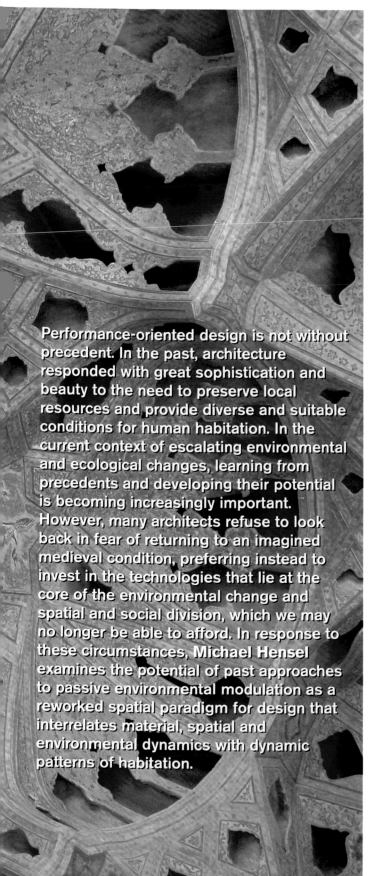

Performance-oriented design is not without precedent. In the past, architecture responded with great sophistication and beauty to the need to preserve local resources and provide diverse and suitable conditions for human habitation. In the current context of escalating environmental and ecological changes, learning from precedents and developing their potential is becoming increasingly important. However, many architects refuse to look back in fear of returning to an imagined medieval condition, preferring instead to invest in the technologies that lie at the core of the environmental change and spatial and social division, which we may no longer be able to afford. In response to these circumstances, Michael Hensel examines the potential of past approaches to passive environmental modulation as a reworked spatial paradigm for design that interrelates material, spatial and environmental dynamics with dynamic patterns of habitation.

It's a bit nippy? Turn on the heating. It's too hot and humid? Turn on the air-con. Jolly good! Except, if your permanent address is Planet Earth you might have heard of climate change and the inconvenient truth seems to be that we accelerate it, heating, cooling and ventilating the hell out of our environment by means of energy-consuming equipment. The extent to which we do this is exorbitant. During last year's hot summer the power grid of California failed at some point due to the vast number of air-conditioning units being used. When the power grid holds up, the carbon footprint is gargantuan. But hey, you hear them say, air-con is a status symbol, a hallmark of modern life, the only way to secure human comfort. Or is it?

It is now widely appreciated that carbon footprints and intensive energy consumption need to be reduced. But the question is how? The bulk of research and legislation in the EU that is geared towards sustainability of the built environment aims for so-called zero-energy buildings. This is pursued by reducing thermal loss or impact through increasing amounts of thermal insulation, electrical thermal regain equipment and the reduction of energy consumption for interior climate modulation. Consequentially, and quite obviously, this approach reinforces the strict dichotomy between interior and exterior that came hand in hand with the emergence of these devices in the first place. We have thus inherited an uncontested solipsistic spatial paradigm that is dictated by and, in turn, dictates the way we think about the homogenous modulation of almost hermetically sealed interior environments.

If, on the other hand, one mentions passive strategies for environmental modulation, it may be welcomed by some as, at best, supplementary to active electrical systems, or condemned by others as a nostalgic reflex that will surely sacrifice comfort at large, turning our built environment back into an infested medieval slum. This fear is quite obviously strategically induced and nourished by energy politics, providers and industries that wish to collect taxes and make profits. Only a few seem to actually consider that updating passive strategies to a contemporary technical context may be a very powerful opportunity for architecture to rethink its preferred spatial paradigm. It thus seems that while we have returned to a preference for heterogeneous space, we are not able to transcend beyond the limit of mere utilitarian environmental consciousness to understand the potential of a broader notion of performativity, as well as the synergy between material arrangements, microclimatic conditioning of space and interrelated migratory activities.

In order to initiate a revised take on this topic, it is necessary to re-evaluate some historical precedents. To pursue a broad account of historical precursors of performative design and passive environmental strategies would vastly exceed the possible scope of this article. Instead only three

Ali Qapu palace in Isfahan, Iran.

The roof of this historic bathhouse in Yazd, Iran, shows the typical domed surface used for self-shading. The air conditioning, which was installed when the building was converted into a coffee house, required the closing of the air vents of the domes, which now only serve to bring light into the interior.

View of a courtyard of traditional residences in Yazd, Iran. The climate is very dry with cold winters and hot summers. The temperature can fluctuate dramatically between night and day and summer and winter. Temperatures of 40°C (104°F) in the summer and -20°C (-68°F) in the winter have been recorded. The city of Yazd is especially well known for its historical architecture, which is uniquely adapted to its desert surroundings. Several passive thermal modulation strategies are simultaneously present in this courtyard setting: the thick brick walls, limited openings towards the perimeter, the tree in the centre, the wind tower, domed roofs and air vents on top of the domes (partly obscured by the tree in the centre). However, these features are in stark contrast to the air-conditioning unit on the left-hand side of the court that renders several of the passive strategies redundant. Performative capacity and passive environmental modulation strategies of such traditional architecture are in this way often obliterated and replaced by energy-consuming electrical devices that have become status symbols in many parts of the world.

areas of perceived potential will be briefly discussed: functional building elements with regard to the articulated surface; heterogeneous spatial arrangements facilitating varied microclimates and gradient thresholds that in turn are related to dynamic modes of habitation; and bodies in space with their own energy signature. It is needless to say that material surfaces already interact with the environment, they partition space in some way and condition it by means of exchange with an environment, and environmental gradients do not only emanate from matter that delimits space as material surfaces, but also from the living bodies that move in space and time. The question is how such strategies can be updated and instrumentalised with regard to the dynamic relationships between subject, object and environment and towards a critical spatial paradigm.

There are many interesting examples in vernacular and representative architecture alike concerning the utilisation of articulated performative surfaces. Great examples are screenwalls, particularly in Islamic architecture. Sophia and Stefan Behling posited that the dream of Mogul architects was to create the ultimate diaphanous wall. 'The multifunctional screens ... allowed the greatest comfort in inside/outside spaces.'[1] Such screenwalls include the Indian *jali* or the Arabic *mashrabiya*. A *jali* is a perforated stone screen, while a *mashrabiya* is a projecting bay window articulated by wood latticework. Visual connection from the interior to the exterior is provided, while visual penetration from the exterior to the interior is prevented, offering privacy to inhabitants. Such screens enable ventilation, provide shading and modulate the luminous environment of the interior. The Behlings argue that Mogul screens are far more sophisticated than modern devices for creating shade. The filigree designs and the dramatic display of light and shadow create virtual spaces within rooms.[2] Screenwalls and similar building elements

have already consolidated what Reyner Banham called the Western tradition of substantial architecture with the non-substantial one of societies who do not build substantial structures [but instead] inhabit a space whose external boundaries are vague, adjustable and rarely regular.[3] Such elements constitute no less than the awesomely beautiful performative synthesis of the delineating material threshold and the environmental gradient.

Contemporary versions of screenwalls range from the sculptural experiments of the Austrian sculptor Erwin Hauer, commencing from the early 1950s, to current non-standard assemblies that utilise parametric associative modelling environments to inform the design of highly performative screenwalls. One interesting move forward would be designs beyond simple flat-screen applications into layered envelopes for entire buildings, as can already be seen in some Mogul architecture. The use of such elements may also not only be constrained to hot climates. Lace villas in northern Europe, so called because of their white-coloured timber latticework which resembles lacework, deploy such screens to provide porches that are protected from wind in the winter while permitting sunlight at a low angle, as well as shading and ventilation in the summer.

Articulated surfaces also include possibilities other than screenwalls; for instance, poche walls or surfaces with non-

The walls and ceiling of the music chamber of the Ali Qapu palace in Isfahan, Iran, have cavities that are set into them with the purpose of reducing reverberation and holding upper and lower tones. In doing so they become an extension of the musical instruments, embedded within the architecture of the music chamber. The plasterwork is fantastically intricate, tapering to 3 millimetres (0.12 inches) thickness towards the edge of each cavity. Such work was possible due to an unprecedented accumulation of craftsmanship in one location.

The photo shows the intricate pattern of light and shadow in the Friday Mosque in Isfahan, Iran, effected by a screenwall that also provides ventilation.

uniform thickness. The Ali Qapu palace located on the western side of Naghsh-i Jahan Square in Isfahan, Iran, built in its initial form by Shah Abbas I in the early 17th century, received under Shah Abbas II a music room on the sixth floor with remarkable walls and ceiling vaults. It contains cavities made from delicate stuccowork that invoke the image of bodies of musical instruments. It is likely that these were intended to reduce reverberation while retaining upper and lower tones. Folklore has it that the music could still be heard long after the musicians had left. While this is obviously quite an exaggeration, it is nevertheless a most remarkable historical precedent to performance-oriented design: an

architecture that is both an extension of musical instruments and an amplifier of musical performance. What has changed since is that due to contemporary means of form-generation, performance analysis and manufacturing, such designs are now affordable for those less fortunate than the then richest man in the known world, the Shah of Persia.

The layering of walls of different thickness or porosity can create a variety of microclimates that can suit individual preferences in terms of comfort and activities. Spatial arrangements and dynamic inhabitation were historically often interrelated. Depending on the time of day or season, activities would shift location in plan or in section. In hot and dry climates, multistorey houses offer the possibility to use the lower floors during the hot day and to sleep on the roof terrace at night where it is coolest. Mogul, Persian and Ottoman pavilions enabled a similar potential for migratory use of space in their careful spatial arrangement in plan.

Seasonal differences in the northern hemisphere might locate activities in the winter on the south-facing side, and in the summer on the north-facing side of the building, and vice versa in the southern hemisphere. Courtyards, loggias, arcades, verandahs and porches are useful elements for this purpose, although they have almost disappeared from contemporary spatial repertoire due to the strict division between exterior and interior that comes hand in hand with electrical air-conditioning and heating. However, combined surface articulation and orientation and layered spatial arrangements can provide for a heterogeneous space and microclimate in which comfort can be found on the basis of individual preferences and needs, contrary to the prescribed homogenously conditioned interior of the age of electrical air-conditioning.

This can be complemented by an understanding of bodies in space as energy emitters.

In cold, mountainous climates, for instance in the Alps, cattle were used as a thermal energy source for the space inhabited by humans. Within the envelope of the building, the cattle were placed in the outer periphery around a second walled-in area reserved for human use, in order to warm up the peripheral space and thus maintain thermal comfort in the inner area. Such strategies were not only used in plan arrangements, but also in section, with the cattle placed on the ground floor and the spaces reserved for human inhabitation placed above. For large auditoria and other such spaces it is relatively common practice today to calculate the heat gain due to the presence of a large number of people. Such methods could be further developed and finely calibrated to differently scaled designs. They may also not only be constrained to thermal modulation, but involve the integration of other organisms for the sake of CO_2 reduction, oxygen provision and so on. This becomes particularly powerful when material properties are once again more carefully, and in a less prejudiced manner, deployed and calibrated to take advantage of their responses to different environmental stimuli.[4]

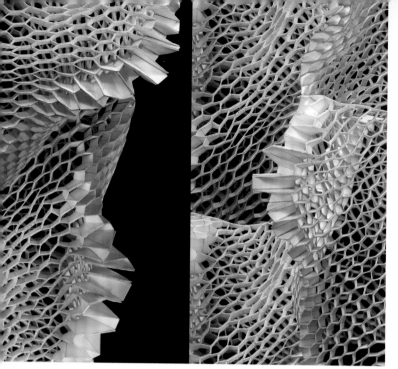

Scaled model of the Manifold screenwall system, designed by Andrew Kudless in 2004, exploring a multiple-layer, double-curved and variable depth honeycomb arrangement to modulate visual transparency, light transmission and ventilation. The design exceeds the typical flat screenwall and can act as layered spatial arrangements and as a porous building envelope.

The Meta-Patch screenwall, designed in 2004 by Joseph Kellner and Dave Newton, is an adaptable assembly. Small timber patches are mounted on to larger ones. The small timber patches are bent and twisted by means of bolts that are used as actuators. Through the incremental actuation of each small patch the larger patches become curved, and thus the assembly acquires the capacity to bear its own self-weight and hold itself in an upright position. Holes are introduced into the larger patches to facilitate airflow and light transmission from one side of the screenwall to the other upon actuation of the timber patches, inducing curvature into the assembly. The interesting aspect here is that the curvature of the screenwall, and therefore its specific performance, can be altered at all times.

The Strip Morphologies screenwall, designed in 2005 by Daniel Coll I Capdevila of OCEAN, explores a multiple-layer, double-curved and variable-depth bent strip arrangement to modulate visual transparency and, luminous, thermal and acoustic performance, and enables layered spatial arrangements by means of a porous envelope.

The Revan Kiosk in the Topkapi palace in Istanbul, Turkey, shows passive cooling strategies similar to the vernacular example in Abyaneh in Iran. The deep open recess on the first floor acts as a shade for the two-storey-high facade. The door on the first floor is shaded by a smaller roof that shades the lower area at lower sun-angles, and accelerates the airflow to and from the interior depending on wind direction.

This traditional building in the famous historic village of Abyaneh, one of the oldest in Iran, is made from the typical red clay of the region. The elevation shows a number of passive environmental modulation strategies: the use of thick clay walls, with deep setbacks on the ground floor to shade window areas, and on the first floor shaded by a wide overhanging roof. All openings have simple screenwalls that enable ventilation while protecting the interior from visual penetration. In this vernacular example, building elements and spatial arrangements operate in synergy and are probably complemented by the migratory pattern of habitation in response to temperature changes at different times of the day and different seasons.

The Membrane Array Canopy, designed and constructed by the Emergent Technologies and Design masters programme in collaboration with structural engineers Buro Happold in 2007 at the Architectural Association, provides a porous canopy that allows views and substantially reduces of horizontal loads while providing shade and protection from rain.

In the case of the discussed strategies for passive environmental modulation and their updating, it will be necessary to develop the material constituents of a dynamic exchange not in isolation, but rather as a condition of energy exchange and environmental modulation. This implies drawing on analytical methods that are available, but not necessarily used in the design process. These might include thermal imaging, digital analysis of environmental conditions, analysis of material behaviour and so on as critical design parameters, rather than post-rationalisation and post-optimisation.

If we return to the two alternatives, the hermetic space and homogenous interior climate of air-conditioned boxes or the porous heterogeneous space of energetic exchange, it would seem odd that the preference should remain with the reductivism of the former. One feels reminded of that scene in Douglas Adams' *Hitchhiker's Guide to the Galaxy* where one character feels locked out from the world when he is in his house. Consequentially he decides to turn his house inside out in order to live in the world. The joke is, of course, on the self-imposed and artificial dichotomy between interior and exterior. This turning on the heating when it is nippy and the air-con when it is too hot and humid is a joke on all of us. Jolly good! ⚙

Notes
1. Sophia and Stefan Behling, *Solar Power: The Evolution of Sustainable Architecture,* Prestel (Munich, London and New York), 2000.
2. Ibid.
3. Reyner Banham, *The Architecture of the Well-Tempered Environment*, University of Chicago Press (Chicago, IL), 1973.
4. See the article on Material Performance in this issue.

Inclusive Performance: Efficiency Versus Effectiveness

Towards a Morpho-Ecological Approach for Design

Towards a Morpho-Ecological Approach for Design

At a time of accelerated global urbanisation and climate change, performance-oriented design has an increasingly important role to play. Here, **Michael Hensel** and **Achim Menges** describe their own 'Morpho-Ecological' approach to design, which challenges some of the most deeply entrenched dogmas of architecture as a material practice, such as the notion of 'efficiency' in design and construction. It focuses specifically on the integral relationship between form-generation, material behaviour and capacity, manufacturing and assembly, environmental modulation and a type of spatial conditioning that is set to deliver a richly heterogeneous space.

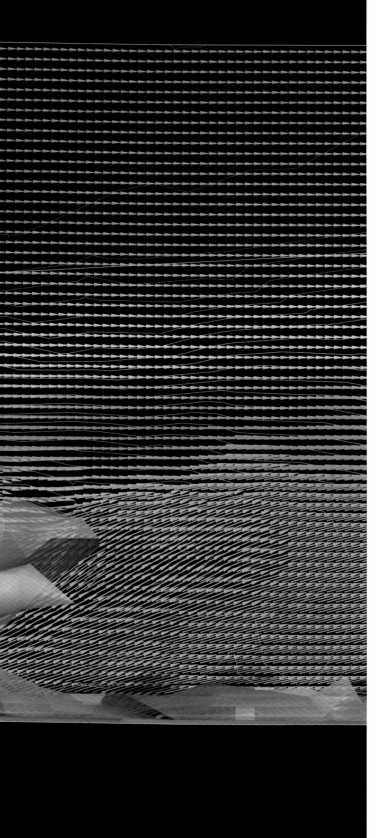

Architecture as a material practice operates through the articulation of spatial, material and energetic interventions within a specific context. Enhanced context-sensitivity of an integral design approach lies at the base of the approach introduced here, entitled 'Morpho-Ecologies'. This approach commences from the unfolding of performative capacities inherent in material systems in relation to the specific environment they are embedded within, as well as an intensively empirical mode based on physical and computational form-generation and analysis methods. Compared with current practice it presents a radically different take on the relation between formal expression and performative capacity of the built environment, as well as a fundamental revision of prevailing approaches to sustainability.

An alternative understanding of performance, one that is based on multiparameter effectiveness rather than single-parameter optimisation and efficiency, must from the start of the design process include both the logics of how material constructions are made and the way they will interact with environmental conditions and stimuli. Computation, in analytical and generative modes, has a key role in both aspects. The underlying logics of computational processes, particularly in combination with computer-controlled manufacturing processes, provide a potential for a much higher level of design synthesis. Yet the current use of CAD-CAM technologies in architecture serves more often than not as the facilitative, and affordable, means to indulge in freeform architecture. Although this may occasionally lead to innovative structures and novel spatial qualities, it is important to recognise that the technology serves merely as an extension of well-rehearsed and established design processes.

Particularly emblematic is the underlying impoverished notion of form-generation, which refers to various digitally driven processes resulting in shapes that remain detached from material and construction logics. In foregrounding the geometry of the eventual outcome as the key feature, these techniques are quintessentially not dissimilar to more conventional and long-established representational techniques for explicit scalar geometric descriptions. As these notational systems are insufficient in integrating means of materialisation, production and construction, they cannot support the evaluation of performative effects, and so these crucial aspects remain invariably pursued as top-down engineered material solutions.

Dae Song Lee, Differentiated Space Frames, Diploma Unit 4, Architectural Association, 2005-06
Through computer fluid dynamics modelling the aerodynamic performance of a local component of the Differentiated Space Frames project can be investigated. The recurrent analyses of system behaviour and performative capacity becomes an integral part of the system's computational generation.

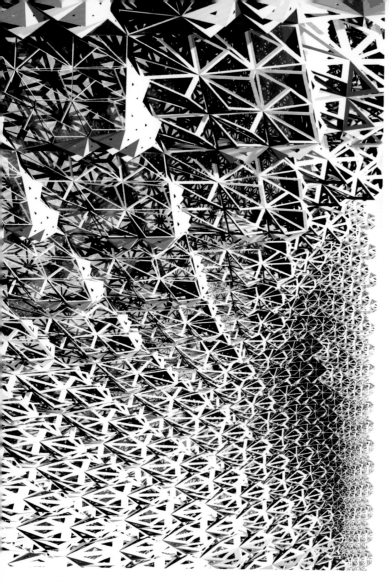

The digital model shows the system's ability to incrementally change from a vector-active space-frame structure to a surface-active structural folded system within one assembly. This enables gradient porosity of the system which can be instrumentalised relative to environmental performance.

This suggests that the latent, but as yet unused, potential of computational design and manufacturing technology may unfold from an alternative approach to design, one that derives morphological complexity and performative capacity without differentiating between form-generation and materialisation processes. The logic of computation strongly suggests such an alternative, in which the geometric rigour and simulation capability of computational modelling can be deployed to integrate manufacturing constraints, assembly logics and material characteristics in the definition of material and construction systems. Furthermore, the development of versatile analysis tools for structure, thermodynamics, light and acoustics provides for integrating feedback loops in evaluating the system's behaviour in interaction with a simulated environment, and can thus become generative drivers in the design process. Such computational models describe behaviour rather than mere shape. This enables the designer to conceive of material and construction systems as the synergetic result of computationally mediating and

instrumentalising the system's intrinsic logics and constraints of making, the system's behaviour and interaction with external forces and environmental influences, as well as the performative effects resulting from these interactions. Thus the understanding of material effects extends beyond the visible effect towards the thermodynamic, acoustic and luminous modulation of the natural and built environment. As these modulations can now be anticipated as actual behaviour rather than textbook principles, the design of space, structure and climate becomes inseparable.

Realising the potential of computational design and computer-controlled fabrication therefore entails two aspects: first, the enabling of a far more immediate relationship between the processes of making and constructing by unfolding intrinsic material capacity and behaviour; and second, the utilisation of this capacity and behaviour as a means of creating spatial arrangements, microclimatic spatial conditioning and also structure.

While the latter aspect may have a profound impact on our conception of spatial organisation, which can now be thought of as differentiated macro- and microclimatic conditions providing a heterogeneous habitat for human activities, the research of the former aspect will first require elaboration.

As this research seeks to develop and employ computational techniques and digital fabrication technologies to unfold intrinsic material capacity and specific performative capacities, it begins with extensive experiments and testing of what we define as material systems. Material systems are considered not so much as derivatives of standardised building systems and elements, but rather as generative drivers in the design process. Extending the concept of material systems by embedding their material characteristics, geometric behaviour, manufacturing constraints and assembly logics within an integral computational model promotes an understanding of form, material, structure and behaviour not as separate elements, but rather as complex interrelations. This initially requires disentangling a number of aspects that later form part of an integral computational setup in which the system evolves.

First of all, the geometric description of material systems, or rather the notation of particular features of the systems' morphology, needs to be established. The designer needs to facilitate the setup of a computational model not as a particular gestalt specified through a number of coordinates, but rather as a framework of possible formations affording further differentiation that remains coherent with the behaviour observed and extracted from physical experiments and explorations of the relevant system; and to inform the data set in addition to specific spatial characteristics, organisations and constraints. This computational framework, which essentially constitutes an open model but will be referred to as a 'framework' here due to the ambiguous notion of 'model' in a design context, is then step by step informed by a series of additional parameters, restrictions and characteristics inferred from material, fabrication and assembly logics and constraints. Principally this includes the specific material and geometric behaviour in formative processes, the size and shape constraints of involved machinery, the procedural logistics of assembly and the sequences of construction. Here, the far-reaching potential of computer-aided manufacturing (CAM) technologies is evident once they turn into one of the defining factors of a design approach seeking the synthesis of form-generation and materialisation processes. At this point the highly specific restrictions and possibilities of manufacturing hardware and controlling software can become generative drivers embedded in the setup and development of the computational framework.

Generally it can be said that the inclusion of what may be referred to as system-intrinsic characteristics and constraints comprises the first crucial constituent of the computational setup, defined through a series of relevant parameters. The definition of the range within which these parameters can be operated, while remaining coherent with the material, fabrication and construction constraints, is the critical task for the designer at this stage.

Analysis plays a critical role during the entire morphogenetic process, not only in establishing and assessing fitness criteria related to structural and environmental capacity, but also in revealing the system's material and geometric behavioural tendencies.

If effectiveness is defined as the extent to which actual performance compares with targeted performance, the inherent need for analysis and diverse and versatile analytical methods becomes immediately clear. The second crucial constituent of the generative computational framework is therefore recurring evaluation cycles that expose the system to embedded analysis tools. Analysis plays a critical role during the entire morphogenetic process, not only in establishing and assessing fitness criteria related to structural and environmental capacity, but also in revealing the system's material and geometric behavioural tendencies. The conditioning relationship between constraint and capacity in concert with the feedback between stimuli and response are consequently operative elements within the computational framework. In this way evaluation protocols serve to track both the coherency of the generative process with the

aforementioned system-intrinsic constraints, and the system's interaction with a simulated environment. Depending on the system's intended environmental modulation capacity, the morphogenetic development process needs to recurrently interface with appropriate analysis applications, for example, multiphysics computer fluid dynamics (CFD) for the investigation of thermodynamic relations or light and acoustic analysis. However, it is important to note that CFD does always only provide a partial insight into the thermodynamic complexity of the actual environment, which is far greater than any computational model can handle at this moment in time. Nonetheless, as the main objective here lies not solely in the prediction of precise data, but mainly in the recognition of behavioural tendencies and patterns, the instrumental contributions of such tools are significant.

In parallel to the environmental factors, continual structural evaluation informs the development process. However, it is imperative to recognise that the computational framework described here does not at all reproduce a technocratic attitude towards an understanding of efficiency based on a minimal material weight to structural capacity ratio. Nor does it embrace the rationale of what 20th-century engineers called 'building correctly'. Structural behaviour here rather becomes one agent within the multifaceted integration process. Overall this necessitates a shift in conceptualising multicriteria evaluation rather than an efficiency model. Biologists, for example, refer to effectiveness as the result of a developmental process comprising a wide range of criteria. Accordingly the robustness of the resulting systems is as much due to the persistent negotiating of divergent and conflicting requirements as their consequential redundancies.

Evaluating a context-specific, differentiated material and spatial arrangement requires taxonomy on the basis of case-specific criteria, yet not inevitably type defined by gestalt. Each family of design solutions can evolve from a specific feedback between material system and environmental context without prejudiced preselection. It is therefore also of great interest to evaluate design solutions for unanticipated spatial arrangements and ultimately also the ensuing potentials for different modes of habitation. If effectiveness is defined as the ability to generate emergent effects, analysis therefore needs to be both quantitative and qualitative (although this artificial dichotomy often comes into the way of more integral modes of analysis), as well as open to questions not a priori defined at the onset of a design process. Morphogenesis driven by analysis thus requires creativity, intelligence and instrumentality in devising integral analytical methods. This necessitates both further research into the setup and running of integral computational design processes, and developing literacy in deploying these processes as well as gaining a new sensitivity in unfolding their inherent design potential. Architectures will always yield multivaried effects; the question is, however, how far designers are able to inform processes of form-generation with desired and emergent effects and effectiveness.

CONTINUOUS LAMINAE

Aleksandra Jaeschke, Diploma Unit 4 (Michael Hensel and Achim Menges), Architectural Association, London, 2004–05

This research started with an interest in the anisotropy of wood, with its specific fibre-directionality and related response-range to environmental stimuli tested against the specific requirements of the context, a coastal sand dune conservation area in which the shifting of sand dunes is critical. Initially the basic elements were finite-length strips made from layers of laminated veneer; rotating the layers against one another allowed an investigation of different fibre-layouts. Shifting the layers of veneer made possible a continuous lamination process, so as to produce a large assembly without construction gaps. A correlated manufacturing strategy was developed, incorporating the possibility of rotating selected sublocations along their long axis. Replacing the moulds with a nodal support system allowed the laminated components to be clamped at the end points and so made them self-organising; that is, able to find their form within the given constraints during the fabrication process.

Achieving a laminar flow by maintaining curvature continuity between the individual elements results in a continuous multiple load-path system that, together with the anisotropic characteristics of timber, helps to maintain the flexibility and integrity of the overall assembly. Furthermore, while the overall assembly consists of finite lengths of veneer strip, the continuous laminae arrangement does not yield a division into elements. The overall assembly becomes a single element, in which each local dimensional change produced by environmental stimuli affects the system at large.

Relating the systematic use of manufacturing-enabled form-finding to extrinsic influences affects the articulation of the sub-locations and the overall system, and their orientation to the sun path and prevailing wind direction. The resulting surface curvatures and varied levels of system porosity can then be used to modulate airflow and related ranges of sand deposition, as well as exposure to sunlight. The overall flexibility of the system – a product of its material elasticity – enables a higher responsiveness to the fluctuations of the wind loads. Several dynamics are thus interrelated: airflow, system deflection and local terrain formation through modulated aggregation, as well as velocity of airflow, airborne sand and abrasion of the material assembly. Ultimately the main concern of this project is the strategic entwining of these time cycles.

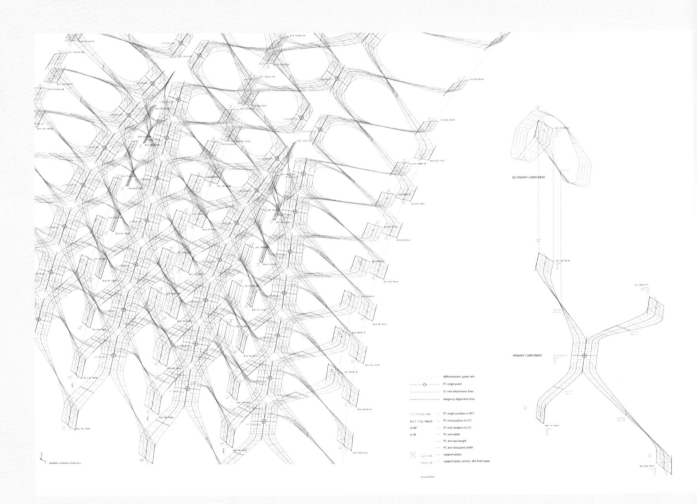

In a larger laminated veneer assembly the insertion points of lamination geometrically vary for each local component. Due to the parametric definition of the component, which embeds the self-forming tendency of the veneer, a range of differentiated morphologies can be produced.

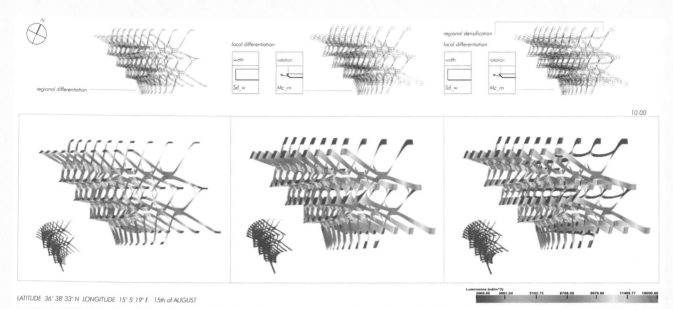

local differentiation

width
Sd_w

rotation
Mc_rn

regional densification
local differentiation

width
Sd_w

rotation
Mc_rn

regional differentiation

10.00

LATITUDE 36° 38' 33" N LONGITUDE 15° 5' 19" E 15th of AUGUST

Luminance (cd/m^2)
3000.00 3881.24 5102.73 6708.55 8678.80 11409.77 15000.00

Three different rapid prototype models produced through selective laser-sintering (top) show the geometric adaptation of a multi-component system in response to particular parametric settings (centre) and the resulting performative capacity of the system interacting with a simulated luminous environment (bottom).

Full-scale prototype manufactured from multiple layers of veneer through processes of continuous lamination.

POROUS CAST

Gabriel Sanchiz Garin, Diploma Unit 4 (Michael Hensel and Achim Menges), Architectural Association, 2005-06

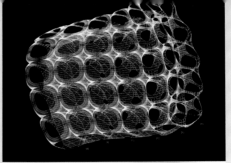

This research was fostered by an interest in the formation process of diatoms and radiolaria. Diatoms are unicellular or colonial algae. The cell is encased by a characteristic and highly differentiated cell wall, which is impregnated with silica. Radiolaria belong to the order of marine planktonic protozoa and feature a central protoplasm comprising a chitinous capsule and siliceous spicules that are perforated by pores. The porous mass of the cell encasements of radiolaria and diatoms delivers an interesting model for differentiated cast walls in architecture that may feature a variety of specific performance capacities.

The initial phase of the material system development focused on producing a skeletal framework articulated through the interstitial spaces left between pressurised containers, so-called pneus. A first series of experiments explored ways of casting plaster between air-filled cushions to achieve the typical shape of the mineralised skeletons between pneus that occurs in nature. Based on different cushion arrangements four-, five- and six-armed configurations were produced and became the basic elements of the material system. Each of these elements is parametrically defined as the relation between pneu organisations and internal pressure by which aspects such as the volume, shape and thickness of each element can be varied. Based on this parametric setup, a series of digital multi-element systems was derived from changing variable inputs. Secondary and tertiary levels of articulation were developed using a series of meso- and micro-pneus to further subdivide the interstitial space between macro-pneumatic cushions. Another series of experiments focused on how it might be possible to gain porosity in the cast form itself.

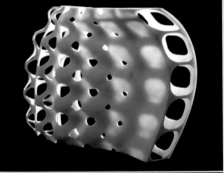

A list of casting materials that feature different thermal characteristics was established. Physical experiments and digital analysis served to establish the possible range of light and airflow modulation relative to morphological features such as the size and density of pores and other characteristics of the material system.

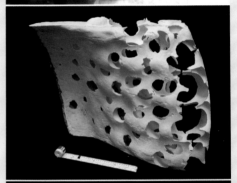

Subsequently a range of manufacturing approaches was tested, resulting in the production of a full-scale prototypical portion of the material system that integrated computer-aided manufacturing processes and pneumatic form-finding as a construction method. A cast form was milled on a 5-axis CNC machine from high-density polystyrene blocks, from which first a fibreglass form and later a cast form from plaster were produced. Air-pressured cushions were distributed into the form and inflated to the defined pressure for each location, and then concrete and other materials were cast into the interstitial spaces between the pneumatic units and the mould.

A second approach focused on strategising a mould that would respond to the casting process and therefore deploy an element of material self-organisation. After several experiments with fabric moulds a rigid frame with an equally rigid back panel was made. The back panel supports an inflatable formwork, with pneus placed between two layers of rubber sheet. The concrete was then cast between the two layers of rubber sheet to fill the space between the pneus. An acrylic inlay in the frame allowed visual control of the casting process and the proper filling of the space between the pneus. The resulting cast is characterised by double-curvature, controlled porosity, and density and mass of the poured material. It can absorb thermal energy and release it to the airflow enabled by the porosity, and the double curvature can be utilised for thermal exposure or self-shading. Moreover, the artificial dichotomy between mass and lightness is brought into an interesting performative synergy.

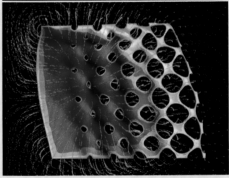

The macro-formwork for casting a parametrically defined prototype structure was milled from a solid high-density Styrofoam block with a 5-axis CNC machine and then equipped with pneumatic cells. The remaining interstitial space was cast with plaster, showing the high-level differentiation and performative capacity previously explored through rapid prototypes and computational fluid dynamics.

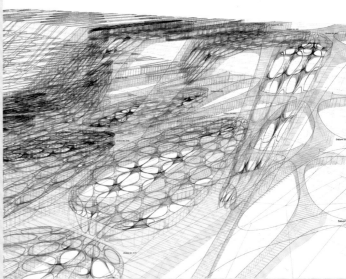

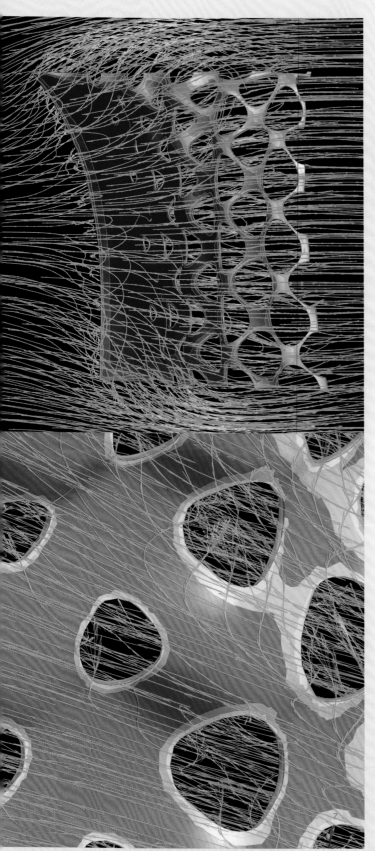

Driven by context-specific information the parametric definition of the system enables an integral setup of the context-specific articulation, responding to a range of performance criteria that include structural, environmental and spatial parameters.

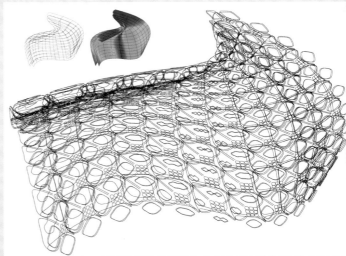

The Porous Cast project is based on manipulation components constituted by the interaction of various pneumatic bodies within a cast system. Through processes of component proliferation and associative adaptation to a mould's shape and curvature, a specific morphology with varying degrees of porosity can be achieved.

The system's performative capacity to modulate airflow through regional (top) and local (bottom) porosity gradation was analysed through computer fluid dynamics modelling.

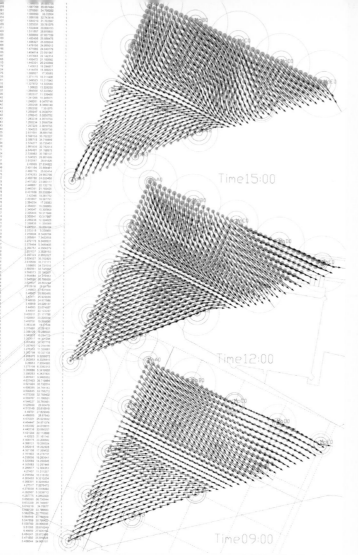

Time15:00

Time12:00

Time09:00

The particular parametric specification of the system is informed by extensive measuring and mapping of thermal, luminous and aeolic conditions across a specific test site. Environmental measurements taken for different times of the day are listed on a data spreadsheet and directly fed into the parametric model.

The parametric components automatically generate associated flat-sheet cutting patterns for laser-cutting processes. For the fabrication and assembly of a scaled prototype, the specific cutting technique of industrial origami allows for flat sheets to be scored from one side only, while making folding possible in both directions.

DIFFERENTIATED SPACE FRAMES

Dae Song Lee, Diploma Unit 4 (Michael Hensel and Achim Menges), Architectural Association, 2005–06

This project examined strategies and methods to incrementally change an assembly from a vector-active to a surface-active structural system. The system has four distinct characteristics: triangular faces of tetrahedrons varied with respect to their porosity; tetrahedral elements that vary in size; hexagonal elements varied in cross-sectional profile thickness relative to structural necessity; or alternatively the multiplication of element layers.

The transition from space-frame to surface morphology offers a range of performative capacities through related changes of porosity. Finite element analysis and computer fluid dynamics analysis were used in order to establish the complex interrelation between the morphology of the system and its structural behaviour and environmental modulation. This process began with basic digital studies that simulated airflow around differently articulated single elements, varying the angles of the faces of the tetrahedrons and the size of aperture in each face, as well as the range of sizes within each element. Configurations consisting of a greater number of differentiated elements were then analysed and the performative capacity of the system documented and notated in a digital protocol. This directly informed subsequent generations of the system in response to a specific climatic and luminous context.

The investigation of geometric-topological articulation and performative capacity was paralleled by an investigation of manufacturing options. Various approaches to unfolding assemblies into flat-sheet patterns for laser cutting were examined and tested in a series of scaled physical models. As a specific cutting technique, an industrial origami method was chosen that allows the flat sheets to be scored from one side only, while folding is possible in both directions. The associative modelling setup was developed so that each assembly was automatically unfolded and laid out for laser- or CNC-cutting. With this manufacturing approach, each profile is hollow unless another material is cast into it in order to increase the self-weight or thermal mass of the element or change subassemblies differentially across the entire system.

Once the issue of cutting and folding had been resolved, the project pursued a second complementary manufacturing strategy in which space-frame-like slender profiles that make up a tetrahedron can be cut as three pieces for each face. This was done to achieve increased self-weight and thermal mass in one production step. Initially elements were cut from Styrofoam and assembled to ensure that the correct cutting angles were defined. Subsequently elements were cut from MDF to produce models for load testing. Physical load tests went hand in hand with digital tests based on the finite element method.

The design was informed by extensive measuring and mapping of thermal, luminous and airflow conditions across a selected test site. Environmental measurements were listed and updated on a data spreadsheet set up to automatically reinterpolate all 20,000 measurement values across the site. This spreadsheet data was linked directly to a map generated within an associative modelling environment. Once the sizes, distribution and orientation of all elements of the material system were established according to the set spatial arrangements, the associative model of the material system could be linked to the mapping setup. This established an instrumental link and a rigorous feedback between material system and environmental conditions. New environmental conditions can now update the design and, in the same way, the environmental impact of the intervention can be visualised, analysed, evaluated and fed back into the design process.

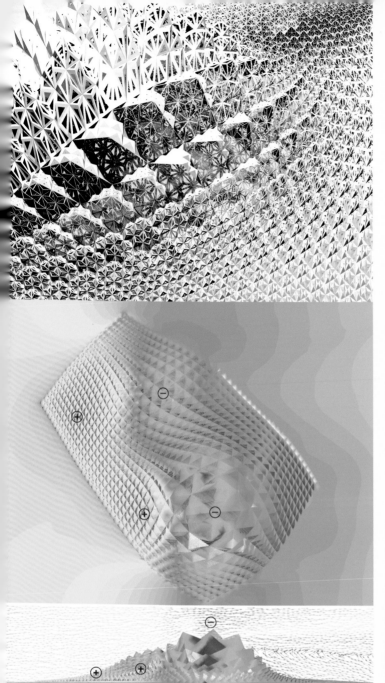

In combination with the analysis of the local component in terms of airflow velocity (top), directional turbulences (centre) and the differential distribution of pressure zones (bottom), a comprehensive data set for further evolutionary steps of the system can be established.

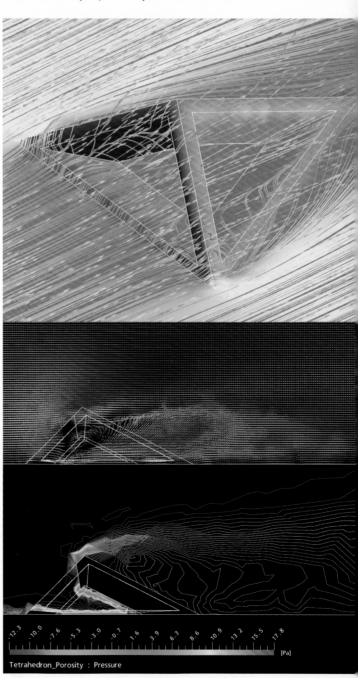

The regional and global articulation (top) is derived through the aerodynamic behaviour of the system tested in computer fluid dynamics. The overall shape emerges according to the particular modulation of high- and low-pressure zones in relation to prevailing wind directions (centre and bottom). ⚙

Tetrahedron_Porosity : Pressure

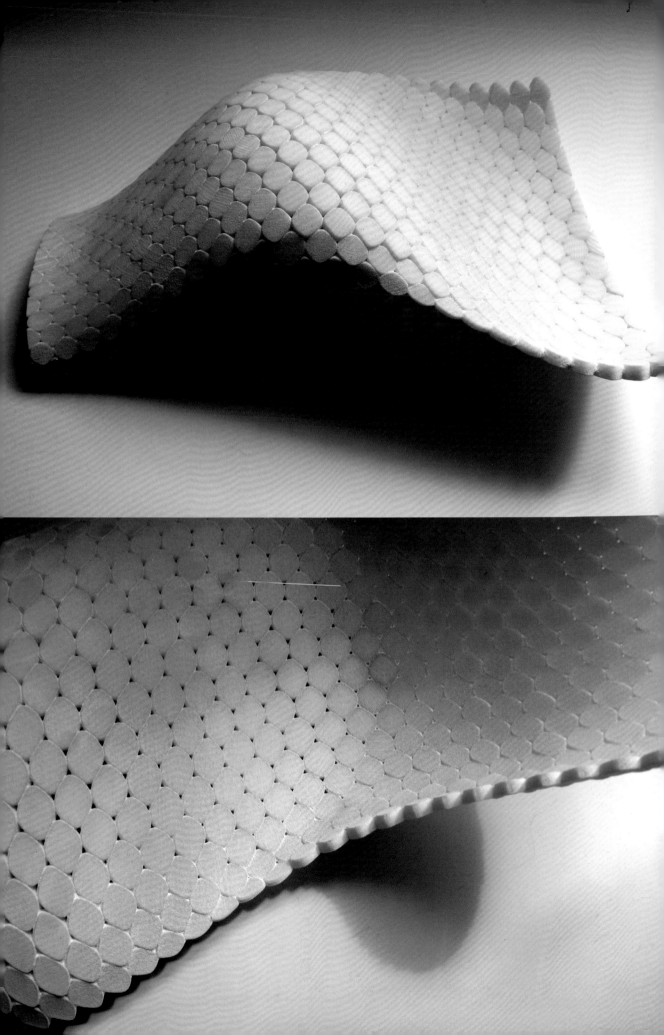

Complex

Brick

Assemblies

Are bricks passé? Or is the contemporary world just failing to realise the innate possibilities of this ancient material? Eladio Dieste once ardently stated that brick is 'a material with unlimited possibilities, almost completely ignored by modern technology.' [1] Dieste's careful inclusion of the word 'almost' here seems to suggest that he suspected some exceptions to the rule – that there may have been some previously untold modern technological dabblings with brick. With this in mind, **Defne Sunguroğlu** acknowledges the innovative uses of brick in the past, and introduces her current research project: Complex Brick Assemblies.

Innovating with Bricks: A Brief History

Bricks are ancient. They have been in use for almost 10,000 years, and so one wonders how they have remained important over such a long period of time, as well as whether there is anything that can still be improved or even innovated with regard to building with bricks. The hypothesis that underlies this inquiry is that the performative capacity of bricks has from the outset been both advanced and feasible. Constant improvements enabled bricks and brick constructions to remain ahead of other types of construction until quite recently, when concrete and steel structures took over, in industrialised contexts, reducing the use of brick more often than not to a form of decorative cladding. Current wisdom has it that constructing with brick in some parts of the world is no longer feasible due to expensive on-site and craft-dependent assembly. While this assessment takes into account resource expenditure in the construction process, it omits a more careful study of the long-term performative gains of brick assemblies. In turn, innovation in the use of brick has become increasingly spare. Nonetheless, some performance-oriented key innovations have taken, and are taking, place that might well usher in a new era of building with brick.

The oldest known bricks were found in southeast Anatolia around 7500 BC. At this time, bricks were shaped by hand and sun-dried. The earliest fired bricks, found in the Middle East, date back to the third millennium BC. Firing bricks at a high temperature hardened them, giving them mechanical strength and making them moisture-proof. The use of brick spread

Defne Sunguroğlu, Complex Brick Assemblies, London, 2006–
Rapid prototyping (selective laser sintering) of selected regions of a complex double-curved brick assembly produced at the Rapid Prototyping Laboratory at the Oslo School of Architecture in collaboration with Professor Steinar Killi. The models confirm the correct geometric definition of the parametric associative model, and enable analysis of the way in which the double-curved surface geometry and porosity modulate the luminous environment.

Eladio Dieste, ADF Wool Warehouse, Juanicó, Uruguay, 1994
Dieste's Gaussian vaults deliver a succinct appearance to the exterior of his designs (top), while resulting in spaces of extraordinary beauty and well-regulated light conditions in the interior (bottom).

from the Middle East and by the beginning of the second millennium AD it was abundant across Europe and Asia. One of the reasons for the success of bricks lies in their format and assembly logic: being small and light they can be picked up by a worker using one hand, while using the trowel with the other. Other typical advantages include high mechanical resistance at a comparatively low cost and passive regulation of environmental humidity; they are lighter in weight and have a smaller elasticity component than concrete, yielding greater adaptability to strain; they also have a long lifespan, good thermal and acoustic performance, good fire resistance and, finally, they are low cost relative to their overall performative capacity. However, while the importance of brick remains undiminished in some parts of the world due to cheap production costs, the brick industry in Western countries finds itself under threat, mostly due to the increasing costs of specialised labour, of being replaced by other industries. Thus brick is now often confined to the outer layer of building envelopes as a decorative measure. So what is the potential of bricks in general and, furthermore, what might innovating with bricks entail?

Improvements in the characteristics of mortar have had a significant impact on innovations in brick technology and construction, creating great potential for design. In order to achieve high performative capacity, bricks as a material system need to be supplemented and augmented with additional materials. Bricks could be laid dry, yet early in the history of brick construction it became apparent that it was better to bond them to improve structural performance, while compensating for tolerances in brick dimensions due to moisture loss in drying or firing. The ancient Egyptians used

mud to bond bricks, and the Mesopotamians used bitumen, while the Romans invented a mortar consisting of sand, cement and water. However, the most significant improvement was prompted in 1824 when Joseph Aspdin patented 'An Improvement in the Mode of Producing An Artificial Stone' (BP 5022), the so-called Portland cement developed from hydraulic limes. It is his son, William Aspdin, however, who is credited with having manufactured the first 'modern' Portland cement. It swiftly became the most common type of cement and the basic ingredient of mortar and concrete due the speed with which it can achieve high strength. It sets in approximately six hours and after 24 hours displays a compressive strength of 8 MPa, and 41 MPa after three months. Besides this impressive structural capacity, it also offers good fire-resistance.

The greater strength of brick structures made possible by mortar that used modern cement was first recognised by the architect and builder Rafael Guastavino, a contemporary of another brick virtuoso, Antoni Gaudí. Guastavino combined this strength with principles deduced from Catalan vaults to develop a new method of constructing with brick. As Jaume Rossell points out, 'It was Guastavino's foresight to associate flat brick masonry with modern cement' that made it possible to combine easy assembly of large-span brick vaults with great structural strength only a few hours after actual assembly.[2] Guastavino categorised two types of masonry structures: the

The Cobogó is a facade element that is assembled into a screenwall thus providing ventilation and shading. One of its most radical applications can be seen in Recife in Brazil, in the application of a second building envelope constructed around an existing building, the Luciano Costa House, an eclectic building from the 1910s that was redesigned in 1959 by the architect Delfim Amorim.

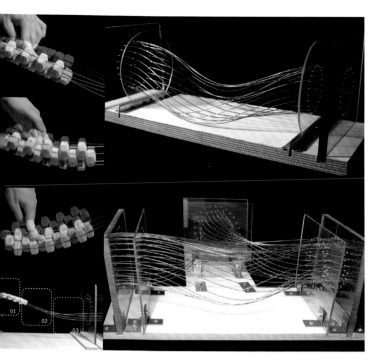

Defne Sunguroğlu, Complex Brick Assemblies, London, 2006–
Empirical physical modelling served to deduce the parameterisation of slender rods under torsional buckling, using them as the means by which to induce prestressing into a complex double-curved brick assembly. The tests included experiments with slender rods and brick-like elements (left), and the instrumental setup for inducing and measuring torsional buckling of slender rods (right).

traditional one that yields structural resistance from self-weight, such as freestanding arches, and 'cohesive systems'. He manifested the latter in the Guastavino tile, patented in 1885, a specific construction technique that deploys standardised terracotta tiles in layers bonded with Portland cement, resulting in very thin self-supporting arches and vaults.

Eladio Dieste, the ingenious Uruguayan engineer, developed ways of constructing with bricks of equal elegance and thinness, which he named *Cerámica Armada*, or reinforced ceramics. Relying entirely on his advanced knowledge of mathematics and physics, Dieste never built any prototypes to test his daring ideas for brick structures. Dependent on mathematical models and proof alone, he embarked on the design, detailing and construction, positing that 'the resistant virtues of the structure that we make depend on their form; it is through their form that they are stable and not because of an awkward accumulation of materials.'[3] Dieste used brick extensively due to the local abundance of the material and the craftsmanship of skilled bricklayers in Uruguay. However, as he introduced prestressing methods he also needed to train his foreman in this new technology. Moreover, he had to invent and fabricate prestressing equipment, which was otherwise not available. His main legacy, though, is the freestanding shells and Gaussian vaults masonry systems.

The evolutionary stages in the development of the freestanding shells include barrel vaults, which deploy reinforcement and prestressing. The cross-section works in compression and prestressing cables run outside the surface from one side of the cross-section to the other, thus fixing the distance between the two sides. Freestanding vaults are also reinforced and prestressed; they utilise arch action in the cross-section and deploy prestressing within the shell by means of a steel mesh within the final layer of screed to avoid flexural tensile stresses on the longitudinal section. Gaussian vaults are characterised by cross-sections that are only one brick deep, prestressed and reinforced. These vaults derive their stiffness and resistance to buckling from a double-curvature catenary arch. In masonry structures, bricks are usually laid in one of two ways: either on edge (freestanding arches) or flat. Dieste used the latter, but modified the section to work for this system.

Depending on the required structural performance and geometry, bricks were either factory produced or handmade by local brick manufacturers, as economy of means and tight project budgets were decisive factors. To further reduce construction costs, Dieste invented movable formwork for repetitive use, as the arches and vaults were constructed sequentially. The architectural qualities of the curved and double-curved brick structures of Dieste are the unique spatiality and light conditions they yield, which are astonishingly beautiful and environmentally work very well, as is evident from his best-known projects, the Church of Jesus Christ the Worker in Atlántida and the J Herrera Y Obes Warehouse in Montevideo harbour, both in Uruguay. Interestingly, the double-curved surfaces echo the use of domes in historical Islamic and Ottoman architecture to provide self-shading for exposed surfaces, and use prevailing wind directions to reduce thermal impact. In this way Dieste's work is truly multiperformative.

Besides being used for structural purposes, brick has been widely used for environmental and spatial performance, for instance for thick walls that provide thermal mass, fire resistance, and so on. But in hot climates its use also began to emulate the screenwalls found in historic Islamic, Arabic and Indian contexts. Noteworthy here is the Cobogó, a contemporary facade element usually made from ceramics or concrete and assembled into a screenwall that provides environmental modulation, such as ventilation and shading, and at the same time regulates visual access. The name of this element is an acronym derived from the names of Coimbra, Boeckmann and Góis, the Brazilian architects and engineers who invented it during the first half of the 20th century. The Cobogó was popularised in Brazilian Modernism first and foremost by Lucio Costa, famous for his plan for Brasília, in projects like Parque Guinle in Rio de Janeiro in 1948. However, one of the most radical applications of the Cobogó is found in Recife in Brazil, in the application of a second building envelope constructed around an existing building.

The Luciano Costa House, an eclectic building triangular in plan and dating from the 1910s, was in dire need of restoration in the 1950s and received a makeover by the architect Delfim

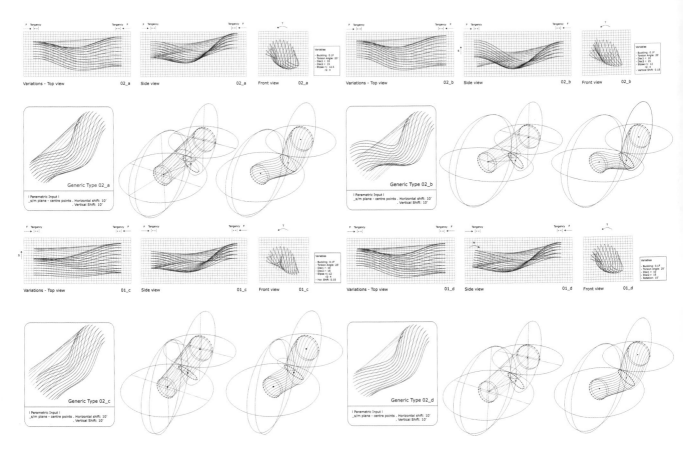

Parametric definition and digital modelling of the slender rods in different torsional buckling modes, examining different arrangements of rods and the amount of force induced.

Amorim in 1959. This included a new perimeter envelope made from a concrete framework with ceramic Cobogó infill. The aim was to provide affordable protection for the building behind the new screen and to use the perimeter envelope for additional environmental modulation. The porous perimeter envelope provides ventilation and shading, and has also resulted in the most idiosyncratic modern building in Recife, so much so that the architectural community stands divided as to whether the house should be restored to its initial eclectic style or whether the Modernist perimeter envelope should be restored. At present it looks as though parts of the eclectic facade will once again be exposed, with parts of the Modernist intervention remaining as well. Whatever the solution, this example helped demonstrate the potential of a perforated perimeter and layered threshold arrangement, with emphasis on the performative capacity of the sum of the interventions that make up buildings.

Innovating with Bricks: An Outlook
Is it possible to combine the structural capacity of double-curved structural brick surfaces with the environmental performance of perforated brick screens, like the Cobogó, for use in hot climates, or to deploy smaller pore sizes and layering of brick surfaces for moderate climates? A solution might be approached in several ways: first by employing and developing double-curved brick surfaces, like those of Eladio Dieste, with perforated bricks; second by using Guastavino's technique of layering terracotta tiles so that openings remain at specific intervals, by drilling through the finished surface without losing the structural strength; and third by omitting mortar and defining the brick geometry so that openings occur between the bricks. The first two approaches may reduce brick's capacity to cope with compressive stresses, while the third will require a reduction in tolerances in the brick geometry, so that brick faces meet in a controlled way to transmit compressive stresses. The research project entitled Complex Brick Assemblies carried out by the author, which commenced in 2006, pursues the third approach, choosing prestressing strategies and double curvature to achieve structural capacity.

In order to enable structural capacity of a brick assembly without mortar it is necessary to use prestressing methods to achieve structurally stable double-curvature surfaces. The project began with an examination of the effects of prestressing with bending rods to achieve double-curved surfaces with synclastic and anticlastic curvature, and pretensioning with cable-nets to achieve anticlastic surface curvature. An initial set of physical experiments examined the behaviour of slender rods under rotational displacement, inducing torsional buckling, to suggest possible ways of prestressing a brick

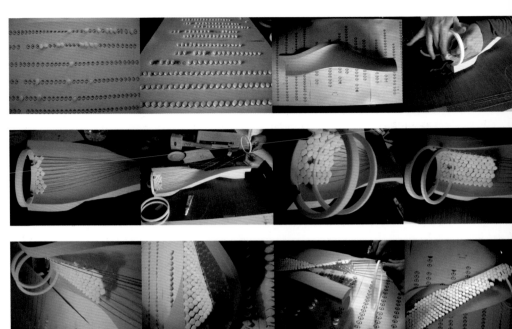

Preparation of a functional model at scale 1:20 to investigate specific assembly methods, induced displacement of the slender rods in buckling once bricks are incrementally added, and the overall behaviour of the assembly . A complex double-curved arrangement was chosen that comprises both positive and negative Gaussian curvature. A formwork was milled on a 5-axis CNC-router and bricks were rapid prototyped (selective laser sintering). The slender rods were fixed at the end positions and the bricks incrementally assembled. In this process the rods undergo torsional buckling and the bricks receive compressive stress. In this way the system self-organises and self-stabilises, reducing the need for a full formwork during the assembly process.

assembly of varied Gaussian curvature. Geometric variation and analysis facilitated the setup of a first parametric definition of the elastically deformed rods. The next set of experiments aimed at stabilising particular geometric configurations by introducing bricks as compression elements, traversed by rods in the longitudinal direction and by an additional set of perpendicular rods that fix the distances between the longitudinal set of rods. The shape of the brick was determined in order to ensure compression transmission and friction between adjacent bricks. A 5-axis CNC-milling machine was then used to produce a formwork for testing the structural behaviour and stability of different types and distributions of bricks in a scaled functional model. The formwork was given a complex double-curved shape, combining synclastic and anticlastic surface curvature with relatively tight radii, so that the most difficult instances could be investigated within a single model. This experiment showed that a full formwork was not necessary during the assembly process: with the incremental assembly of bricks on to the slender rods, the resultant incremental bending and torsion in the rods assumed the final form due to the specific geometry of the bricks and the consequential equilibrium between pre-stressing and compression. In parallel with this investigation, the finite element method was used to digitally analyse the stress patterns occurring in the bricks upon prestressing and further loading, in order to ensure that the areas of compression transmission were correctly placed, shaped and sized.

The second line of inquiry focused on pretensioning as a way of stabilising a double-curved brick assembly without the use of mortar, deploying hyperbolic-paraboloid surface geometry. The hyperbolic-paraboloid surface acts as an arch in compression between the two corners that meet the ground datum, and as cantilevers in the axis of the two raised corners. Pretensioning is achieved by means of a cable-net, in the first generation model, with cables running perpendicular to the edge of the surface. A 1:10 scale functional model served to develop both prestressing and brick assembly strategies, where the cable-net was also used as the formwork to lay the brick elements. A 1:5 prototype of this version is currently in development.

Environmental performance analysis for both sets of structural solutions focused on the filtering of light and modulation of airflow resulting from the gaps between bricks, as well as the thermal behaviour of the brick surface. With knowledge of the stress pattern of bricks in each region of the assembly, it is possible to reduce the brick shape to the minimum necessary for transmitting load while allowing for a certain range of possible gap sizes, from zero to the maximum opening that can still facilitate sufficient load transmission. Thermal behaviour is directly related to this manipulation: presence or absence of material also implies presence or absence of thermal mass. However, two additional variables can be introduced here: the porosity of the material itself, and the amount of air trapped within the material. The

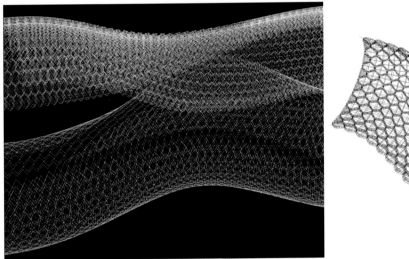

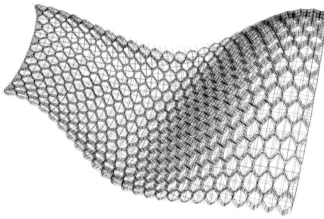

Parametrically defined digital models of double-curved brick asemblies.

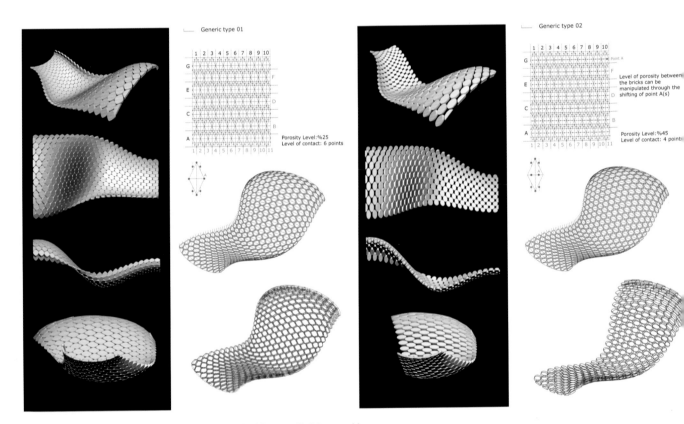

Generic type 01

Porosity Level:%25
Level of contact: 6 points

Generic type 02

Level of porosity between
the bricks can be
manipulated through the
shifting of point A(s)

Porosity Level:%45
Level of contact: 4 points

Parametrically defined and varied digital model of a double-curved brick assembly.

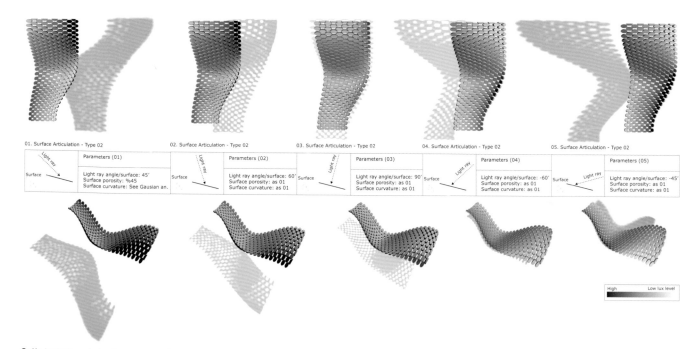

01. Surface Articulation - Type 02		02. Surface Articulation - Type 02		03. Surface Articulation - Type 02		04. Surface Articulation - Type 02		05. Surface Articulation - Type 02	
Parameters (01)		Parameters (02)		Parameters (03)		Parameters (04)		Parameters (05)	
Light ray angle/surface: 45' Surface porosity: %45 Surface curvature: See Gausian an.		Light ray angle/surface: 60' Surface porosity: as 01 Surface curvature: as 01		Light ray angle/surface: 90' Surface porosity: as 01 Surface curvature: as 01		Light ray angle/surface: -60' Surface porosity: as 01 Surface curvature: as 01		Light ray angle/surface: -45' Surface porosity: as 01 Surface curvature: as 01	

High   Low lux level

Self-shading and shading pattern of a specific double-curved and porous brick surface at five different times on 21 June at a specific location. This type of analysis enables context-specific articulations of material assemblies that accomplish the desired range of environmental modulation.

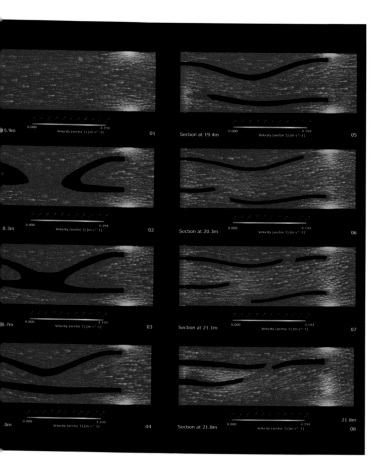

Fluid dynamics analysis of overall surface curvatures, investigating aerodynamic behaviour for the purpose of passive cooling in a hot and humid environment.

former influences the thermal exchange between the two sides of the material, while the latter determines its insulation capacity or thermal energy transmission from one side of the material to the other. On the whole, the use of the double curvature is twofold: curvature yields structural capacity and curvature helps orient surface area towards or away from environmental impact, so as to gain thermal energy or to self-shade, to accelerate or break airflow, and to increase or decrease light and visual penetration.

There are certain questions to be asked regarding the exact material make-up of the brick and its manufacturing to required tolerances. The first might benefit from research into natural systems, such as is conducted in the field of biomimetic engineering. The second question addresses current and projected advancements in brick manufacturing methods and technologies. Bricks are made up of clay and water and are anisotropic: their material has directionality. This directionality is due to air channels that are trapped within the material as a result of the fabrication methods, such as extrusion or throwing. The porosity level of the brick depends on the size of grain that makes up the material and the firing process. Current research within the field of mineralised crystal or ceramic material structures includes porous materials with regard to pillaring reactions. The latter greatly improve the diversity of clay catalysts. The technique is used to manipulate the clay microstructure to control pore channels and to engineer the level of porosity within the material. Research into microporous materials serves to develop porous solids whose pore sizes and shapes can be engineered.

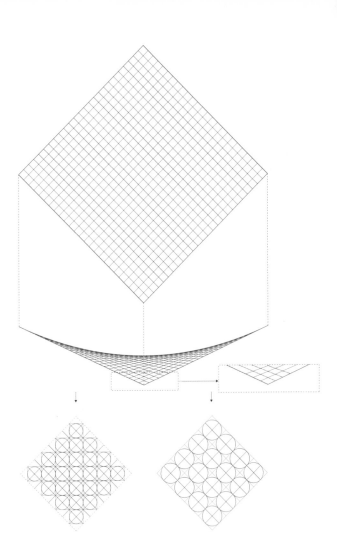

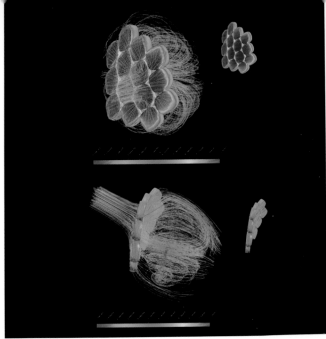

Fluid dynamics analysis of a selected portion of a complex brick assembly, showing airflow perpendicular to the surface and the resulting turbulent flow on the reverse side of the porous surface. The types of airflow that result from the surface curvature, surface porosity and thermal mass can be strategised as passive means of environmental modulation, towards greater environmental sustainability.

Parametric digital model of saddle-shape or hyperbolic-paraboloid pretensioned brick assembly. The model served for the investigation of the repercussion of symmetry on the production of standardised or non-standard bricks, as well as for the fabrication of a prototype in 1:10 scale.

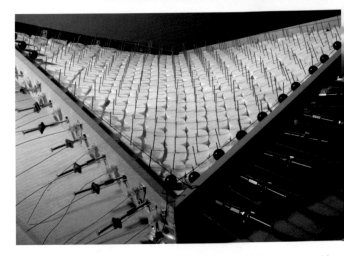

Plan view of the digital model of the 1:10 prototype of a hyperbolic-paraboloid brick assembly showing the anticipated stress distribution within the system.

A functional prototype scale 1:10 of a hyperbolic-paraboloid brick assembly enabled the investigation of different cable-net arrangements for pretensioning the assembly to obtain structural equilibrium. The bricks were laser-sintered at the Rapid Prototyping Laboratory at the Oslo School of Architecture in collaboration with Professor Steinar Killi.

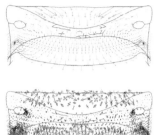

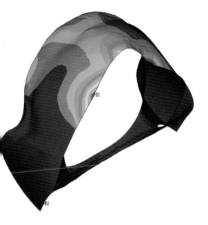

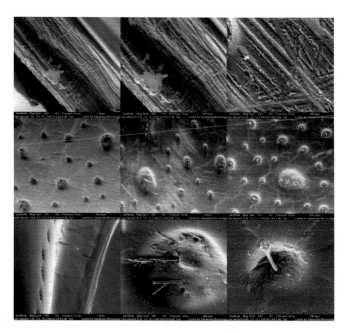

Defne Sunguroğlu and Karola Dierichs, Structural Behaviour and Material Make-up of an Abdominal Shell of a Lobster, London, 2007
An abdominal shell of a lobster was digitally modelled and analysed in terms of its capacity to bear different directional loads. Finite element analysis served to deduce loads and loading directions to be subsequently compared with the intrinsic directional material make-up of the shell segment.

Electron-microscopic imaging of the abdominal shell of a lobster was undertaken in collaboration with Dr Emma Johnson at the Centre of Advanced Microscopy, part of the Centre of Biomimetic Engineering at the University of Reading. The research showed that the shell is a multiphase nano-composite tissue that is organised as a protein-chitin fibre matrix, which also embeds biominerals, mainly calcite. From the electron-microscopic imaging it can be discerned that there are two different types of fibre organisations. Fibres and pore channels are oriented to best cope with the constant mechanical stresses and strains acting on them.

Anisotropy is often seen as disadvantageous, as it results in variable behaviour. If, however, varied performance becomes a central design concern for performance-oriented design, directionality in material may be a tremendous potential and gain. Natural systems display fibre directionality specific to environmental stimuli and forces. A research project conducted by the author with Karola Dierichs and in collaboration with Dr Emma Johnson of the Centre of Biomimetic Engineering at the University of Reading focused on the interrelation between structural capacity and fibre distribution in the abdominal shells of lobsters. It showed that the shell is a multiphase nano-composite tissue that is organised as a protein-chitin fibre matrix, which also embeds biominerals, mainly calcite. This exoskeleton is hard and inelastic. Using electron-microscopic imaging it can be discerned that there are two different types of fibre organisation, parallel as well as the helicoidal arrangement of the protein-chitin matrix. Fibres and pore channels are oriented to best cope with the constant mechanical stresses and strains acting on them. A varied fibre-composite enables continuous variation in structural morphology and topology: a surface can transform seamlessly into a beam or an opening. The insights and future research opportunities that can be deduced from this are that the anisotropic material

make-up and property of bricks could be enhanced to cope more specifically with local stresses in bricks and across regions of brick assemblies, and that the material properties could be varied to yield a greater scope of mechanical and environmental properties.

One issue that still requires extensive research is the high emission and carbon footprint resulting from producing fired brick and Portland cement, although brick can be recycled and is biodegradable. However, given the outstanding performance capacity of the material, investment in this and other areas of research is bound to bring desirable results, as our understanding and utilisation of the performative capacity of complex brick assemblies has only just begun. Yes, bricks are ancient, but they are far from exhausted. △

Notes
1. Exhibition catalogue, *Eladio Dieste: 1943–1996*, Junta de Andalucía, 1996.
2. Salvador Tarragó (ed), *Guastavino Co. (1885–1962): Catalogue of Works in Catalonia and America*, COAC – Collegi d'Arquitectes de Catalunya, ACTAR (Barcelona), 2002.
3. Remo Pedreschi, *Eladio Dieste: The Engineer's Contribution to Contemporary Architecture*, RIBA Publications, Thomas Telford (London), 2000.

Membrane Spaces

Membrane structures are becoming increasingly popular in architectural design. This is exemplified by mechanically pretensioned systems, such as Foster + Partner's roof for Dresden Station and even by large-scale art installations, such as Anish Kapoor's *Tarantantara* or *MARSYAS*; and also by pneumatically pretensioned systems, such as Herzog & de Meuron's Allianz Arena in Munich or PTW's Watercube in Beijing. But how might membrane systems and their performative potential be developed further? Here, **Michael Hensel** and **Achim Menges** discuss the findings of a series of membrane-research studios that they conducted at the Architectural Association in London and the Rotterdam Academy of Architecture and Urban Design.

Building with membranes is emerging from the shadow of the early pioneering achievements. Several decades of practical experience have led to a technology that is future oriented and that deserves to be more widely established.

Klaus-Michael Koch, *Membrane Structures*, 2004[1]

A membrane is a thin, synthetic or natural, pliable material that constitutes the lightest material means for spatial organisation and environmental modulation. Membranes therefore have great potential to be used in circumstances in which lightweight solutions to spatial arrangement and environmental performance are required. Structurally membranes belong to form-active tension systems: they transmit only tensile forces, shape according to the applied forces into minimal surfaces, and more specifically double-curved anticlastic or saddle-shape surfaces, and register manipulations throughout the entire system. In order for a membrane to be in tension and thus structurally active, there needs to be equilibrium of tensile forces throughout the system: if this is not the case, the membrane will typically show flat or wrinkled regions. This implies that the membrane's shape and extent must be established as part of the solution, and specifically that membrane systems must be form-found, utilising the self-organisational behaviour of membranes under extrinsic influences such as by applying tensile forces, and by constraining the membrane via specifically chosen control points. In these points the tensile forces are collected and transmitted. Membranes are therefore defined through the displacement of particular boundary points and the pre-tensioning forces, which are directly correlated with the material form. The form of a membrane can thus be found as the state of equilibrium of internal resistances and external forces.

Techniques for physically form-finding form-active tension systems have been developed by Frei Otto and his collaborators at the Institute of Lightweight Structures in Stuttgart for the task of the optimisation of lightweight structures. Today form-finding processes include both physical form-finding models and digital modelling by means of dynamic relaxation. Dynamic relaxation is a finite element method involving a digital mesh that settles into an equilibrium state through iterative calculations based on the specific elasticity and material properties of the membrane, combined with the designation of boundary points and related forces.

Form-finding as a design method can now be extended beyond single optimisation and can begin to facilitate the design of more complex performative arrangements. Complex arrangements can acquire hierarchies of articulation, for instance in combination with other systems, such as cable-nets with arrays of membranes set within, leading to multiple-hierarchy form-finding. The combination of several performance criteria into a form-finding process introduces the second crucial extension to traditional form-finding techniques: multiple-objective form-finding. The combination of the two contributions is then multiple-objective form-finding across multiple hierarchies that define a complex system. Membrane systems are particularly suited for teaching and research purposes in this line of inquiry, since their inherent logic is easily comprehended, both on an intuitive and an intellectual level. Moreover, the use of membrane systems in densely built-up areas is immense due

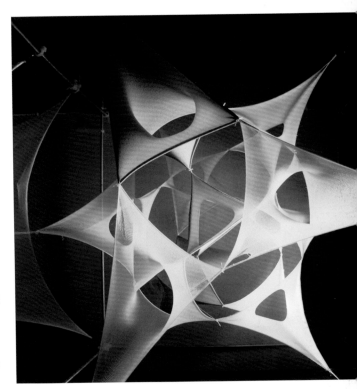

Ralph Doggen, Membrane Spaces GPA 02 Studio, 2005
The physical form-finding model of a complex membrane arrangement based on triangular cutting patterns with minimal holes.

to the lightness of the system. In today's context of sparse resources in hot climates, urban heat islands and general global-warming, membrane systems might serve as a first inroad to remedy some of the worst problems. It is with this in mind that we pursued our research into membrane systems. Following are four projects selected from the research undertaken in the 'Membrane Spaces' studios.

Note
1. Klaus-Michael Koch, *Membrane Structures*, Prestel (Munich, Berlin, London and New York), 2004, p 8.

Ralph Doggen, Membrane Spaces GPA 02 Studio (Michael Hensel and Achim Menges), Rotterdam Academy of Architecture and Urban Design, The Netherlands, 2005
The physical form-finding model of a complex membrane arrangement based on four-sided membrane components settling into the saddle-shape hyperbolic paraboloids (hypars).

MEMBRANE INTERCONNECTION

Rene Toet, Membrane Spaces GPA 02 Studio (Michael Hensel and Achim Menges), Rotterdam Academy of Architecture and Urban Design, The Netherlands, 2005

The research focused on achieving membrane systems with a complex geometric surface articulation created by connecting the membrane with itself, implying increased membrane articulation without increased connections to compression elements. This alternative approach is of particular interest for contexts that do not offer many attachment points for membrane systems, for instance between existing buildings that do not have the structural capacity to receive tensile loads.

The research commenced with a set of experiments that investigated different cutting patterns for membrane patches and the way in which different patches can be connected by means of minimal holes, V-shaped cuts that provide an additional control point at the end of the resulting flap. The introduction of minimal holes makes it possible to achieve more definition, with the membrane being connected to itself rather than to the external frame. It is also possible to nest smaller minimal holes within larger ones. This approach enables the integration of self-similar manipulations of the form-active tension system which helps, in turn, to achieve varying degrees of permeability of the membrane and exposure of the spaces beyond it. Membranes can either be connected by joining the flaps of minimal holes or by directly sewing and welding membranes to each other. Both aspects are defined by the cutting pattern of membranes and their form-found geometry.

A second set of experiments focused on connecting membrane patches by sewing them together in a continuous strip and investigating the possibility of directional changes of the membrane in tension. This resulted in the articulation of a larger system consisting of 14 patches that were strategically connected and pretensioned according to a digitally defined protocol. The resulting membrane morphology indicates the possibility of arriving at variable degrees of enclosure and visual control through multiplication of the boundary threshold, or greater levels of porosity by means of introducing more minimal holes.

The physical form-finding of eight different membrane component and connection types (eight columns of four images each, from left to right and top to bottom) indicates different component proliferation possibilities.

Dynamic relaxation processes enable the digital form-finding of membrane morphologies.

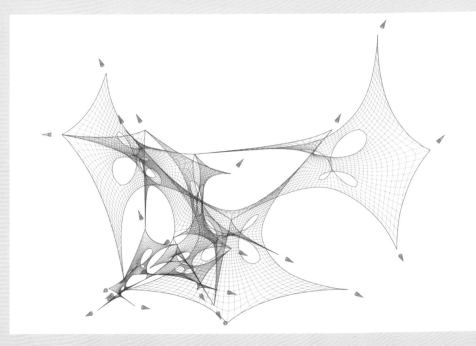

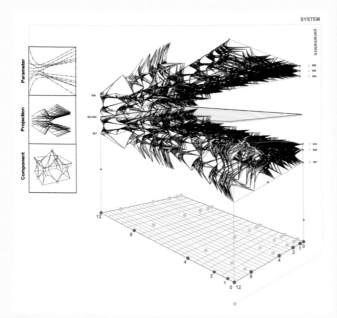

A parametric framework enables the definition, rapid generation and evaluation of various local and overall system configurations exploring varying degrees of porosity and related performative capacities.

Digital proliferation tests indicate the adaptation of each dynamically relaxed membrane component within a larger parametric framework defined in an associative modelling application.

MEMBRANE ARRAYS

Pavlos Sideris, Diploma Unit 4 (Michael Hensel and Achim Menges), Architectural Association, London, 2005–06

This research combines two form-active tension systems in an integral manner: a layered cable-net arrangement and an array of membrane patches suspended between the layers of the cable-net. Both systems derive their specific articulation in space through applying tension and, more specifically, the distribution of bearing points and the direction of the tension force applied. Since the specific articulation of the membrane patches is dependent on the way they are suspended between the layers of the cable-net, it can be said that the overall assembly consists of two hierarchically related systems.

Combining the two systems into a complex field of arrayed membranes enables careful environmental modulation beyond the capacity of the typical large membrane roof. Arraying smaller membrane patches reduces horizontal wind loads and the local acceleration or deceleration of airflow. Likewise it also serves to achieve differentiated patterns of shading and self-shading. Physical and digital form-finding go hand in hand in the design process.

Once the interaction between cable-net and arrayed membrane patches is established in a series of physical tests, it is possible to elaborate the differentiated assembly through continuous variation in a parametric associative modelling environment, utilising a dynamic relaxation function that through an iterative mathematical process approaches the minimal surface geometry of form-active tension systems. The output of this process was subsequently evaluated and ranked through advanced digital analysis (computer fluid dynamics) with regard to the modulation of airflow. Specific instances of the system articulation were then tested through a series of scaled prototypes, culminating in a full-scale assembly at the Architectural Association.

Full-scale prototype of a performative membrane organisation constructed for the 'AA Projects Review Exhibition', 2006.

LAYERED MEMBRANES AND ARRAYED MEMBRANE FEATURES

Kazutaka Fuji, LMU Diploma Unit 9 (Michael Hensel, Daniel Coll I Capdevila and Mattia Gambardella), London Metropolitan University, 2006–07

The research focused on the possibility to span continuous membranes between layers of metal grid that serve as a frame, while introducing cuts and minimal holes as an array of features that articulates the membrane geometry and therefore its performance on a local scale.

Thus, while the frame is entirely generic the membrane layers spanned between the layers of metal grid begin to acquire a high degree of differentiation through the location and size of minimal hole and varying distance between the membrane layers. Two performance criteria informed the elaboration of the system: airflow and sunlight. The latter concerned the way in which light and shadow patterns are distributed on the various layers of the membranes and the space and surfaces beyond the assembly. The orientation of the membrane assembly to the sun path and the prevailing wind direction is therefore crucial. Extensive physical tests and the construction of full-scale prototypes were conducted to map the shadow pattern and airflow conditions relative to the degree of exposure, rotating the assembly relative to the direction of the environmental input and mapping the resulting conditions. This made it possible to relate the distribution of the bearing points of the membrane and the direction of tension force applied to the membrane and the minimal holes to the specifically resultant conditions with regards to airflow, light and [self-]shading pattern. Through simple modifications of the material system it was possible to achieve and regulate an extremely fine grading of effects.

The performative capacity of the membrane field to modulate the transmission of light tested with a full-scale prototype.

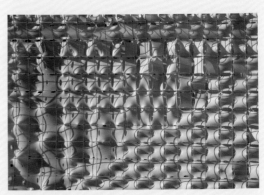

Study of the differentiated modulation of light and shadow on the surface of the membrane field.

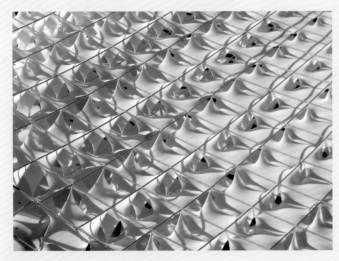

A field of differentiated membrane components constructed within a grid framework.

A large number of tests were conducted to catalogue the relationship between the definition of tying patterns and the related shadow cast.

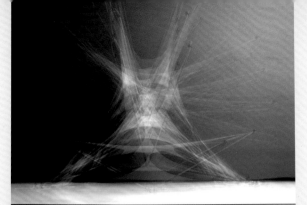

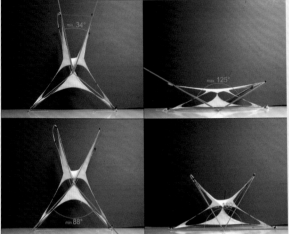

The membrane component assembled from membrane patches and frame elements provides for a number of adjustments within a defined range of possible reconfiguration geometry.

MEMBRANE FRAME KINETICS

Jaap Baselmans, Membrane Spaces GPA 02 Studio (Michael Hensel and Achim Menges), Rotterdam Academy of Architecture and Urban Design, 2005

Although form-finding methods use elastic membranes, membranes with low elasticity are used for full-scale constructions. Low-elasticity membranes are pretensioned, much like a drum skin, in order to be able to bear loads. If, however, the requirements were such that elastic membranes could be used it would be possible to change their configurations into multiple stable states. In other words, elastic membranes are shape adaptable for as long as they are shaped by equal tension into minimal surfaces when the bearing points are displaced. This would introduce form-active systems to a full construction scale.

In order to pursue this possibility, a set of initial experiments was aimed at establishing membrane and frame relations in which a multitude of stable states can be achieved. Subsequent experiments involved the frame in the kinetic setup. The frame, too, became reconfigurable, with the degree and direction of movability being informed by the vectors of displacement of the bearing points of the membranes. Calibrating the movement of membrane and frame so that equal tension was retained in all membrane patches included establishing the relationship between the membrane boundary points on the frame, the locations of the joints and the axes and extent of rotational movement. Once this was accomplished it was possible to model these relationships in an associative parametric modelling environment and to digitally analyse the performative capacity of different stable states. A scaled prototype for an adaptable membrane canopy concluded the research.

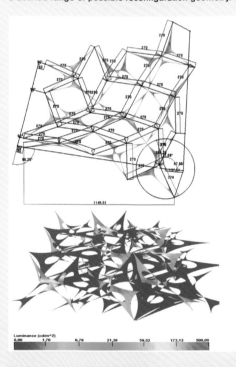

Luminance (cd/m^2)
0,00   1,70   6,78   21,38   59,52   173,13   500,00

The location and relationship between pin joints and members of the adjustable framework are modelled in constraint-solving software (top). This allows for testing various possible configurations and, after the digital membrane relaxation (in red), investigating related performative capacities of the membrane system (bottom). △

A digital membrane component set up through combined processes of digital dynamic relaxation and parametric modelling. The geometric constraints of the component are derived through the mapping of possible adjustment ranges of the related physical model.

Aggregates

In their bound form, aggregates are by far the most ubiquitous materials in architectural construction. However, there are few precedents for using loose aggregates in any significant way, despite their ability to swiftly interact with a given environment. Michael Hensel and Achim Menges argue for a better understanding of the behaviour of such materials in order that they can be used in their loose form. Aggregates are formed not through the connection of elements with joints or a binding matrix, but through the loose accumulation of separate elements. This approach therefore requires a radical departure from architectural design based on assemblies and assembly processes.

Aggregates are loosely compacted masses of particles or granules that are in contact. Particles aggregate into heaps under the influence of extrinsic influences such as gravity and wind, and develop as a state of equilibrium between dead weight and internal friction resistances.

The building industry makes use of aggregates as materials for construction, mainly in their bound state with cement to form concrete, bitumen to form asphalt, or aggregate filling for composite materials. This utilisation of aggregates has a long history; for instance, the use of loose aggregates as an essential ingredient of mortar, consisting of sand cement and water, dates back to Roman times. There are a few interesting exceptions, such as the use of sand hydraulics, used by the ancient Egyptians for moving very large blocks of stone with great precision. However, in such cases the loose aggregate was exclusively used to facilitate construction processes. Other exceptions include the use of sand beds under the foundations of stone temples as a way of damping the impact of earthquakes, as employed by the ancient Greeks, or the use of aggregates as a loose filling between walls or floor and ceiling panels to absorb vibration and acoustic impact.

The common use of bound aggregates, however, is rooted in a technological history based on imposing shape on material constructs with a high degree of control. Conceiving of aggregates in this way, as shapeless materials to be controlled by elaborate enclosing formwork, disregards their innate capacity of pattern formation according to specific influences and constraints. The greatest potential of aggregates may lie in not assigning such a subordinate role to granular substances, but, instead, in utilising the way in which granular substances shift between liquid and stable states.

Liquefaction, the change from solid to liquid matter and behaviour, is a particularly interesting property of aggregates. While aggregates are composed of solid grains, they are able to display liquid-like behaviour. This characteristic could be their greatest architectural potential: easy (re)shape-ability based on state shifts between temporary equilibriums found by the aggregate itself. When aggregates are bound into solid materials they cannot be reshaped without major energy expenditure, but when they remain loose the flow of air, water, any impact of solid objects, or the pouring of more particles under the influence of gravity leads to immediate formations. A sand pile, or dune, for instance, is a dynamically stable shape as it retains the inclination of its slope during the process of the accumulation of granules. Such systems are non-equilibrium dissipative structures, in which, as Philip Ball describes, 'the spatial scale of the pattern formation bears no

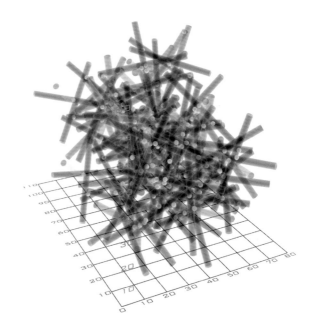

Eichi Matsuda, Designed Particles and Aggregation Strategies 01, Diploma Unit 4, Architectural Association, 2003-04
Computational experiments conducted in a physics simulation environment indicate the distribution of aggregates under the influence of gravity. This simulation enables the tracing of the contact points between the individual aggregate elements as well as their formation tendencies and structural behaviour.

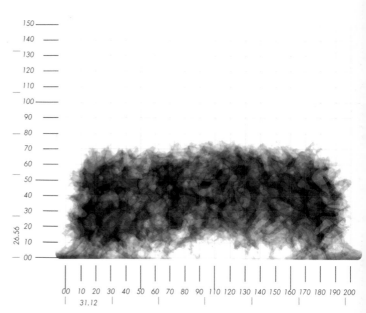

A digital composite-imaging technique allows the density-distribution tendencies across a large number of aggregate experiments conducted using the same setup to be registered.

Full-scale aggregate system exhibited in the 'Modulations' exhibition at Rice School of Architecture, Houston, Texas, 2004.

relation to the size of its constituents',[2] displaying robustness throughout perturbations. Transient disturbances can disrupt dissipative structures momentarily, with sand piles collapsing when a critical threshold is reached, but eventually the same formative pattern will reoccur and the sand pile will start building up again.

The ability of aggregates to 'flow' and to settle into self-stabilising formations that can support themselves and external loads, as well as resist shearing stresses, is of particular interest for the development of an alternative design and construction approach in architecture based on deploying granular behaviour. Equally promising is the particular load-bearing behaviour displayed by granular substances. For example, while in most substances the pressure at the bottom of a column of matter is directly related to its height, the pressure that results from a tall column of sand is independent from its height. Another interesting aspect is the stress distribution below piles of sand, for instance where the stress is minimal below the highest point of the pile. Granular materials are also generally anisotropic; that is, they show variable behaviour in different directions, either due to the mode of deposition or induced by irreversible deformations caused by stresses. Anisotropy resulting from arrangement entails anisotropy of mechanical behaviour. This characteristic can be instrumentalised in designing with aggregates.

The specific load-bearing behaviour, particular mass distribution, spatial organisation, surface textures and granular thresholds are a strong incentive for design research on aggregates.

The specific load-bearing behaviour, particular mass distribution, spatial organisation, surface textures and granular thresholds are a strong incentive for design research on aggregates. However, when dealing with granular substances the focus of the designer must shift from precise control of shape, location and connection of the tectonics elements defined through representational notation systems towards pattern recognition and methods of exploiting particular behavioural tendencies. This requires not only a very different take on the design process, but also different analysis and design tools.

In order to better understand and utilise granular behaviour, current research frequently combines several complementary approaches: experimental analysis by means of material experiments that serve to directly observe granular behaviour; numerical modelling through the discrete element method (DEM) as a means of micromechanical analysis that serves to investigate and model local behaviour of granular behaviour; and numerical modelling through the finite element method to investigate and model boundary problems,[3] combined with computational models that simulate granular dynamics.[4] Not as well known in architectural engineering as finite element analysis, DEM enables the computation of the motion of large numbers of particles and encompasses a number of different methods serving this purpose.

However, there is still scientific controversy over phenomena such as convective flow in granular media and particle size segregation in aggregate accumulations during the fluid state. While aggregate structures of limited size can be computationally modelled, the more immediate and, arguably, more accurate design approach relies strongly on empirical methods and physical testing. Conducting tests for each alteration to critical design parameters, such as element shape and size, emission path, pouring speed and time and so on, enables the designer to establish a catalogue of behavioural tendencies and performative capacities that can then be instrumentalised in the subsequent design process.

Furthermore, no aggregate state can ever be conceived of as final. Instead, what is required is an acceptance of a dynamic of perpetual alteration and regulative measures embedded in the aggregate, boundary conditions and other constraints and influences such as gravity, wind and water as catalysts of change rather than conditions to be resisted. Aggregates may be highly porous or dense depending on the geometry and number of the particles. Environmental modulation, such as airflow or thermal behaviour, can in this way be regulated with great ease. Thus the dynamics of material formation and environmental modulation are interrelated and interdependent. On the whole, this demarcates a decisive shift from design of static arrangements towards reconfigurable and self-organising structures with multiple stable states, transient spatial conditions, variable connectivity and granular, differentially porous thresholds and boundaries. Herein lies the intellectual challenge for designers who wish to explore the potential of loose aggregates.

Notes
1. Philip Ball, *The Self-Made Tapestry: Pattern Formation in Nature*, Oxford University Press (Oxford, New York and Tokyo), 1999, p 199.
2. Ibid, p 203.
3. For detailed elaboration see, for instance, Bernard Cambou, *Behaviour of Granular Materials*, Springer (Vienna and New York), 1998.
4. Thorsten Pöschel and T Schwager, *Computational Granular Dynamics: Models and Algorithms*, Springer (Heidelberg, London and New York), 1999.

Further Reading
Ralph A Bagnold, *The Physics of Blown Sand and Desert Dunes*, Methuen (London), 1954.
Bernard Cambou, *Behaviour of Granular Materials*, Springer (Vienna and New York), 1998.
Jaques Duran, PG de Gennes and A Reisinger, *Sands, Powders and Grains: An Introduction to the Physics of Granular Materials*, Springer (Heidelberg, London and New York), 1999.
RM Nedderman, *Statics and Kinematics of Granular Materials*, Cambridge University Press (Cambridge), 2005.
Thorsten Pöschel and T Schwager, *Computational Granular Dynamics: Models and Algorithms*, Springer (Heidelberg, London and New York), 1999.

Time: 00 sec   Time: 01 sec   Time: 05 sec

The image sequence shows a sand formation under the influence of frequency over a period of 6 seconds (from left to right).

Different periodic sand textures emerge in response to changes in frequency.

PERIODIC TEXTURES: FREQUENCY-INDUCED AGGREGATE FORMATIONS

Karola Dierichs, Emergent Technologies and Design Programme (Michael Hensel, Achim Menges and Michael Weinstock), Architectural Association, 2006–07

In this examination of the formations of aggregates under vibration, different types of aggregates placed on a vibrating plate showed specific patterns depending on the design of the individual aggregate unit, enabling various time-dependent aggregate formations to be developed.

This field of research was initiated by the Swiss physician and natural scientist Hans Jenny (1904–72). Based on the findings of Ernst Chladni (1756–1827) and other researchers, Jenny coined the term 'Cymatics', derived from the Greek word '*ta kymatika*', meaning 'matters pertaining to waves', and explored a wide variety of experimental setups in order to test aggregate behaviour under vibration.

The experiments conducted at the AA were based on the basic setup of Chladni plates, whereby a metal plate covered by sand is excited by sine waves, which results in the sand assembling itself on the so-called nodal lines – the areas of the plate that do not experience deformation under resonance. This basic principle was maintained, but using different kinds of granules. The aggregate material, its absolute size and its size in relation to the exciting wave as well as its aspect ratio were varied in order to test how such parameters affect the behaviour of the aggregate and how specific configurations can be achieved. The variation of the aggregate unit thus leads to different configurations under the same boundary conditions. These formations generally reach a stable state; that is, a distribution on the plate under which the aggregate experiences no further reorganisation. However, the stable states are adjustable; if the exciting frequency changes, the aggregate takes on a new distribution. The formation itself is a time-dependent process that allows the observation of various intermediate states before it reaches its stable point.

A series of experiments indicates the relationship between pouring or draining sand and geometric rules that underlie the sand-pile formations. Variables include the angle of the base surface as well as the amount of sand to be poured or drained, pouring speed, and funnel size and configuration. During the process of pouring or draining. different sand formations emerge.

DEPLOYING NATURAL GRANULES AND AGGREGATION PROCESSES 01

Gen Takahashi, Diploma Unit 4 (Michael Hensel and Achim Menges), Architectural Association, London, 2005–06

Based on the research on natural aggregation undertaken by Frei Otto and his team at the Institute for Lightweight Structures in Stuttgart, and by Ralph A Bagnold on the physics of blown sand and desert dunes, this project examined processes of sand formation for deployment in design. In nature, such processes are observable in dune and ripple formations shaped by airflow and water and, moreover, the interaction between aggregate and environment. Initial experiments focused on sand pouring and draining formations. Variables included the amount of sand, pouring speed, funnel size for pouring or draining, the angle and roughness of the receiving surface, and extrinsic influences such as gravity and airflow. Geometrically differentiated lattice structures were then introduced to study their impact on pattern formation in relation to the inclination, orientation and distance between lattice members and distribution and sizes of openings. Wind-blown sand in part drained through layered lattices resulted in aggregate formations on and below the lattice datum, where sand was captured, resulting in terrains of varied topography and texture, cavernous spaces and different degrees of exposure to extrinsic influences. The orientation of sand formations relative to prevailing wind directions is significant with regard to the further formative process, and the sun path is of importance with regard to thermal performance and self-shading. A desired relationship between aggregate and prevailing wind direction and sun path can inform the placement of specifically articulated lattices and therefore the distribution of specific aggregation patterns. In addition, the closure of drain channels can be achieved locally through small pneumatic cushions that shut off single lattice fields to prevent sand passing through.

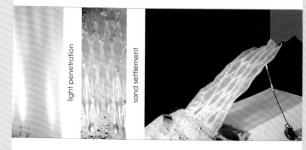

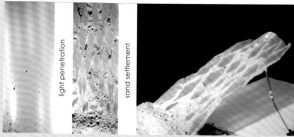

(Image labels, repeated: light penetration / sand settlement)

DEPLOYING NATURAL GRANULES AND AGGREGATION PROCESSES 02

Hani Fallaha, Diploma Unit 4 (Michael Hensel and Achim Menges), Architectural Association, 2003–04

This research delivered a design for a rapidly deployable refugee shelter in a sand desert environment subjected to strong winds. The units consist of low-cost pneumatic assemblies that become functional only in interaction with their environment, utilising wind-blown sand. The sectional articulation of the shelter units is based on aerodynamics, modulating airflow and creating zones of pressure differential to remove sand or deliver it to and from specific areas of the shelter surface, so as to stabilise the units structurally against horizontal wind load by increasing the self-load, and also to achieve thermal mass and shading of the interior. Small sand-collector pockets welded into the leading edges of the pneumatic cushion face the direction of either airflow or slide-off of wind-blown sand deposited on the pneumatic surface of the shelter units. The distribution pattern of the sand-collector pockets serves to modulate thermal mass, solar penetration and visual exposure. The distance between shelter units takes into account sand saltation (the properties of sand movement), and secondary overflow (how far wind-blown sand will carry past an obstacle), so as to establish optimum shelter distances.

Different trapeze-form articulations of pneumatic elements are tested in relation to sand collection under the influence of changing angles of inclination and wind directions. The sand-collection patterns allow for modulating solar penetration and degree of privacy as well as protecting the skin from sandstorms.

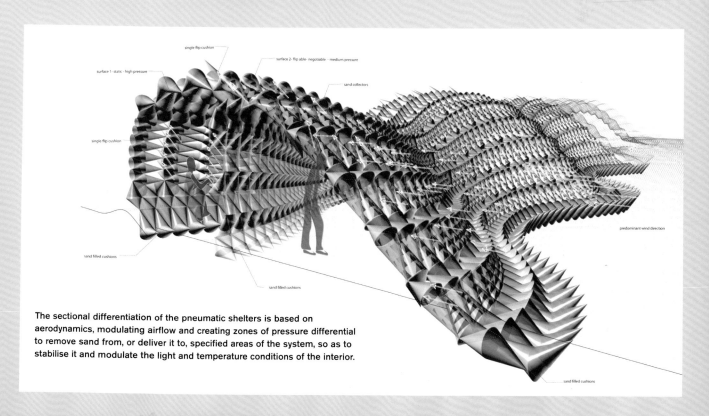

The sectional differentiation of the pneumatic shelters is based on aerodynamics, modulating airflow and creating zones of pressure differential to remove sand from, or deliver it to, specified areas of the system, so as to stabilise it and modulate the light and temperature conditions of the interior.

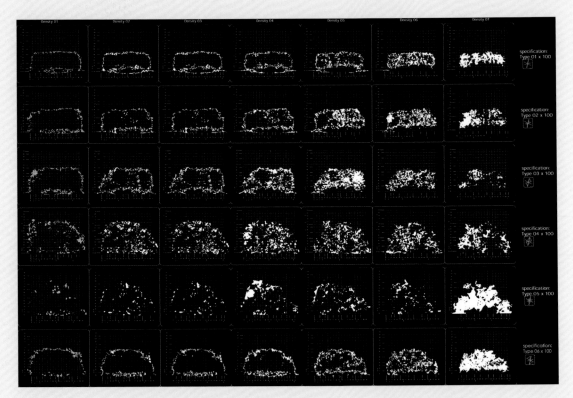

The table shows the distribution of zones of increasing aggregate density (from left to right) for six different aggregate particle types (from top to bottom).

Aggregates have the ability to form a self-supporting structure over a cavity produced by an inflated formwork. This was tested in a series of experiments by pouring designed aggregate elements into a test container filled with a pneu that was subsequently deflated (left). Cavernous spaces emerge as a result of the aggregate's related self-stabilising process (right).

DESIGNED PARTICLES AND AGGREGATION STRATEGIES 01

Eiichi Matsuda, Diploma Unit 4 (Michael Hensel and Achim Menges), Architectural Association, 2003–04

The aim of this study was to design aggregate particles and develop an aggregation process based on their behavioural tendencies in order to discover inherent potentials for spatial arrangements. Ten thousand 3-axial elements were produced and colour-marked in order to make visible aggregation patterns resulting from different aggregation strategies. Initial aggregation experiments were constrained only by a horizontal surface. Variables included the number of elements per experiment, element geometry, pouring speed, pouring height, and the roughness, and thus the degree of friction provided by the horizontal surface. Experiments focused on establishing maximum pile height and footprint for each element geometry before critical mass was reached and the pile collapsed. Also important was the density of elements in each pile. For each experiment the resulting variation in density and porosity of the aggregate was mapped. The constraining surface arrangements were then changed. The next set of experiments introduced inflatable formwork that could be easily removed after the aggregation process set within permanent perimeter constraints. The elements were poured with the formwork inflated. Once the aggregate had settled, the formwork was deflated and the aggregate underwent a secondary cycle of liquefaction, while resettling into the next stable state, resulting in cavernous spaces where the formwork was located. Regulating geometries and size ranges of elements and their pouring sequence helped to enhance the self-stabilisation through the interlocking of elements, with different degrees of porosity of the granular thresholds contributing to a fine modulation of airflow, luminous and thermal environment within the cavernous space that resulted from the pouring process.

DESIGNED PARTICLES AND AGGREGATION STRATEGIES 02

Anne Hawkins and Catie Newell, GPA Studio (Michael Hensel and Achim Menges), Rice University, Houston, Texas, 2004

This study investigated the design of an aggregate on a human scale that is easy to manipulate so that specific formations and related environmental conditions can be achieved quickly by just a few people. Three categories of variables were identified. The first category comprised the geometric articulation and material characteristics of the individual aggregate element, resulting in two geometric types at variable sizes and weights. The second category involved the aggregation process including the emission path, pouring speed and time. The third category included the particular boundary conditions that constrain the pouring area and aggregation process. Tests were conducted for each category and combinations of categories. From these experiments the density or porosity of different aggregations and sublocations of each aggregate were measured and mapped.

To test the capacity for light modulation, the aggregate was poured into formwork consisting of removable panels and a tall windowpane. The density and porosity variations resulting from specific manipulations of the aggregation process were then analysed in relation to the transmission of daylight over several days. The resulting light conditions were recorded at 15-minute intervals in order to map the specific luminosity modulation. To test the capacity to bear their self-weight, aggregates were poured into wall, arch, half-vault and vault configurations. Other experiments focused on the removal of elements to the point of collapse, in order to assess and utilise redundancies of load paths. All experiments were carried out by hand in order to assure ease of manipulation, with each pouring process taking no longer than 30 minutes. ⚿

The aggregate's performative capacity to modulate luminous flow was investigated through a larger system constructed by pouring the aggregate into formwork consisting of removable panels and a tall windowpane. Different degrees of porosity resulting from specific manipulations of the aggregation process enable differential modulation of light transmission across various sublocations of the system.

Various aggregation processes were tested in a series of experiments in order to explore, notate and understand the interrelated influences of the element type, the pouring conditions and the articulation or use of existing external constraints in relation to the aggregate's capacity to modulate luminous conditions.

Environmental Intensifiers

Fibre-reinforced composite materials have significant potential in performance-oriented design. Composites enable seamless transitions between material make-up, characteristics and effects, and fibre directionality can yield variable context-specific behaviour. Such materials are the closest to those in living nature and could be further developed to mimic or optimise natural processes. **Aleksandra Jaeschke** examines developments in this field at the Department of Form Generation and Materialisation at the Hochschule für Gestaltung (HfG) in Offenbach, Germany, led by Achim Menges. She also looks at the specific ways in which integrated form-generation and materialisation are being used in design that engages with composites.

There is nothing deeper than skin.
Paul Valéry, *Idée Fixe: The Collected Works of Paul Valéry*, 1957[1]

Surfaces have been explored extensively by architects and designers of the digital era as topologically fascinating models of spatial organisation. The material systems developed at the Department of Form Generation and Materialisation at the HfG in Offenbach continue this line of research, yet go beyond the superficiality of surface to focus on its depth. They explore functional and structural potentials of surfaces exploiting the versatility of fibre-reinforced composite materials. At the HfG department they seamlessly integrate form-generation with its subsequent fabrication modes emulating conditions existing in natural systems and using advanced computational techniques. A kind of intensive dermatology can be articulated as one tries to analyse the make-up and performance of these highly articulated surfaces.

The functionality of many living organisms relies on interrelated systems distributed across seamlessly connected strata. The Lounge Landscape and Intensifier 01 and 02 projects are such surfaces – they constitute complex, multilayered organisations. The Offenbach surfaces develop from simple principles, offering specific opportunities into increasingly complex multifunctional systems in order to reach a state of equilibrium between structure and function. They satisfy multiple structural and functional requirements through careful combination of the performative capacity offered by simple elements. The 3-D spacer textile employed in the Lounge Landscape and Intensifier 01 projects, or the continuous glass-fibre bands utilised in Intensifier 02, both suggest numerous possible configurations of material arrangements. The simplicity and flexibility of these basic elements are a source of potential diversity in their articulations within more complex assemblies. All of the presented examples are adaptable forms and structures that can easily respond to global changes through locally applied manipulations.

In the Offenbach experiments, design proceeds through making. The findings are triggered by contingencies and the work unfolds as a resonance between the intrinsic material qualities and their emergent performative potentials in exchange with the external influences. The physical form-finding techniques offer a method of exploring the self-organising tendencies of structural systems under specific external pressures, be they structural or environmental forces. In the Offenbach projects, manipulations applied during the form-finding experiments are not aimed at obtaining the final form, but at triggering local opportunities for adjustment through incremental changes. This makes the systems open and adaptable. Novel performative synergies emerge from the investigation of differentiated morphologies based on thorough understanding and rigorous management of environmental conditions. Throughout the entire process, material properties interact with the dynamic forces of a hosting environment.

This evolution is a time-based computational procedure in which valid solutions emerge through a series of mutually informed material and computational tests and evaluations. It is a process framed by specific parameters, yet it is full of intricate loops. Successive iterations strengthen the integration between materials, geometries and manufacturing techniques towards a performance-driven balance. Operations are performed on numerical and sensorial data. Performance-related discoveries are translated into rigorous, rule-based procedures. This approach bounds the eventual formal and material expression to the creativity of the design process, and shifts importance from preconceived formal ideas towards the validity and ingenuity of applied techniques. The adopted design methods oscillate between emergent tactics acting nonlinearly bottom-up and analytical strategies operating linearly top-down.

The seamlessness of the design process is strongly related to the way the project findings are notated and communicated. The computational tools are not used in order to represent the evolving forms, but to describe and manage the underlying parametric relationships of systems with the aim of elaborating and transferring data across design stages. Operative, parameter-based geometries are an instrument for classifying and correlating diverse inputs, allowing for internal feedback and migration across domains and scales. Specific to each project, rigorous and flexible notation methods are gradually built up to manage the project and to eventually govern the manufacturing and assembly. In this sense there is no distinction between the design phase and the eventual manufacturing. The building process starts with the very first experiments.

The complexity of the Offenbach forms is a result of negotiation between structural stability, various functional requirements and the technologies used in the process of materialisation. The aim of the research is to develop multi-performative systems avoiding the typical post-design problem-solving and optimisation. Through careful exploitation of opportunities offered by the basic components and their proliferation, the Lounge Landscape and the Intensifiers combine material, structural, functional and environmental performance in one integral system.

Most living organisms depend for load-bearing on an internal skeleton. However, nature suggests a variety of possible solutions. Hard, self-supporting exoskeletons, for instance, offer another model of structural organisation. Both the Intensifiers and the Lounge Landscape constitute such

**Nico Reinhardt, Intensifier 01, Department of Form Generation and Materialisation
(Achim Menges), Hochschule für Gestaltung (HfG), Offenbach, Germany, 2006–07**
A full-scale surface prototype demonstrates the high level of articulation and structural capacity enabled by the manipulation of 3-D spacer-textile composite surfaces through specifically developed gathering techniques.

INTENSIFIER 01

Nico Reinhardt, Department of Form Generation and Materialisation (Achim Menges), Hochschule für Gestaltung (HfG), Offenbach, Germany, 2006–07

The Intensifier 01 project investigated ways of instrumentalising local form-finding processes to differentiate continuous 3-D textile glass-fibre composite surfaces. Form-finding is a design technique that utilises the self-organisation of material systems under the influence of extrinsic forces or manipulations. In other words, material form can be found as the state of equilibrium of internal resistances and external forces. Contrary to most form-finding processes, which are concerned with the global morphology of a system, this project aimed at exploring local manipulations to elaborate the mathematically defined geometry of 3-D textile glass-fibre composite surfaces. A series of manipulation techniques was developed as the specific distribution of parametric manipulation components defining the vectors and distances of gathering particular points on a three-dimensional spacer textile. Numerous experiments were conducted exploring the behaviour of gathering sequence and kind, emerging surface articulation and overall morphology. This led to a catalogue of specific local manipulations, applied through simple procedures of point-gathering following computationally derived protocols, which enable overall double curvature and considerably increase the structural depth and bending stiffness of the system. The local manipulations were then correlated with the possibility of integrating a glass-fibre-reinforced skin and the mathematics of defining formwork geometry in order to produce a series of full-scale prototypes.

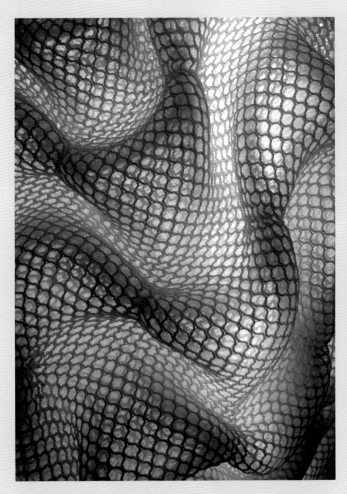

The parametric definition of gathering techniques of a 3-D spacer textile allows for the differential manipulation of primary surface geometry in relation to secondary surface articulation.

A close-up view of a full-scale prototype shows how local spacer-textile manipulations can be embedded in a glass-fibre composite. The resulting surface integrates both the load-bearing capacity of the structure and the environmental modulation of the skin.

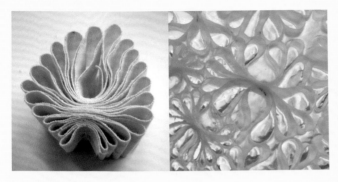

A glass-fibre band manipulated through a parametric gathering technique is the basic component (left) within a larger composite surface structure (right).

INTENSIFIER 02

Elena Burggraf, Department of Form Generation and Materialisation (Achim Menges), HfG, Offenbach, 2006–07

Intensifier 02 aimed at exploring the performative capacity of topological exactitude found in systems consisting of elements that find their position and alignments as an alternative to the geometric precision of highly defined component assemblies. The project started with the investigation of the behaviour of a basic element: glass-fibre band. By pulling a thread stitched through the band in defined distances, a specific loop pattern emerges due to the gathering action. In numerous physical tests the related parameters of band width, length and cut pattern, and stitch distance as well as tensile force induced in the gathering process were explored in relation to the resultant components behaviour of adapting to formwork curvature and, once hardened by resin, structural capacity. As the taxonomy of the observed component behaviour was established, this could be related to the principal stress analyses of specific formwork geometry within a computational setup. The relationship between local curvature and structural requirements determined through the formwork geometry then defines the specific distribution of parametrically varied components. The component layout is then transferred from the computational realm to the actual formwork via a specially developed projection technique. As the components are laid out in the soft state, the alignment of adjacent components providing for subsequent connections happens by itself. Although the initial distribution focuses only on component size, depth, orientation and spacing in correspondence with structural criteria, the application of resin and related adhesive forces combined with the self-forming capacity of the strips produces a highly defined material system.

Top right: Through the application of highly transparent resin and its related adhesive forces combined with the self-forming capacity of the glass-fibre components, a full-scale continuous surface prototype can be constructed.

Right: In response to structural and environmental criteria, each component's basic parameters, such as band width, length and cut pattern, stitch distance as well as tensile force induced in the gathering process, is differentiated in order to construct a full-scale, performative prototype surface.

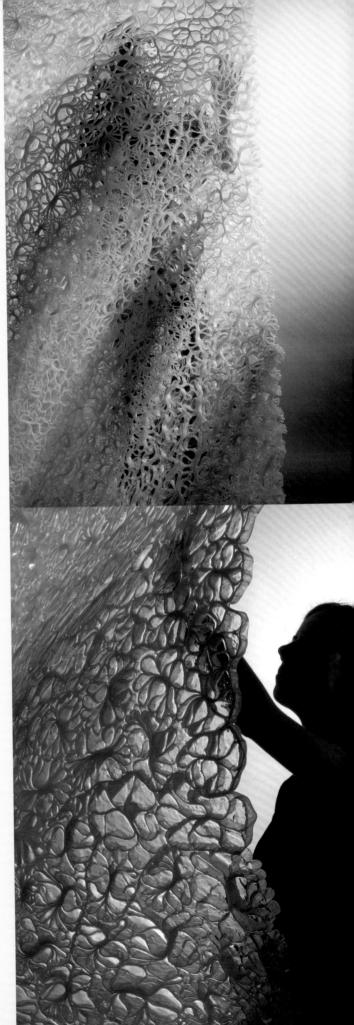

LOUNGE LANDSCAPE

**Nicola Burggraf, Susanne Hoffmann, Steffen Reichert, Nico Reinhardt, Yanbo Xu,
Department of Form Generation and Materialisation (Achim Menges), HfG, Offenbach, 2007**

The Lounge Landscape was instigated by the university's commission to design and manufacture seating furniture, for its 175th anniversary celebrations, reflecting the school's design and prototyping expertise. In collaboration with the relevant manufacturing industry, the project began with the development of a novel composite material system consisting of a 3-D spacer textile sandwiched in a stressed glass-fibre skin. The nonelastic textile's capacity to differentially stretch and contract through geometric deformation offers the possibility to articulate double-curved surfaces without the need for seams or cut patterns. This specific material behaviour was encoded in a custom-programmed analysis application linked with form-generation processes based on mathematical equations. This enabled a morphological evolution of iteratively testing and evaluating parametric variants of the mathematical definition based on the innate possibilities and constraints of the 3-D textile to form seamless double-curved surfaces. The resulting form was CNC manufactured as a mother mould, facilitating the production of a multitude of individual, geometrically different furniture morphologies all remaining material specific and stackable. More importantly, this integral approach to form, material, structure and manufacturing also provides an inroad for rethinking surface articulation as a means of differentiating possible body–surface interaction. Each Lounge Landscape furniture piece provides for a multitude of anticipated as well as divergent activities by up to seven people at a time. The open-endedness of possible uses and loose-fit ergonomics, and the concurrent erosion of clearly demarcated functional zones of more conventional seating furniture, demands a conscious (re)positioning of the user within the landscape-like articulation and its microsocial context, prompting an intensified individual and collective experience.

The mother mould, from which all six geometrically variant individual surfaces were built, is CNC milled from high-density polystyrene blocks, reinforced with glass-fibre mats and finished with glossy, jet-black paint in order to achieve the high-quality composite surface finish of the furniture pieces.

The individual Lounge Landscape furniture pieces are constructed from novel composite material systems consisting of a 3-D spacer textile sandwiched in a stressed glass-fibre skin. The integral approach to form, material, structure and manufacturing provides an inroad for rethinking surface articulation as a means of differentiating possible body–surface interaction.

In combination with an animated illumination, each individual, translucent Lounge Landscape furniture piece provides for a wide range of possible uses through its loose-fit ergonomics. This demands a conscious (re)positioning of the user within the landscape-like articulation and its microsocial context.

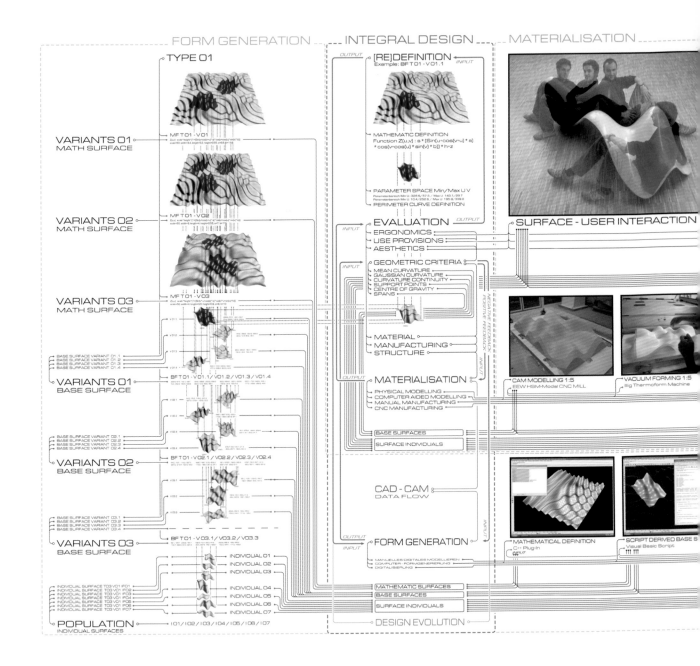

multifunctional respiring body armours. In each case a different configuration of fibres helps constitute the structural core of each surface. In the Lounge Landscape, a nonelastic 3-D textile is manipulated to form global structural undulations. The Intensifier 01 is stiffened through local gathering of the same nonelastic 3-D spacer textile in order to add structural depth. In the Intensifier 02, the inner stratum is formed by seamlessly interconnected loops of fibre-glass bands that actively adapt to the geometry of pre-established moulds. In all cases the core stratum is sandwiched in stress-bearing layers of resin matrix. The choice of fibre composites helps achieve continuous surfaces avoiding stitches and joints. The structural forces are continuously distributed along multiple paths and continuous surfaces, reducing stresses normally concentrating around point connections.

The organisational principles responsible for the structural performance of the discussed projects are simultaneously explored in terms of their functional capacities. The Offenbach surfaces act as multifunctional interfaces. The differentiated reticular webs developed in Intensifiers 01 and 02 simultaneously offer enclosure and filter light. In both cases, local variations in material distribution create zones of differentiated luminous conditions and areas of greater or lesser exposure. In a similar way, the undulating surface of the Lounge Landscape offers a variety of possible ways of space and surface occupation, while simultaneously ensuring structural integrity. The integration of different functions in one system is open ended and it can potentially involve an increasing number of additional parameters. In the case of Intensifiers 01 and 02, the porous configuration of fibres is se

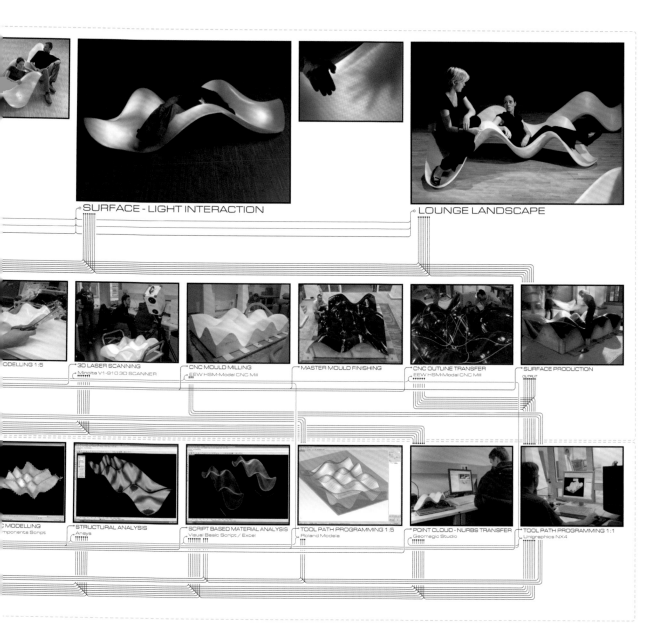

SURFACE - LIGHT INTERACTION

LOUNGE LANDSCAPE

ODELLING 1:5

3D LASER SCANNING
Minolta V1-910 3D SCANNER

CNC MOULD MILLING
EEW HSM-Model CNC Mill

MASTER MOULD FINISHING

CNC OUTLINE TRANSFER
EEW HSM-Model CNC Mill

SURFACE PRODUCTION
OUTPUT

C MODELLING
omponents Script

STRUCTURAL ANALYSIS
Ansys

SCRIPT BASED MATERIAL ANALYSIS
Visual Basic Script / Excel

TOOL PATH PROGRAMMING 1:5
Roland Models

POINT CLOUD - NURBS TRANSFER
Geomagic Studio

TOOL PATH PROGRAMMING 1:1
Unigraphics NX4

to filter light and regulate views. Although its capacity to control airflow is still to be explored, the parametric control of relations established between material properties, geometry and performance allows for readjustments and incorporation of new factors. One can, for instance, imagine potential iterations of the Lounge Landscape in which the system evolves from flexible seating furniture into an extensive landscape capable of hosting a variety of other activities.

The integration of advanced fibre-composite materials, open-ended computing protocols and tightly interlinked formation and materialisation modes makes the Offenbach forms closer to biological rather than mechanical development and design processes. The Offenbach surfaces append to existing environments establishing intensive climatic (see Intensifier 01 and 02) and ergonomic (see Lounge Landscape) relationships with their milieus. The role of these semi-autonomous projections is to augment ambient intensities and to suggest new ways of space occupation. Opportunities emerge from explored geometries to impose clear and immediate patterns of articulation. Potential architectures germinate in each exploration celebrating the expressive power of materials and their capacity to suggest organisational patterns. ∆

Note
1. Quoted in Paul Valéry, *Idée Fixe: The Collected Works of Paul Valéry*, Vol 5, The Bollingen Series, Princeton University Press (Princeton, NJ), 1957.

Engineering Ecologies

New Forms of Settlements, Associative Design & Synthetic Vernacular research programme (directed by Peter Trummer), Berlage Institute, Rotterdam, The Netherlands, 2006–07
Associative Design is a research programme in the production of disciplinary knowledge of computational techniques in the domain of urbanisation. In opposition to the practice of typological thinking, the research applies what in biology is called population thinking. The aim of the research is to project new neighbourhood models driven by the forces of contemporary urban regimes.

Engineering disciplines have, historically, been strongly dominated by physics. Structural and civil engineering are still based on the notion of controlling the forces of physics within our material world. However, a shift from physics to biology as the underlying paradigm of engineering is on the horizon, and with it a fundamental change in the way we conceive and practise architecture. Peter Trummer speculates on the possibilities and potential repercussions of 'engineering ecologies', which will be inherent to such a paradigm shift, by investigating a broad palette of contemporary design disciplines aimed at the careful modulation of environments and ecologies.

It has become part of the accepted wisdom to say that the twentieth century was the century of physics and the twenty-first century will be the century of biology. Two facts about the coming century are agreed on by almost everyone. Biology is now bigger than physics, as measured by the size of budgets, by the size of the workforce, or by the output of major discoveries; and biology is likely to remain the biggest part of science through the twenty-first century. Biology is also more important than physics, as measured by its economic consequences, by its ethical implication, or by its effects on human welfare.

Freeman Dyson, 'Our Biotech Future', 2007[1]

In his article, Freeman Dyson sketched out the future of our domestic biotechnology as the creation of new fauna and flora by means of genetic engineering. In the future, according to Dyson, people will have access to do-it-yourself kits for gardening that make possible genetic engineering to breed new varieties of roses and orchids, or even kits to breed new varieties of pet. Moreover, Carl Woese, in his article 'A new biology for a new century', [2] declared reductionist biology, with its assumption that biological processes can be understood by studying genes and molecules, obsolete. What is needed instead, argues Woese, is a new synthetic biology based on emergent patterns of organisation. He posits that the time of merely seeking to understand existing nature has come to an end, and that our future will be about projecting new natures.

Since their inception in the 19th century, engineering disciplines have been strongly dominated by physics. The professions of structural and civil engineering were and still are based on the knowledge of controlling the forces of physics within our material world. And so the question arises: If our future will be determined by biological processes, what will this entail for architecture and engineering practices? What will it mean to our ideas and creativity?

Before we can imagine a practice of engineering ecology, we must clarify how we define the term 'ecology'.

In his tremendously visionary book *The Three Ecologies*, written in 1989, Felix Guattari described a landmark experiment by Alain Bombard, a doctor, biologist and senior member of the European Parliament, who has dedicated his life to the study of marine biology, and established and presided over several marine laboratories. He once conducted the following experiment on television. Of two glass tanks, one contained polluted water and a healthy and thriving octopus, and the other contained clear and unpolluted water. When the octopus was transferred from the polluted to the unpolluted water, it almost immediately sank to the bottom and died.[3] This example delivers a good image of what ecologies actually are.

Theo Jansen, Strandbeest, IJmuiden, The Netherlands, 2005
Jansen's walking skeletons, made out of yellow electricity tubes, can be understood as new forms of material organisations that could not exist without their particular environment – the Dutch coastline.

Theo Jansen, Animaris Rhinoceros, Amsterdam/Geuzenveld, The Netherlands, 2004
The lightweight skeletons of Jansen's artificial beach animals are wind powered and their structures create a walking behaviour in response to the specific ground conditions: from dry sand on summer days to wed mud in other seasons.

The general definition of ecology has hardly changed from the one Ernst Haeckel described at the end of the 19th century when he defined it as the relationship between a species or an object and its environment. This relationship is like that of the orchid and the wasp: the wasp becomes part of the orchid's reproductive apparatus while at the same time the orchid becomes the sexual organ of the wasp. The one not only needs the other, like an object needs its environment; it is part of the same process of becoming. To become is not to imitate, nor is it to conform to an existing model.[4]

Guattari's example says it all. In addition to his attempt to give an understanding of how ecology works, he demonstrates the way in which our understanding of ecology is misguided by preconceptions, formed by typological thought and reduction to averages or simple reductivist views, in which the richness of stimuli and forces is obliterated in order to derive and apply recognisable objective types of ideas and understandings. This is a technique or *modus operandi* that collapses differences into a homogenous view of environments in order to engineer them with simple and reductive laws, regulations and methods.

To engineer ideas, we distinguish reality by means of the possible and the real. Possible is what we can imagine. It is that which we want to realise. Such practices deal with two essential rules: one is to resemble or to imitate, and the other is limitation, the conformation to existing models. But ecologies cannot be engineered by ideas of such types. Rather they work by means of actualisation. Ecologies cannot be seen in terms of the possible and the real. They are virtual environments in which all species and objects are actualised, meaning that within our ecologies there are possible worlds, things, objects that are not yet real but are waiting to be actualised.[5] Such processes of actualisation cannot rely on pre-established ideas, but rather on rules of difference or divergence and creation.

It is this process of actualisation that is interesting when we talk about engineering ecologies. Until today, architectural practices applied the notion of engineered ecology from the viewpoint of the object. The design of architecture had to perform in relation to its physical environment dominated by gravity, climate, airflows or hydraulics. But can we imagine an architectural practice that starts from the virtual potential of an environment, and if so, what is its actualising potential?

Below are three examples that may help in understanding what has been described above. Each has been chosen to give an insight into the variety of material practices and the variations of what these practices actualise, from novel cultural landscape to new forms of behaviour.

Emerging landscapes: Fraser Island off Australia's Queensland coast is just one kind of emerging land formation driven by the environmental forces of wind and water. The sedimentation process of such islands is never fixed and therefore their configuration, size and formation change constantly.

Processes of Actualisation

Emerging Landscape

From the beginning of the 1990s, the Dutch policy of coastal defence against flooding changed radically. The protection of the Dutch landscape from the sea by dikes reached its engineering limits. To build even higher dikes, to resist the physical forces of sea water, became an obsolete idea. Instead, institutions such as the Rijkswaterstaat started what we can call engineering ecology. The Dutch intervened in the natural process of dike production by filling up the coastline with layers of sand. Wind and water did the rest. The dynamic handling of the coastline was mainly used to increase the strength of the existing dikes,[6] but eventually nature's morphological processes caused different effects. In recent years new forms of sandbanks have emerged. Instead of just providing physical protection, the process of intervening in the ecological process of coastal morphologies has actualised a new landscape. The potential of these new cultural landscapes is not yet realised, but they will eventually transform the economic, environmental and cultural future of the Netherlands.

Material Organisations

What for the Dutch Ministry of Water and Infrastructure is a form of defence, for Dutch artist Theo Jansen is the potential to generate new material organisations. Jansen studied physics

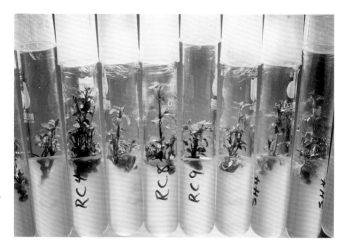

Genetically modified plants grow from tissue culture in growth medium at Cornell University.

at the University of Delft, and over the last 15 years has been developing artificial beach animals. At first glance the strangely moving vehicles or kinetic objects with names like Animaris Rhinoceros or Strandbeest look like creatures from a science-fiction movie.[7] But these walking skeletons, made out of yellow electricity tubes, can actually be understood as new forms of material organisations that could not exist without their particular environment – the Dutch coastline. The lightweight skeletons are wind powered and their structures create a walking behaviour in response to the specific ground conditions: from dry sand in summer days to wed mud in other seasons. These objects owe their existence to the condition of their environment. They are context-specific.

Forms of behaviour

Who has ever thought of surfing in Munich? Who could ever imagine experiencing a surf-wave on the river Isar, which runs through Munich's inner city? Tube 6, a German new-wave technologist group, has developed a perfect breaking wave in running water in cooperation with the city's technical university. What appears to be engineered by means of external energy resources is actually based on geometrical features, an underwater structure that generates aqua-dynamic conditions.

The geometrically varied underwater hill formations can yield different waves for different water sports.[8] Tube 6 thus produces variations of wave geometries, expressed in terms of 'wave shoulders' and 'wave tubes'. For instance, one type of the wave produced by Tube 6 intervention is a powerful hollow-breaking wave, with a deep tube and fast shoulder, which corresponds to the classic tube found in fine reef-breaks that is ideal for short-board and body-board, advanced surfers and professionals. In the case of the river Isar, the artificial modification of the river bed via pneumatic cushions creates waves in the process of breaking and becoming hollow. The tube of such waves is small, not very powerful, with a broad shoulder and a flat run-out area. This is the most popular ocean wave, often found on sandy beaches, and is ideal for all types of boards, manoeuvres and skill levels.

Another form of wave is the flat wave without any lip. This corresponds to so-called build-up waves in the sea and is ideal for long boarders, beginners and kids. Yet another type, so-called foam-bals, are ocean waves with powerful steep shoulders that are ideal for rodeo kayak, short boards and advanced surfers. This type of wave forms a churning white-water barrel with a smaller shoulder perfect for kayakers.

Markus Gruber and Dr Markus Aufleger, Tube 6 technology, Technical University of Munich, Germany, 2005
The Tube 6 technology was developed by Markus Gruber in collaboration with Dr Markus Aufleger from the Technical University of Munich, Germany. The effects of the waves were generated by an interrelated process of 'computational engineering' on the one hand and physical tests on the other, whereby computational fluid dynamic modelling was tested and simulated in water laboratories. The top image shows a possible urban application of Tube 6 technology on the river Isar in Munich. The other images show several test runs of various breaking waves with a flexible tube or bag, simulating a riff condition.

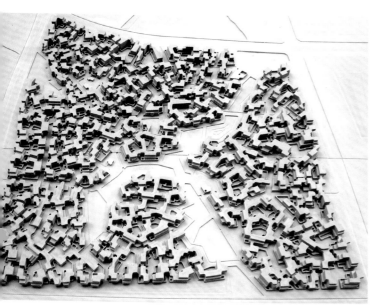

Luming Wang and Zhenfrei Wang, Associative Design & Synthetic Vernacular research programme (directed by Peter Trummer), Berlage Institute, Rotterdam, The Netherlands, 2006–07
Projected neighbourhood models as an alternative to contemporary Chinese urbanisation in the Jiangnan River Delta in Shanghai. Learning from biological systems, the urban pattern is based on the growth logic, whereby the accumulation of cells generates various urban tissues. The topology of the urban network is similar to self-generated structures in nature and can accommodate changes due to the economic forces of the housing development.

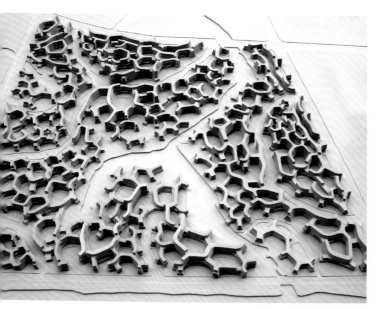

Ming-Ying Tsai and Sheng-Ming Wu, Associative Design & Synthetic Vernacular research programme (directed by Peter Trummer), Berlage Institute, Rotterdam, The Netherlands, 2006–07
Learning from nonplanned urban settlements, the projected urban fabric is based on a growth logic similar to the Chinese vernaculars. Over 3,000 years, urban fabrics within the Jiangnan River Delta have emerged through the interrelationship of economic forces and the water landscape as its main infrastructural network.

All these forms of behaviour are actualised by constructing an artificial environment. These water sports would never be able to occur in nature in the same context, since each of the waves either belongs to the performance of another context, for instance the sea and its specific sea-floor articulation, or river ravines and white water. In Munich they are actualised as the virtual potential of the engineered ecology.

All three of the examples above can be understood as engineered ecologies, as practices of actualisation. But what they actualise is not just a new thing, a new environment; it is a cultural product through context-specific intervention in environmental ecologies.

The implications for future architectural practices and the necessity to engage with ecologies as the potential of artificial natures seem even more important when we listen to Freeman Dyson's conclusion to his predicted biotechnical future:

> Biology gave birth to village communities ten thousand years ago, starting from the domestication of plants and animals, the invention of agriculture, the breeding of goats and sheeps and horses and cows and pigs, the manufacture of textile and cheese and wine. Physics and chemistry is the technology that gave birth to the cities and empires five thousand years later, starting from forging of bronze and iron, the invention of wheeled vehicles and paved roads, the building of ships and war chariots, the manufacture of swords and guns and bombs. It produced steel plows, tractors, reapers, and processing plant that made agriculture more productive and transformed much of the resulting wealth from village-based farmers to city-based corporations.[9]

Participating in the new synthetic biological paradigm by actualising new forms of cultural environments is in the hands of the architect. Engineering ecologies can then become the practice to unfold new forms of material environments for living, new neighbourhood models[10] or new kinds of urban landscape or material organisms. In the future, the success of architectural practice is likely to be measured in terms of processing the virtual potential of our synthetic worlds. ⟁

Notes

1. Freeman Dyson, 'Our Biotech Future', *The New York Review*, Vol LIV, No 12, NYREV (New York), 2007, pp 4–8.
2. Carl R Woese, 'A new biology for a new century', *Microbiology and Molecular Biology Reviews*, Vol 68, No 2, June 2004, pp 173–86.
3. Felix Guattari, *The Three Ecologies*, Continuum (New York) and the Athlone Press (London), 2000, first published in France in 1989 by Editions Galilée, pp 42–3.
4. The example is taken from Gilles Deleuze and Claire Parnet, *Dialogues II*, Continuum (New York) and the Athlone Press (London), 2000, p 2, first published in France in 1977 by Flammarion, Paris.
5. See Gilles Deleuze, *Bergsonism*, Zone Books (New York), 2001, pp 96–7.
6. In Dutch this methodology is called 'zandsuppletie'; see www.rikz.nl and www.delta.tudelft.nl.
7. See www.strandbeest.com.
8. www.tube6.de.
9. Dyson, op cit.
10. See the second-year research programme by Peter Trummer on Associative Design II and III at the Berlage Institute in Rotterdam, the Netherlands.

Designing Morpho-Ecologies
Versatility and Vicissitude of Heterogeneous Space

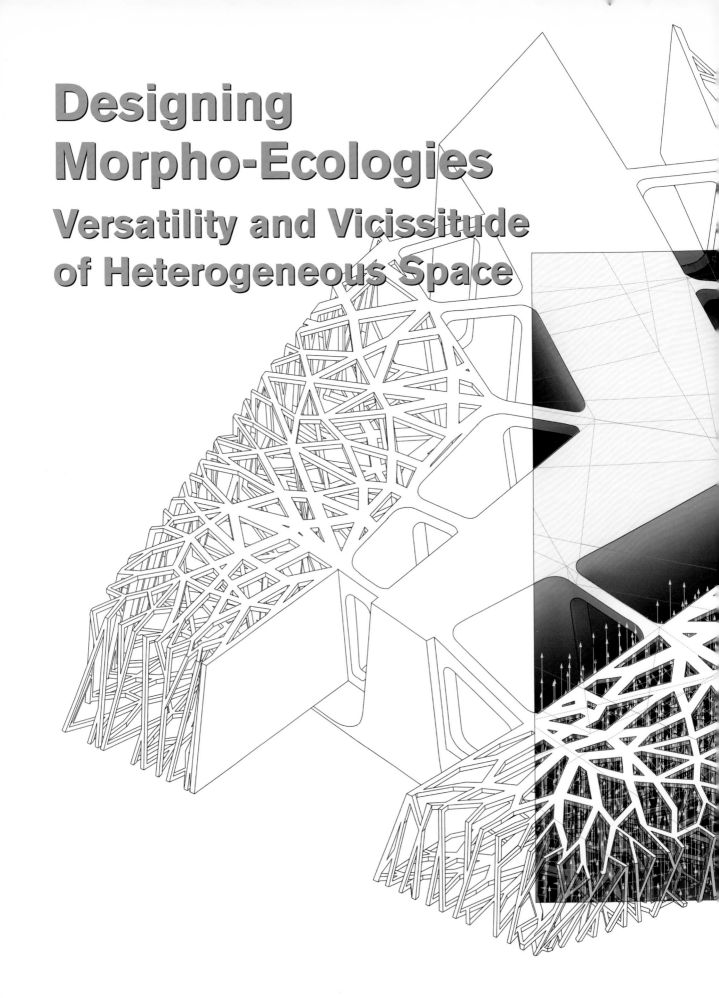

'Morpho-Ecology' is a concept and design approach that combines the notion of 'morphology', and thus intrinsically 'morphogenesis', with the notion of 'ecology'. In the early 19th century, in the context of his studies in botany, the poet and writer Goethe defined morphology as the study of forms; he combined the study of 'Gestalt', or structured form, with the process of 'Bildung', or formation, which acts continuously upon form.[1] Later on in the century, the term 'ecology' was coined by the German physician and zoologist Ernst Haeckel, who defined it as the science of relationships between organisms and their environment.[2] Here **Michael Hensel** and **Achim Menges** outline their theoretical and methodological framework for 'morpho-ecological design' in architecture, illustrating it further with two projects that combine research and design.

OCEAN and Scheffler + Partner, New Czech National Library, Prague, 2006
The growth of the library's tectonic envelope is driven by computational processes that derive the specific articulation of each tectonic element's dimensions, angle and orientation in response to recurrent analyses of structural, spatial and environmental parameters. The resulting structure synthesises form, load-bearing behaviour, microclimatic provisions and organisational capacity within the differentiation of the envelope.

Ecological systems are open systems that maintain themselves far from thermodynamic equilibrium by the uptake and transformation of energy and the exchange of organisms and matter across their arbitrary boundaries.

James H Brown, 'Complex ecological systems', 2004[3]

Throughout architectural history an astonishingly large number of spatial strategies and arrangements and related modes of habitation have emerged. Cellular, labyrinthine and universal spatial arrangements have been developed: *plan libre* (Le Corbusier) and *raumplan* (Loos) evolved from Modernist discourse, and more recently concepts such as deep (Venturi), interstitial (Tschumi), smooth (Eisenman), vast (Kipnis) and liquid space have been explored. However, the current repertoire of spatial arrangement that characterises the vast amount of architecture today is, in comparison with this rich history of exploration, rather impoverished. Two main arrangements prevail: the corridor and cellular room arrangement, and the open plan. The former increases the number of internal thresholds so as to separate circulation from controlled access rooms, while the latter reduces thresholds to perimeter conditions that, in an

The late Robin Evans argued that 'the cumulative effect of architecture during the last two centuries has been like that of a general lobotomy performed on society at large, obliterating vast areas of social experience'

extreme situation, are condensed into an outer building envelope. What is common to both, however, is the reduction of an understanding of space mainly to the surfaces and thresholds that delimit regions of space. We argue that this is an impoverished paradigm that needs to be expended to include the specific environment within which a material intervention is set and interacting with, and also the subject that likewise interacts with both. We have called this expended notion, and the related instrumental approach to design, 'Morpho-Ecology'.

The late Robin Evans argued that 'the cumulative effect of architecture during the last two centuries has been like that of a general lobotomy performed on society at large, obliterating vast areas of social experience'.[4] Evans criticised that the relentless partitioning of space along the corridor and cellular room arrangement has reduced the possibility of richly varied social formations by means of segregation and for the sake of privacy and security. The

result is an excessively partitioned space that in its constituents, characteristics and effect is both homogenous and homogenising in many respects. This was not always seen as negative. For instance, certain Modernists postulated homogenous universal space as democratic space. The glorification of the open plan as the sole enabler of equal opportunities for inhabitation resulted in its organisational dominance seeking its idealised extension into an infinite grid, or at least to the maximum reduction of boundary thresholds.

Both the tectonics of intensely partitioned space (with its preference for opacity) and its other, the Modernist universal space (with its preference for transparency) have eventually led to intensive standardisation and modularisation of building elements in such a way that the mass-produced elements and systems are optimised for performing one principal function (for example, primary structure, secondary structure, sun shading, rain cover or climate envelope) with utmost efficiency. Within this single-objective optimisation paradigm, efficiency is postulated as the ratio of using a minimum amount of material and energy to achieve maximum projected performance.

The German philosopher Peter Sloterdijk has argued that a dramatic shift occurred when in early 19th-century England hothouses began to emerge that provided a suitable environment for non-native plants.[5] According to Sloterdijk, this development was possible and accelerated by the invention of bent glass and the prefabrication of standardised glass and steel elements. Sloterdijk posited that one 'encounters the materialisation of a new view of building by virtue of which climatic factors were taken into account in the very structures made'.[6] While this significant change in the purpose and performance of such structures took place, it was, in turn, ultimately reduced to little variability due to the standardisation of its constituent parts. The dominance of a certain notion of efficiency thus prevented the emergence of one of multivaried effectiveness, as discussed earlier in this issue.

It is interesting, in this regard, to recall Reyner Banham's succinct analysis of two architectural traditions: the Western tradition of substantial structures that articulates the boundary threshold as a material condition, and the tradition of nonsubstantiality that operates through the opportunistic use of environmental gradients, such as a campfire around which social formation and individual opportunistic appropriation are dynamically driven by individual preferences, social interaction and hierarchy set within an equally dynamic environment of microclimatic differentiation.[7] Surely such gradient spatial conditioning seems initially diametrically opposed to the familiar dichotomous definition of space that divides exterior from interior, and one space from another. However, we argue that these traditions can and must be consolidated. In fact, they can actually never truly be separated. Yet the question is whether or not the ensuing feedback relation between the substantial, material interventions and environmental dynamics has been instrumentalised to serve the purpose of a richly varied heterogeneous space that provides choice for the individual and helps to sustain individual and collective itineraries of habitation that can also evolve over time in tune with the dynamics that facilitate them.

The morpho-ecological approach therefore aims for a more integral design approach to correlate object, environment and subject into a synergetic dynamic relationship. The theoretical and methodological framework concerns itself with intensive differentiation of material and energetic interventions that are evolved from their specific behavioural tendencies in a given environment and with regards to their mutual feedback relationship, passive modulation strategies that are sustainable, and speculation on the resultant relationship between spatial and social arrangements and habitational pattern and potentials.

We aim to extend Evans' concerns about the relationship between spatial and social arrangements, consolidating Banham's notion of substantial and nonsubstantial architectures into the synergetic relationship it has always been in ways not dissimilar to Peter Sloterdijk's succinct analysis of early hothouses that anticipate structures that incorporate climatic factors into their correlated formation and materialisation. The intention is to achieve richly varied heterogeneous spatial arrangements, profusely conditioned by microclimatic variation, that provide for migratory human activities and dynamic social formations. The following two schemes by OCEAN were aimed at developing morpho-ecological design strategies and methods in architecture.

OCEAN and Scheffler + Partner, New Czech National Library, Prague, 2006

The shift from programme as design-defining towards design as programme-evolving that is emblematic for our morpho-ecological design approach has implications across all levels of the deeply entrenched concepts and operations that characterise the vast majority of architecture and architectural practice today. The aim of the project here was to explore the possibilities of gradually eroding exclusive programmatic and hard threshold alignments in favour of heterogeneous spatial arrangements and environmental gradients within the constraints of a competition entry for one of the most functionally regulated and programmatically determined building typologies.

The competition proposal for the New Czech National Library in Prague, a collaborative project between OCEAN and Scheffler + Partner, seeks to provide both a singular monolithic appearance for one of the country's key cultural buildings, as well as a continuous and gradient spatial experience of the building and adjacent landscape of the site. The overall building volume is organised as a large object that is at the same time contained and open, confined and continuous, providing differentiated spatial experiences for both visitors and employees. The scheme is understood as one of several landscaped sites that together form a network of

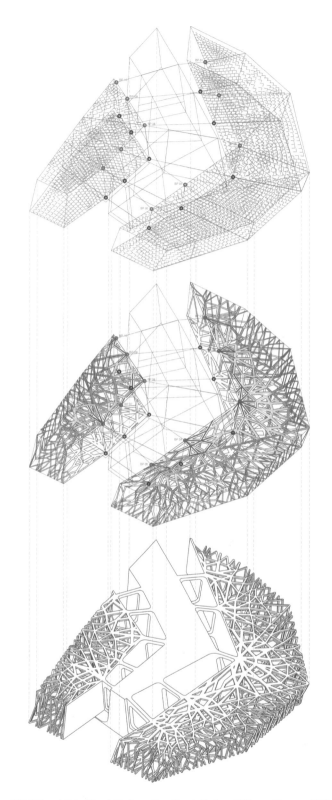

OCEAN and Scheffler + Partner, New Czech National Library, Prague, 2006
An analytic computational procedure indicates the stress distribution within the envelope of the new library's cantilevering volumes which is evaluated and mapped as a vector field of principal forces (top). According to this structural information, combined with other parameters such as for instance the angle of incident of sunlight, view axes and spatial characteristics, a network of merging branches is derived (centre), which is developed into a structural envelope of the volumes cantilevering from the central national archive (bottom).

Exterior view of the library situated in Letenské Park showing the intricate branching structure derived through an integral computational form-generation process.

Night view of the southern facade showing the various interrelated levels of the reading rooms overlooking Letenské Park.

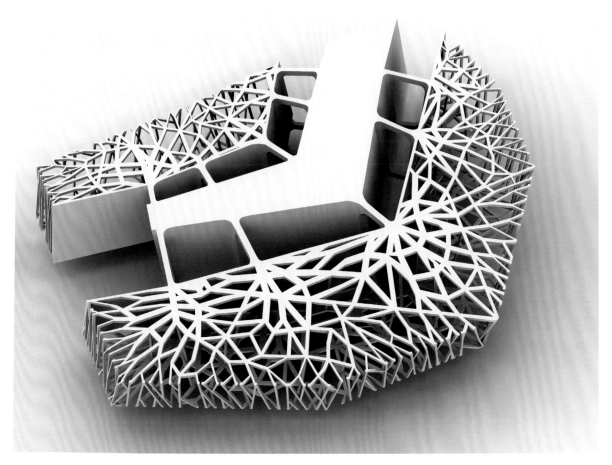

The distinctive tectonic articulation of the library's cantilevering volumes is developed through generative computational processes driven by spatial and structural criteria.

adjacent events, differentiated spatial provisions and scenic spots. It was therefore important to provide suitable spatial and visual links between the various locations of the landscape network.

The national archive, the core of the library housing one copy of all of the books published in the Czech Republic during the last century, constitutes a central volume that organises a smooth connection between Milady Horákové Avenue and Letenské Park. On both sides of this massive structure cantilever are the volumes that contain the administrative functions and reading rooms within a branching structure. Below these, at ground-floor level, a continuous public landscape mediates between the urban edge of the boulevard and the adjacent park, providing an articulated, continuous connection. The main challenge of the project was the generation of a material and tectonic system possessing the organisational capacity of a smooth transition from the highly functional, unit-based zones required for an effective library service to the reading areas of a condition-based, individual literature and space experience. Furthermore, the gradual shift from channelled to undirected circulatory zones enabled different modes of searching and browsing.

The distinctive tectonic articulation of the cantilevering volumes is developed through generative computational processes driven by spatial and structural criteria. In an analytic procedure, the stress distribution within the envelope of a specified volume is evaluated and mapped as a vector field of principal forces. A network of merging branches is derived according to this structural information, combined with other parameters such as the angle of incident of sunlight, view axes and spatial characteristics. Concentrating at the five support points, the flux of forces within the planes of the envelope is complex due to the irregular geometry and the extreme cantilever at both the street and park sides of the volumes. As all parameters need to be understood as interrelated, the generative process recurrently analyses the structural behaviour in relation to the other input parameters and responds by adjusting the specific articulation of each element's dimensions, angle and orientation during the growth process. Inherent variations of structural input data and parameters lead to the generation of a differentiated, tectonic envelope in which the interrelation of form, load-bearing behaviour and organisational capacity is synthesised. Thus the tectonic articulation becomes integral to the spatial organisation. This is manifested, for example, in the gradient

Interior view of the library's various levels of reading rooms enclosed by the differentiated branching network of the cantilevering envelope.

Model indicating the changing opacity and permeability of the building envelope that ranges from the opaque and solid national archive to the gradient density of the cantilevered envelopes' structural skin.

transition from controlled and channelled circulation concentrated at the support points of the cantilevering volumes towards open zones of individual movement and inhabitation in the reading areas at the perimeter of the volumes.

The interstitial space between the central opaque volume and the two cantilevering volumes is particularly important. It delivers the means of passive environmental modulations of the areas that do not require highly specific controlled interior climates and the transitional microclimates between all adjacent spaces. In order to do so, the distance and degree of inclination between facing surfaces is crucial. An associative parametric model served to determine an effective setup that serves the modulation of thermal, airflow and luminous conditioning of the different areas according to their required performance profiles. In addition, the changing opacity and permeability of the building envelope, which ranges from the opaque and solid national archive to the gradient density of the cantilevered envelopes' structural skin and the open access to public landscape, provides a wide range of spatial and microclimatic situations that facilitate and enable both the high level of organisational control required for a library building, and the heterogeneous conditions enabling zones of migrating activities and the intensified individual experience of inhabiting space and enjoying the various media and social dynamic of the library.

OCEAN and Scheffler + Partner, German Pavilion, Prague Quadrennial International Exhibition of Scenography and Theatre Architecture, 2007

Taking place every four years, the Prague Quadrennial is one of the most important theatre festivals in the world, with more than 50 nations showcasing contemporary approaches to the design of the spatial and scenic elements, light and aural aspects that make up the theatrical event.

This design study for a pavilion commissioned by the exhibition's German curator was constrained by its 10 x 8 metre (32.8 x 26.2 foot) site on a prominent spot within the main international exhibition hall. In contrast to most other pavilions that exhibit stage sets and theatre architecture, as well as related lighting, sound, projections, décors and costumes, the curator envisioned the pavilion as a performance environment of deliberately ambiguous relationships between space, time and the convergence of protagonist and playgoer. This ambition of blurring the role of actor and audience manifested itself in the curator's concept of not showing any exhibits except the pavilion structure itself and the multitude of effects it generated.

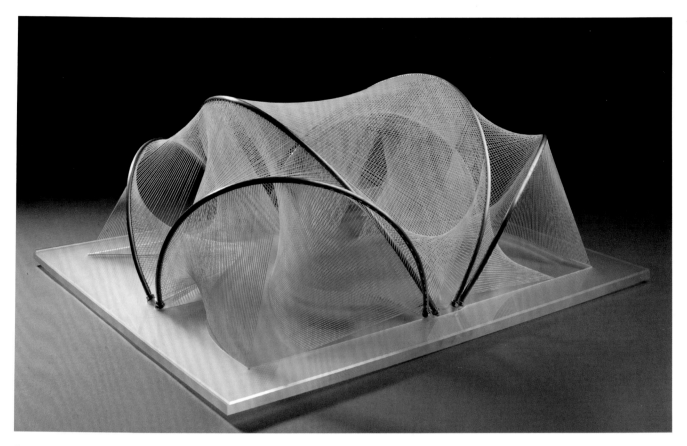

OCEAN and Scheffler + Partner, German Pavilion, Prague Quadrennial International Exhibition of Scenography and Theatre Architecture, 2007
A 1:20 scale model of the pavilion proposal showing the relationship between the intensification and filtering of visual conditions resulting from changes to the density and orientation of rulings dependent on the definition of base curves and the increment of material ruling interpretations.

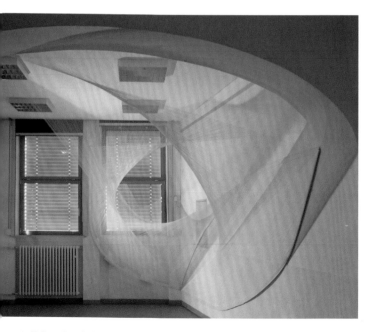

Full-scale ruled surface thread installation as constructed at the Hochschule für Gestaltung (HfG) in Offenbach, Germany, showing the relationship between varying degrees of transparency and the geometric articulation of base curves and 'thread' rulings.

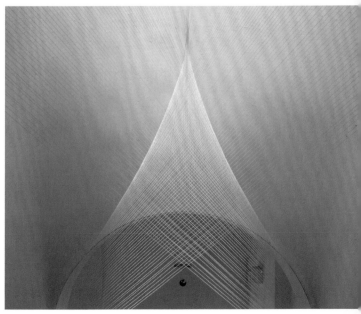

Ruled surfaces spanning between the base and director curves are constituted by straight lines called rulings, which can be materialised as elastic threads to articulate complex surfaces with different degrees of transparency and light filtration.

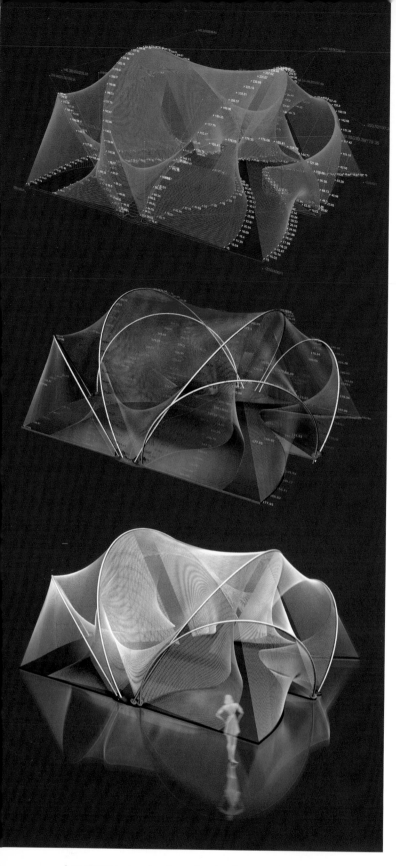

A computational process is employed to derive each individual ruled surface configuration as a sequence of base curve coordinates and related rulings (top). In this generative process, structural criteria are embedded and recurrently analysed in order to maintain an equilibrium state within the overall system (centre). In addition to the structural criteria, the parameters governing the complex relationship between space, body, movement and the emergent visual as well as luminous environment drive the design evolution (bottom).

There are no actors performing a rehearsed play. The visitors become actors for one another without noticing, perceiving the presence and movement of other visitors as a play of bodies in space that yield effects. Rather than the well-rehearsed spatial division between stage and ranks of the modern theatre, here the division between actors and theatregoers is eroded through a space of differentiated exposure, filtered and intensified by the pavilion structure itself.

A particular challenge in the design process was the development of a material and structural system with the capacity to provide differentiated conditions that result from the calibration and negotiation of multiple input parameters, while at the same time adhering to the very limited budget.

The project began with the definition of a material system based on ruled surfaces. In geometry, surfaces that can be swept out by moving a line in space are referred to as ruled surfaces. These surfaces spanning between the base and director curves are constituted by straight lines called rulings. In this design study, the surfaces were reduced to the materialisation of the rulings as elastic strings, which are guided by a system of articulated base curves. As demonstrated in a number of full-scale installations developed at the Hochschule für Gestaltung (HfG) in Offenbach, Germany, and constructed from several kilometres of elastic strings, these surfaces of rulings can be employed to modulate levels of transparency, exposure and enclosure as well as to manipulate visual and physical connectivity. The emergent moiré effects can be instrumentalised to expose or veil visitors navigating their way through the structure, as an individual's presence between overlapping layers limits the effect locally and creates a flickering silhouette.

The relation between the intensification and filtering of circulatory and visual conditions and various geometric parameters was explored using iterative digital and physical tests; for instance, the density and orientation of rulings dependent on the definition of base curves and the increment of material ruling interpretations. Beyond the parameters influencing conditions that affect the complex relationship between space, body, movement and the emergent visual as well as luminous environment, the structural capacity is also an integral aspect of the system. Due to the necessity to create a self-supporting system that does not rely on the listed exhibition hall except for resting on the ground, the articulation of the base curve follows structural criteria in such a way that the considerable accumulation of forces of all individual strings leads to an equilibrium state within the overall system.

The design culminates in a labyrinthine space of varied transparency and light effects that is animated by the visitors, a space with vague boundaries that enables a smooth flow from the exhibition hall into and through the pavilion. Each individual visitor's response to these conditions, and their resultant positioning and navigation through the space, becomes part of a transient inhabitation that is at the same time an active and passive constituent of the performance environment.

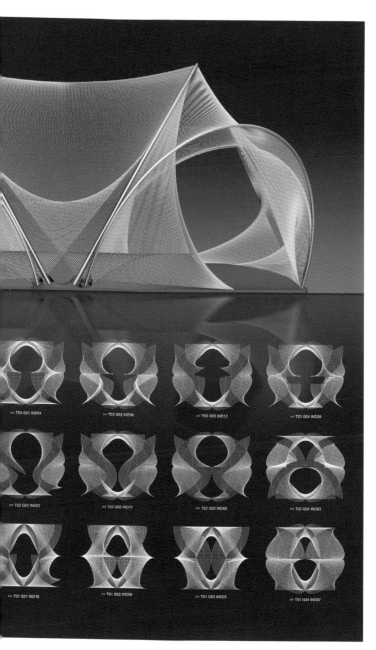

The design proposal is based on ruled surface geometry articulated through thread rulings (top). The geometry is derived through an evolutionary process of generating and evaluating different types of ruled surface configurations over a large number of generations and individuals, of which 12 individual articulations are shown here (bottom).

increasingly complex in terms of their context-specific performative capacities. The context for this work is provided by an operative correlation between practice, research and education that has been developed with leading institutions, experts and industries. Without doubt these efforts take place under time pressure, as effective and feasible responses to current unsustainable social and environmental problems are in dire need. Nevertheless, we are also facing a very exciting moment where architecture can leave behind both mindless standardisation fetishism and current hapless formal caprioles, and instead take on a new significance through intelligence, performance and beauty. ◬

Notes

1. See, for instance, 'Die Absicht ist eingeleitet', written in 1807, published in 1817, in Erich Trunz et al (eds), *Goethes Werke*, Hamburger Ausgabe Vol 13, Wegner (Hamburg), 1948–60, pp 54–6.
2. The term 'Oekologie' occurs first in Ernst Haeckel's *General Morphology*, in 1866.
3. James H Brown, 'Complex ecological systems', in George A Cowan, David Meltzer and David Pines (eds), *Complexity: Metaphors, Models and Reality*; Santa Fe Institute, Perseus Books (Reading, MA), 1994.
4. Robin Evans, 'Figures, doors and passages', in *Translations from Drawings to Buildings and Other Essays*, AA Documents 2, Architectural Association (London), 1997.
5. Peter Sloterdijk, 'Atmospheric politics', in Bruno Latour and Peter Weibel, *Making Things Public: Atmospheres of Democracy*, MIT Press (Cambridge, MA), 2005, pp 944–51.
6. Sloterdijk op cit, p 945.
7. Reyner Banham, *The Architecture of the Well-tempered Environment*, University of Chicago Press (Chicago, IL), 1973.
8. We aim to elaborate the shift from a Modernist preference for homogenous space to a contemporary preference for heterogeneous space in a forthcoming book entitled *Heterogeneous Space Readers*; eds Michael Hensel, Christopher Hight and Achim Menges, John Wiley & Sons (London), Spring 2009.

Project credits
New Czech National Library in Prague
OCEAN and Scheffler + Partner
Michael Hensel and Achim Menges (project coordinators); Andrea Di Stefano, Aleksandra Jaeschke, Steinar Killi, Eva Scheffler, Birger Sevaldson, Defne Sunguroğlu with Guillem Barraut, Mattia Gambardella, Pavel Hladik, Gabriel Sanchiz (project team); Bollinger + Grohmann Consulting Engineers (engineering consultants); Thom Roelly (landscape consultant).
German Pavilion for the Prague Quadrennial
International Exhibition of Scenography and Theatre Architecture
OCEAN and Scheffler + Partner
Achim Menges (project coordinator); Eva Scheffler, Steffen Reichert, Jochen Schütz (project team); Ruled Surface Installations: Hochschule für Gestaltung (HfG), Department of Form Generation and Materialisation (Professor Achim Menges with Marc Bischoff, Lisa Kelso, Albertus Niko, Sabrina Spee, Cristopher Brückner, Raphael Krug, Daniel Kussmaul, Lukas Methner, Cristoph Prenzel).

Epilogue
At the end of this issue we are left with the question as to what will be the way forward for the outlined morpho-ecological approach to design. We will look back in time to better understand the emergence of a preference for heterogeneous space[8] so as to inform the developing theoretical framework of the approach. We will also analyse existing and historical performative architectures in order to stock up on strategies for context-specific passive environmental modulation and related dynamic modes of habitation in order to update them and embed them in a range of contemporary technological, social and cultural contexts. And finally we will continue to design and construct full-scale prototypes and pilot projects that will become

Contributors

Klaus Bollinger and **Manfred Grohmann** established their practice Bollinger + Grohmann in Darmstadt in 1983 and are currently located in Frankfurt am Main, Vienna and Paris. The internationally operating consulting engineers are collaborating with a large variety of architects including Coop Himmelb(l)au, SANAA, Dominique Perrault, Zaha Hadid, Peter Cook, Frank O Gehry, Hans Hollein, Toyo Ito, Claude Vasconi and Christoph Mäckler. The scope of their projects includes residential buildings, office and commercial buildings, public buildings, exhibition and event structures and classical structural engineering for bridges, roofs and towers. Both engineers also teach at architectural faculties: Klaus Bollinger at the University for Applied Arts in Vienna and Manfred Grohmann at Kassel University. **Oliver Tessmann** is currently doing a PhD on collaborative design techniques at the University of Kassel and is working with Bollinger + Grohmann. After graduating in Kassel in 2001 he worked as an architect in Germany, Austria and Mexico. He has published in Europe, the US und Asia.

Michael Hensel is an architect, writer and principal researcher in OCEAN and the Emergence and Design Group, as well as a board member of BIONIS (the Biomimetic Network for Industrial Sustainability), and co-founder and co-director of the Emergent Technologies and Design masters programme at the Architectural Association School of Architecture. He is also on the editorial boards of *AD* and *JBE* (the Journal for Bionic Engineering). Recent publications include *AD Emergence: Morphogenetic Design Strategies* (2004), *AD Techniques and Technologies in Morphogenetic Design* (2006), and *Morpho-Ecologies* (AA Publications, 2006). Forthcoming publications include a book entitled *Heterogeneous Space Reader*, which he is co-editing with Professor Christopher Hight and Professor Achim Menges, to be published by John Wiley and Sons in early 2009. He is currently working on the concept and content for a peer-reviewed architectural research journal that will focus on research by design.

Achim Menges is an architect and partner in OCEAN and the Emergence and Design Group. He studied at the Technical University Darmstadt and graduated from the Architectural Association with honours. He has taught at the AA as studio master of the Emergent Technologies and Design masters programme since 2002 and as unit master of Diploma Unit 4 from 2003 to 2006. Since 2005 he has been professor of form generation and materialisation at the HfG Offenbach University for Art and Design in Germany. He has recently been appointed as professor at Stuttgart University leading an institute for computational design. His research focuses on the development of integral design processes at the intersection of evolutionary computation, parametric design, biomimetic engineering and computer aided manufacturing that enable a highly articulated, performative built environment (www.achimmenges.net). His research projects have been published and exhibited in Europe, Asia and the US. He received the FEIDAD (Far Eastern International Digital Architectural Design) Outstanding Design Award in 2002, the FEIDAD Design Merit Award in 2003, the Archiprix International Award 2003, RIBA Tutor Prize 2004, the International Bentley Educator of the Year Award 2005 and the ACADIA 2007 Award for Emerging Digital Practice.

Aleksandra Jaeschke is an architect, graphic designer and principal researcher in OCEAN. Born in Poland, she graduated from the Architectural Association in London and worked in the UK, Spain and Italy. Together with Andrea Di Stefano, she leads the Rome-based architectural practice AION and the Italian branch of the research and design network OCEAN. Investigating the essential relationship between structural and functional performance across scales and domains, her work focuses on processes of formation leading towards novel models of material organisation. Among other publications, she provided the graphic design of *Morpho-Ecologies* (AA Publications, 2006).

Remo Pedreschi holds the chair of architectural technology at the University of Edinburgh, and joined the university after a period in the construction industry. He is interested in the relationship between technology and design and was editor of the book series *The Engineer's Contribution to Contemporary Architecture*, to which he also contributed the monograph on the Uruguayan engineer Eladio Dieste. He is currently working on novel systems for stone construction, steel and plywood composite systems and fabrics as formwork for concrete. The methodology often involves the interaction of formal research and student-led projects as a device for both detailed and exploratory study leading to the construction of full-scale prototypes.

Defne Sunguroğlu is an architect, interior architect and principal researcher in OCEAN. She studied interior architecture and Architecture Part I at Kent University and completed her Diploma degree at the Architectural Association. She received the Buro Happold Studentship in 2006 and the CERAM Industrial Category Award in 2007 to pursue her research into complex brick assemblies, the Holloway Trust Award 2006 for an outstanding contribution to the construction industry, and the Anthony Pott Memorial Award 2006 to fund her research on Eladio Dieste's work. She is currently working on a book on innovating with brick, including the works of Guastavino, Dieste and an outline of her own current research.

Peter Trummer is an architect and researcher. Since 2005 he has been studio professor of the second-year Associative Design research programme at the Berlage Institute in Rotterdam, a postgraduate laboratory for architecture. He is also currently a PhD candidate at the institute, doing design research on the topic of 'population thinking' in architecture. He was born in Graz, Austria, and obtained his university diploma at the Technical University of Graz in 1994. He moved to Amsterdam in 1995, and finished his postgraduate study at the Berlage Institute in 1997. He became project architect at UN-Studio and was co-founder of offshore architects in 2001. He started his own practice in 2004. He is currently a guest professor at the Technical University in Munich and was a guest professor at the Academy of Arts in Nuremberg, Germany. He lectures, teaches and publishes internationally, including at the Berlage Institute and Academy of Architecture, the Architectural Association in London and Rice University in Houston.

Michael Weinstock is an architect. Born in Germany, he lived as a child in the Far East and then West Africa, and attended an English public school. He ran away to sea at the age of 17 after reading Conrad, and had years at sea in traditional sailing ships, with shipyard and shipbuilding experience. He studied architecture at the Architectural Association and has taught at the AA School of Architecture since 1989 as, variously, unit master, master of technical studies and academic head. He is a founder and co-director, with Michael Hensel, of the Emergent Technologies masters programme, and a founder member of the Emergence and Design Group. His research interests lie in exploring the convergence of biomimetic engineering, emergence and material sciences. He is currently working on the book *The Architecture of Emergence: The Evolution of Form in Nature and Civilisation*, to be published by Wiley-Academy in 2008.

C O N T E N T S

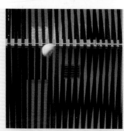

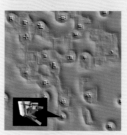

Craftsteak, New York

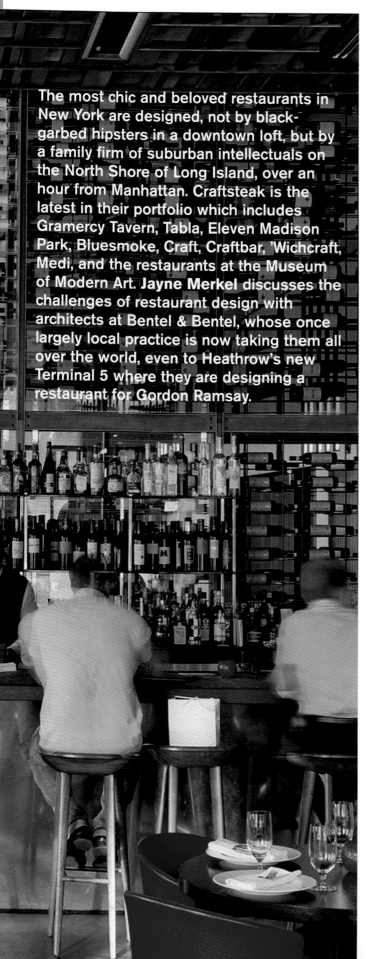

The most chic and beloved restaurants in New York are designed, not by black-garbed hipsters in a downtown loft, but by a family firm of suburban intellectuals on the North Shore of Long Island, over an hour from Manhattan. Craftsteak is the latest in their portfolio which includes Gramercy Tavern, Tabla, Eleven Madison Park, Bluesmoke, Craft, Craftbar, 'Wichcraft, Medi, and the restaurants at the Museum of Modern Art. Jayne Merkel discusses the challenges of restaurant design with architects at Bentel & Bentel, whose once largely local practice is now taking them all over the world, even to Heathrow's new Terminal 5 where they are designing a restaurant for Gordon Ramsay.

Paul Bentel, his brother Peter Bentel, their wives Carol Rusche Bentel and Susan Nagle, and their father Frederick R Bentel, work out of a woodsy, skylit, multilevel studio that Frederick carved out of a 19th-century house and then expanded with his wife and first partner. Maria Azzarone Bentel, an early graduate of MIT and professor of architecture at the New York Institute of Technology, died in 2000. Now the rest of her family carries on the practice which was devoted largely to institutional buildings – libraries, schools, churches, synagogues – until 1992 when a contractor recommended them to Danny Meyer, who was about to become the most successful restaurateur in New York. The contractor was doing some work on Meyer's apartment. He thought Bentel & Bentel would be the right people to help the young entrepreneur expand his already successful Union Square Café, which had been designed by Larry Bogdanow, the restaurant designer of the moment.

Bentel & Bentel were a strange choice. They didn't even live in the city, let alone the neighbourhood (Gramercy Park) where all Meyer's restaurants were located. Although they had won numerous Long Island design awards, the Bentels were not very interested in fashion, and most restaurants at the time were designed as stage sets. As Paul Bentel puts it: 'The "Wow Look" is all that mattered.' He and his partners were working on PhDs in architectural theory at MIT and happiest doing libraries.

But Meyer, who now owns the two most highly rated restaurants in New York City (the Union Square Café and Gramercy Tavern), was not a typical restaurateur. He wanted to make his customers feel welcome and at home, not lucky to have been let in and proud of having the best table in a glittery place. He was not a chef, but an entrepreneur, whose father in St Louis had been in the travel business, seeing the hospitality industry from the customer's side.

When they started talking to Meyer, the Bentels realised that their experience was more relevant than one might have thought. 'We had a longstanding tradition of institutional work which involves translating ideas about what people want into architecture,' Peter notes.

'Computerised bibliographic systems came out at the same time as the use of computers in restaurants,' adds Paul. 'The circulation desk is similar to the maître d' stand in a restaurant, and the idea is the same – to make things seem effortless.' Also, earlier in his career Meyer had been the top salesman in a company that made library book detection systems, so he didn't even mind if they lapsed into library lingo.

Meyer's restaurants, like the Bentels' public buildings on Long Island, have a distinctive sense of place. The *New York Times'* Bryan Miller described Union Square Café as 'a part of the neighborhood but not imposed on it'. Big windows allow passers-by to look in on happy diners glowing under little

---

Bentel & Bentel, Craftsteak, New York, 2006
The front room of Craftsteak, like those at Danny Meyer's restaurants, is devoted to a bar and casual dining. This one has a raw seafood bar and a bar for drinks that is framed by a two-storey glass and blackened-steel wine vault. A riveted column is left as raw as the oysters on the half shell to the right.

Craftsteak, New York, 2006
The west wall of the main dining room, which obscures a view of the Hudson River, is adorned with a mural-sized Stephen Hannock painting of the High Line which is visible at the east end of the bar room. The mural depicts the neighbourhood under development. Frank Gehry's IAC office building is shown under construction, but new apartment towers by a host of star architects that are now under way are not yet visible.

halogen pin lights. All Meyer's restaurants are in old buildings that set the cues for their decor. The goal is to make them part of the fabric but also 'transporting'.

When he opened Gramercy Tavern, Meyer, who had once worked as a tour guide in Rome, sent the Bentels to visit a number of restaurants in Italy that he and his father knew. (It is hard work but somebody's got to do it.) They were particularly impressed by Antica Osteria del Ponte, a several-hundred-year-old inn outside Milan where 'what they were willing to do to achieve a level of hospitality was amazing'. There were even little red stools at each table for diners' handbags. The architects noticed that the rooms were about 6 x 6.4 metres (20 x 21 feet), their widths determined by the lengths of the chestnut ceiling beams. The resulting dimension made it possible to have small tables along the sides and a long one in the centre that could accommodate large groups.

Bentel & Bentel, Gramercy Tavern, New York, 1994
A gastronomically inspired mural by Robert Kushner surrounds the bar in the front room of Gramercy Tavern where informal meals are served within view of people walking down the street. Views into the vaulted formal dining room from the bar are echoed on the side as rooms unfold into one another, providing partially enclosed intimate spaces that also seem to be a part of a lively larger scene.

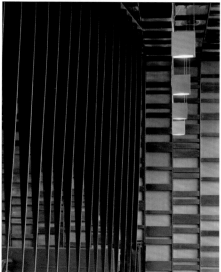

Craftsteak, New York, 2006
Curved acoustic panels wrap around the private dining room located directly off the kitchen since service there is all-at-once and separate from regular restaurant operations. On the west wall is a pixilated painting in blues and greens suggestive of the Hudson River which is just behind, but invisible from, the restaurant.

Twisted steel fins divide the entry from the bar room nearby. The sidewall (and ceilings elsewhere) are covered in acoustic panelling sheathed with bronze insect screening and blackened-steel strips in an irregular jazz-beat pattern inspired by the old bakery ceilings in the main dining room.

They employed the same dimensions at Gramercy Tavern, but made it possible to look from one room to the next. They also made the most of the very tall space to create vaulted ceilings that unify each room, and used original works of art that give character to each area, as they would again and again. A colourful mural commissioned from artist Robert Kushner wraps around the upper walls in the bar room at the front, unifying the space, which is visible (and inviting) from the street.

At Gramercy Tavern, the architects met the chef, Tom Colicchio, who went on to open several highly rated restaurants of his own and asked the Bentels to design them. Craftsteak, in New York's trendy Meat Packing District, is the latest. Here there are views out, but none in because the space, which once belonged to the National Biscuit Company, is 1.8 metres (6 feet) above street level so that baked goods could be transferred directly into vehicles for transport. The major work of art here is a mural by Stephen Hannock, portraying the nearby High Line, a new 2.4-kilometre (1.5-mile) long park across the street being designed by Diller, Scofidio + Renfro with Field Operations on an elevated railroad track, which is actually visible on the east side of the restaurant.

At Craftsteak the architects took their cues both from the existing space, as they always do, and from the chef's philosophy. Colicchio believes in serving artisan-raised ingredients unadorned to express their full flavour. Bentel & Bentel therefore used, as the main inspiration for the design, the riveted steel I-beam columns in their raw states throughout the restaurant, and the old, slightly arched concrete ceilings with steel channel equipment hangers on them in the main dining room. They employed the irregular rhythm of these old bakery ceilings in carpet patterns and in

other areas where they installed acoustic ceilings of bronze insect screening, blackened oak slats and steel edging. The black, white and red colour scheme comes from the white plaster, black steel and red brick interior walls that were there when they arrived. Wood floors and wall panels have been blackened and steel beams painted black. The height of the space is emphasised by a new two-storey glass-walled wine vault, which is accessed by a steel spiral staircase. Throughout, the architects have reinforced the connection between what you see and how it was made, as chef Colicchio does in his straightforward food.

The bold black-steel elements, refined here by careful proportions and elegant complementary furnishings, relate to the High Line.

No one could have predicted that Peter and Paul Bentel would end up designing the most fashionable restaurants in the hottest Manhattan locations when their parents left the city in 1956 to settle in an artists' colony with Josep Lluís Sert, Richard Lippold, Alexander Calder and even, briefly, Leger and Le Corbusier. Maria and Frederick Bentel came hoping to build schools and other public institutions in the newly developing communities on the North Shore. A generation later, when their sons and their wives joined them in the practice, the action was back in Manhattan. It was only the hunch of a contractor who appreciated Bentel & Bentel's way of putting things together that led to a practice they could not have planned for if they had stayed in the city and set their sights on this kind stardom. Life has a curious way of mixing up the stew. △+

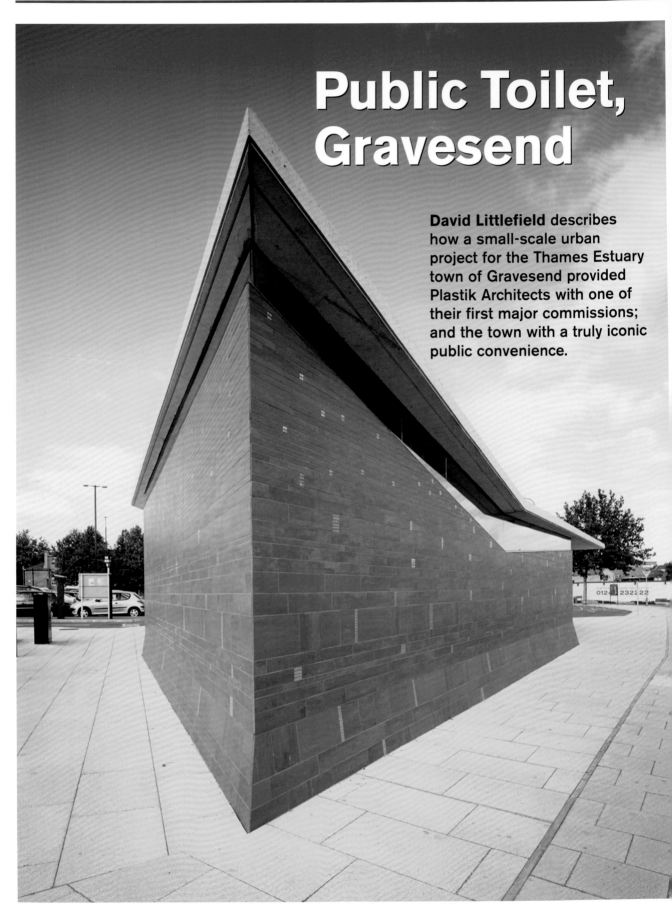

Public Toilet, Gravesend

David Littlefield describes how a small-scale urban project for the Thames Estuary town of Gravesend provided Plastik Architects with one of their first major commissions; and the town with a truly iconic public convenience.

Is there such a thing as 'virgin territory', a landscape so devoid of reference points that there is nothing worth translating into an architectural language? There is always, surely, some redeeming quality about a place (a shape, a history, even plain old-fashioned context) one can grab hold of and amplify, or use as a starting point for a design journey. John Davies, a director of Plastik Architects, had always assumed that architects could hunt, like detectives, for clues from which a design solution could spring. That was until he found himself designing a public toilet in Gravesend.

master plan. Some smart housing is going up and the town centre looks like it might benefit from a dose of predetermined order in lieu of an accumulation of second-rate bits and bobs. Which is where the toilets come in.

The newly emerging street plan for this quarter of Gravesend seemed to suggest what Davies described as a 'node point', a position within the master plan that cried out for something (anything) to act as a landmark, a beacon, an urban punctuation mark. As the public loo had disappeared with one of the car parks, a new facility seemed like a good

The long elevation of the building; from this angle, the purpose of the structure is unknowable.

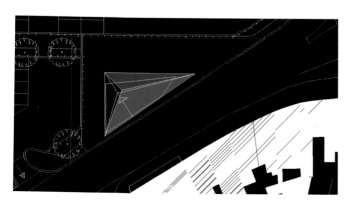

Site plan showing the public toilet as an event between the open space of the car park to the north, and buildings to the south. 'This was about giving something to the town, rather than pushing some sort of personal agenda,' says John Davies of Plastik Architects.

Gravesend is not, in fact, as dead-end a place as its name suggests. Forty-five minutes east from London Bridge railway station – past Woolwich, past Bexley, past Dartford – Gravesend lies in the scruffy urban nothingness that is north Kent. With medieval roots (and the place where Pocahontas died), this estuarine town is not unloved – just knocked about a bit and subject to piecemeal developments that add up to very little. However, the local authority has a certain ambition for the place and has demolished a couple of multistorey car parks to make way for a Penoyre & Prasad

idea. The local authority even set aside £300,000 for the project.

Originally, the contract went to Penoyre & Prasad, falling within the remit of one of their senior architects, Richard Owers. But when Owers decided to leave the practice and take up a directorship at the brand-new firm of Plastik Architects, he asked if he could take the loo project with him. His former bosses obliged, and Plastik found themselves with one of their first jobs.

The finished product is a curious affair, and one that is atypical of everything else that Plastik have produced since setting up four years ago. Which comes down to this matter of virgin territory. There is no contemporary archetype for the public toilet, other than that they are often 'pretty dark and pretty smelly,' says Davies, who also describes the site as 'dreary'. With a grade-level car park on one side and a row of unremarkable shops on the other (no less than five places to get your hair cut, a pub, a Chinese takeaway and an Afro-Caribbean café), there was nothing in the immediate vicinity that Plastik felt deserved anything like a poetic response.

But there was one thing that provided a prompt for a creative move – the slab of new pavement on which this little pavilion sits is triangular. Plastik, having at last found something to cling on to, exploited this happy accident for all it was worth. The result is a freeform piece of public art, all angles and asymmetry; a structure that is deliberately self-referential and even a little alien.

Plastik Architects, Public Toilet, Gravesend, Kent, 2007
The toilets were conceived as a consciously angular piece of public art – a design move that emerged from the triangular site.

The concrete roof is given an edge detail that creates a line of shadow, reinforcing the angularity of the structure – a detail inspired by the work of Carlo Scarpa.

The building sits like a heavy-duty trireme, a concrete and ceramic wedge idling in a sea of paving slabs. But it is delightful. On a sunny day last October, the toilet attendant, an elderly man called Robert, was mopping the floor in a very business-like manner and cheerfully telling anyone who cared to listen that the building had, he thought, won Toilet of the Year.

The fundamental constructional/conceptual idea driving this building is that of a floating canopy, hovering above the walls to admit light into what is otherwise (almost) a windowless structure. Four load-bearing walls (picked out in primary colours) support the inverted pyramid of a roof, the underside of which is washed dramatically in light. The building was imagined more as a set of simple surfaces assembled with the minimum amount of detail, and it was a strategy that almost worked.

Davies and Owers briefly considered omitting the perimeter walls in favour of treating the facility as 'a settlement of cubicles sitting under a protective sculptural roof' defined by the structural walls alone. This would have eliminated the need for ventilation, but the client considered this arrangement to be

difficult to manage and maintain. The whole ensemble therefore came to be enclosed within a heavyweight, faceted wall upon which the roof sits via a 'brittle glazed strip' that zigzags its way around the building above head height. The glass and its framing material sit within slots cast into the concrete structure. This detailing has not been terribly well executed and, worse, retrofitted lighting units look exactly that – an afterthought (not by the architects). However, considering the project came to be about 'the extent to which a public toilet can become a piece of public sculpture,' as Davies says, Plastik has managed to pull off an idea with few compromises.

That said, this public toilet is the most alluring architectural object for a very long time. Outside, its appearance changes radically with even a slight change of one's viewpoint, while randomly spaced glass tiles catch the light intermittently like cat's-eyes or sequins. Inside, the brightly coloured concrete, the three-dimensional angularity (like a set for a German Expressionist film), the grooves that emphasise the folds of the roof, all combine to create a place that makes you want to linger for far longer than is seemly in a building of this type.

Interior of the Gravesend toilet, showing the pink-edged skylight and the blue figures indicating the direction of the male and female facilities.

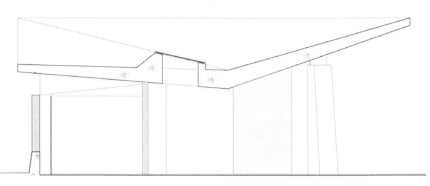

Short section through the building. The roof slab reduces to 200 millimetres (7.9 inches) – about as thin as the engineer would allow.

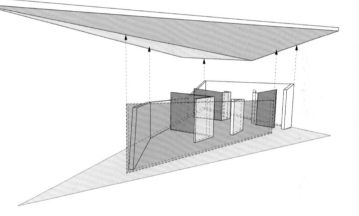

3-D model showing the handful of construction elements: floor slab, load-bearing walls, facades and roof.

This little building is constructed of few materials and colours. Yellow is glimpsed through the entrance; once inside, there is blue, pink and orange.

Gravesend's public toilet is a piece of whimsy. And why not? It is generous also: with three cubicles for women and three for men (plus urinals), little offices for two attendants and a storeroom. There can be few public facilities boasting such largesse.

Certainly, the locals seem to like it – although the building bears the scuffs of skateboarders' attentions, it has attracted little or no graffiti. Soon after the building first opened, council officials observed two old ladies pause, uncertainly, before entering; when they exited shortly afterwards, they were giggling. If the giggles were down to the virtues of the building alone, Plastik have done their work very well indeed. **Δ+**

David Littlefield is an architectural writer. He has written and edited a number of books, including *Architectural Voices: Listening to Old Buildings*, published by Wiley in October 2007. He is also curating the exhibition 'Unseen Hands: 100 Years of Structural Engineering' which will run at the Victoria & Albert Museum from March to October 2008. He has taught at Chelsea College of Art & Design and the University of Bath.

A retrofitted lighting installation, which disturbs the clarity of the concrete edges during the daytime, at night emphasises dramatically the angular cut between the facades.

m3architecture

The m3architecture practice in Brisbane combines experience with youth: in practice now for a decade, all four partners remain under forty. **Mark Taylor** describes how in its work the office has developed a 'social and cultural agenda and site-driven approach' that eschews the oversimplification of a house style while motivating the architects to continue questioning every project on a first-principles basis.

The office of m3architecture is located far from other Brisbane architectural offices in a gritty semi-industrial district a few doors along from a 'nude' car wash and surrounded by a number of small traders. Formed 10 years ago, the partnership of Michael Banney, Michael Christensen, Michael Lavery and Ben Vielle (former graduates of Queensland University of Technology) is now comfortably accommodated in a remodelled older-style timber house. Painted silver-grey on the outside, the interior separates this colour into a white upper-level office space with individual work areas and a lower-level entryway and conference room that is predominantly black. Such experiments between form, colour and visibility are present in several of the practice's projects, as is a concern that Modernism's insistence on clarity and purity of form generates a discordant relation to the reality of the built environment.

For some projects, this idea is used to create architecture that responds to the lived traces of inhabitation, a serious concern for more than one partner in this practice where all four are under the age of 40. This is perhaps a generational attitude to their collective education in a city that has tended to characterise 'subtropical' design through overhanging monopitch roofs, the shading of windows, and open timber screens to allow air movement and prevent heat gain. Moreover, the presence of a few very successful local practices tends to establish a direction that without critical appraisal quickly becomes an easily assimilated 'style'. Resistant to such simplifications, m3architecture's social and cultural agenda and site-driven approach is, as Michael Banney suggests, a place to question pervading assumptions from first principles. For example, they have taken Michael Christensen's expertise in laboratory design and fused it with a programme-specific social/artistic intention, completely altering our perception of such spaces.

It is clear from their approach that when producing architecture that is geographically distant from Europe (as in this case), the search for connections and crossings as a catalyst for intellectual inquiry is measured by the desire to generate architecture that is intimate to its discipline and distant from convention. That is, m3architecture's work is a visible reminder that lines of culture, local environment, material production and climatic difference are just some of the factors that enable the emergence of differentiated architectural form and new geometries of living. Concomitant with these is an understanding that the practices and procedures of one social/cultural situation are not easily placed in another context, irrespective of how wellintentioned might be the translation of ideas or how wellinformed and receptive the audience.

Many of the practice's projects, as speculations on architecture, engage dynamic or 'emergent' properties derived from an individual basis, and emanating from the

Armstrong Residence, Brisbane, 2002
Set on a steep site with dense vegetation, the alterations to this house included a pavilion in the garden, a room seamlessly integrated into the house, and a connecting space. For the garden pavilion, a reflective glass surface dematerialises the building's presence while the pebble-covered roof extends the landscape from above.

personal ideological positions of those involved. Such procedures remove any tendency towards an identifiable 'house style' or promotion of a particular agenda, providing a looser uncentred condition allowing for an idiosyncratic discovery of architecture. Perhaps the only idea that transcends is an understanding that each project exists within a continuum – having a 'before' and an 'after'. That is, by departing from framed Modernist spatial thinking, it is possible to discover some conditions *prior* to the emergent form, while speculating that *subsequent* conditions invoke another architectural distribution.

These latter ideas also speak to the firm's commitment to local 'vernacular' architecture, the typological and quintessential Queenslander house, and a desire to retain its visibility as market forces demand it is altered to accommodate modern living. Many such projects have been undertaken by m3architecture throughout Brisbane, retaining as much of the existing building as possible while carefully orchestrating new accommodation into clearly defined additions. One example is the Armstrong Residence, where a reflective glass pavilion is placed beyond the main house clearly identifying the new against the existing. This action

Creative Learning Centre, Brisbane Girls Grammar School, 2007

Human Movement Pavilion, Queensland University of Technology, Brisbane, 2005
Rather than construct a separate structure alongside an existing proprietary industrial tractor shed and lighting tower, the proposal amalgamates both into the new work in an attempt to validate the ordinary. A fascia extends across both new and existing, and includes elements that change appearance depending upon field position and human movement. As a collaboration between artist and architect, the south elevation also registers the passage of time by season, day, hour and instant.

forces the appearance of a dematerialised architecture that mimics the immediate forest landscape and is evidenced only by the thick edge of a concrete roofline. This foundational idea of invisibility is countered by the evidential presence of the new lower-level interior spaces excavated beneath the existing building and exposed to the garden. Colour in the form of red light radiating through a translucent white plastic surface indicates a moment of inflection – when the plan becomes section – and the invitation to ascend a staircase.

The importance of this project and other work is that they do not delimit architecture to recognisable representations and style (although they operate through the frame of both), but instead generate sensations never before experienced. Such work reminds me of Elizabeth Grosz's proposition that it is from the whirling chaos that is nature, materiality and force that the artist makes a selection or parenthesises various elements that allow art to evolve.[1] It is a progression that rises beyond movements and styles, when these are considered as the continued replacement of fundamentally unstable effects, to reveal a distribution that concerns becoming artistic – a state of self-transformation. This selection, a consequence of cultural difference, brings forth the unpredictability of taste, so that the artistic response partitions space and frames a field or territory into a compositional plane concerned with affect, sensation and intensity.

For example, the Human Movement Pavilion for Queensland University of Technology proposes a translation between industrialised product and artistic practice. Here the existing proprietary tractor shed and floodlighting pole are located on the edge of a sports field formed by cutting and filling a sloping hillside. Respectful of this change in ground condition, the project engages with these conditions rather than ignoring their potential. The architectural proposition establishes the pavilion as a ground-floor extension comprising teaching, changing and storage facilities with a predominantly white upper-level fascia stretching across the front of the lighting pole. The fascia was conceived, working with artist Dirk Yates, as a register of time catalysed by the sun's daily path through summer and winter, as well as artificial lighting at night. Constructed from a palette of 'ordinary' materials with differing reflective, translucent and colour properties, it exceeds the bare requirements of its bodily form, self-transforming and evolving – becoming artistic.

Designed to be read from the playing field as well as from afar, the brilliance of the white fascia under the summer sunshine is activated at one end by shadows cast from an irregular pattern of angle brackets and a diagonal fold reminiscent of the original hillside. However, in winter, when the sun is in the northern hemisphere, the fascia is backlit, rendering the front green. Moreover, when moving around the building subtle changes momentarily destabilise any sense of permanence.

More recently, m3architecture completed the Creative Learning Centre at Brisbane Girls Grammar School, a private institution with a strong academic reputation. This is an interesting and opportunistic project and is the practice's largest commission to date. Beginning as a much less ambitious proposal, it is a testament to the client for having faith in a younger practice as the scope of the project expanded. This time the architecture frames the territory of movement, so that one facade includes a combination of material arrangement and surface graphics to generate the tension found in moiré patterns. Using a combination of repetitive figures with similar spacing, and overlapping them at a small angle, creates an optical illusion whereby various points of intersection on the superimposed grids create interesting effects that the eye is unable to determine.

The tension and effect created by moiré are confined to the west wall where movement is not simply self-referential but mimics aspects of the local environment. Viewed from a

Creative Learning Centre, Brisbane Girls Grammar School, 2007
Located on the edge of an urban freeway and rail corridor, the west facade utilises a combination of material arrangement and surface graphics to generate the tension and effect found in moiré patterns. Against this gesture, the central interior void contributes significantly to the social spaces in the school, facilitating connections within and without the immediacy of its locale. A connection back to the main administrative building is articulated as a crease, a rotational deformation expressed through the use of 'k' section columns.

Chemistry Laboratory Interiors, University of Queensland, Brisbane, 2007
This refurbishment of levels 6 and 10 escapes Modernist homogenised commercial space by generating designs that respond to the programmatic requirements of individual floor occupancy and activity. The often conflicting spatial and material requirements of offices and research labs are diagrammed relative to each other rather than to any preconceived idea. Points of contact between both areas lead to extraordinary spatial and perceptual experiences such as bifurcated or infinite space.

distance (for example from Brisbane's inner-city bypass and local railway line), radial patterns reminiscent of nearby arched windows pulsate as the rulings interact with their own distorted 'shadows'. Drawing closer, the visual distortion caused by lines at variance is no less powerful, particularly as the underlying black-and-white painted parallel grid becomes discernible. It is only when viewed up close and obliquely that it collapses into a flat planar surface and the static capacity of the bronze anodised aluminium 'screen' is exposed. Touching the illusory surface confirms the flattened face is not in motion, but discloses a relationship between the animate and the material, and the diagrammatic and the representational that is also central to experimentation in the digital realm. Challenges to the conventions of surface and substrate by architects such as Herzog & de Meuron are also present, in that virtual movement is indicated through materiality. The surface manipulation of the Creative Learning Centre illuminates what Michael Ostwald identified as the 'philosophically contested territory of the surface ... wherein the form of the building and the impression generated by its skin are most at variance'.[2]

As the site of exchange between architecture and 'other', materials and motion graphics translate this face into something nonrepresentational. That is, the diagrammatic surface represents nothing yet opposes the figurative. Moreover, this outer material face resists projection across all surfaces, in a hermetic manner, to realise the interior 'void' as a volumetric effect generated through horizontal and vertical systems. However, to speak of 'the volume effect' is to recognise the relation between dividing surfaces and flowing space, between material presence and intangibility. In this case the dematerialisation of enclosing walls to three sides of the notional cubic form announces that conventional functional distribution has been reprogrammed. Spatial and material definition is manifested through the partially transparent roof, literally a productive or performing surface operating as both diagram and material.

The general entry concourse aligning with the axially orientated main administration building of the centre is on level four, midway up the building. This eastern edge is more open, conducive to informal learning activities and student-generated events including music, drama and recitals. It is announced through the building volume as an incision, or 'crease' – a rotational deformation that induces tension between the incidence of the outer world (the urban) and private life (the school). Beneath the roofline, the central area or eroded void is nonhierarchical, boundary-less and, to some extent, has a labyrinthine-like terrain comprising stairs and balconies negotiable in several ways. The dynamic of this space is further increased by carefully programming various activities as visible acts of architectural extension. For example, the lower-level co-curricular music rooms are not amorphous spaces hidden from view. They are allowed to distribute other foundational architectural ideas such as the way transparency raises visibility and furthers the inside as

Micro Health Laboratory, University of Queensland, Brisbane, 2001
As the first built stage of a new pedestrian spine through the Gatton campus, this project for a 40-seat laboratory counters the code-derived, regulated sterile interior with a richly textured exterior surface. Working collaboratively with Ashley Paine, the unpredictability of an artistic intention was translated through contemporary techniques and technologies to create a pixilated line diagram as a precursor to the brickwork drawing. To some extent the project invokes abstraction in an attempt to transcend the figurative.

labyrinth, while consistent materiality collapses the interior–exterior dichotomy and inflates the requirements of individual and community.

To some extent the inner hard, raw 'industrial' aesthetic performs as traditional architecture; not that the floor is made in a traditional manner, but the floor surface grounds occupants within this large space. Resisting the temptation to revitalise traditional material and social hierarchical divisions, terrace becomes stair becomes balcony becomes studio. However, the use of achromatic surfaces and natural materials are, as observed by William Braham, 'deemed masculine by virtue of their authenticity (or are they authentic by virtue of their masculinity)?'[3] Colour (the fear of taste affiliated with irrationality and the feminine) is applied to bathroom floors and cubicle doors, strategic internal walls, and as radial patterns to the underside of floor slabs indicating areas of informal activity. In each case their emphasis is not the tension between decorative urge and material, but is argued as a coding system.

Diagrammed this way, colour might just transcend gender stratification in this women-orientated environment; rather than the continuation of modern architecture's excising of colour, a gendered discourse that aligns ornament and applied colours to the traditional practice of feminine interior design/decoration. And while we can argue chromophobia as one problematic of modern architecture (rather than a specific concern of the Creative Learning Centre), m3architecture do, as indicated, tend to engage material and colour palettes on an individual basis, often acting as agents, or indicators, of programmatic intention. Moreover, their ability to engage with the immanence of lived spatiality, the body's movement, and sensations that contribute to an affective space sets them apart from other practices, both locally and internationally. ∆+

Mark Taylor is a senior lecturer at Queensland University of Technology, Australia, where he researches and lectures on spatial theory and the designed interior. He is also a research fellow at RMIT's Spatial Information Architecture Laboratory and a board member of *Architectural Design Research*. He guest-edited the *Surface Consciousness* issue of *Architectural Design* in 2003, and was co-editor, with Julieanna Preston, of the book *Intimus: Interior Design Theory Reader* (John Wiley & Sons, 2006).

Notes
1. Elizabeth Grosz, 'Chaos, territory and art: Deleuze and the framing of the earth', *IDEA Journal*, 2005, pp 15–28.
2. Michael Ostwald, 'Seduction, subversion and predation: Surface characteristics', in Mark Taylor (ed), *Surface Consciousness*, *Architectural Design*, Vol 73, No 2, 2003, p 77.
3. William W Braham, 'A wall of books: The gender of natural colors in modern architecture', *Journal of Architectural Education*, Vol 53, No 1, September 1999, p 13.

Renewable Types and the Urban Plan

CONTROL = HOMOGENEITY?   FREEDOM = DIVERSITY?

The notion of designing according to building type for some might imply constraint, or even a reversion to convention. In Diploma Unit 6 at the AA in London, **Christopher Lee** and **Sam Jacoby** have proved typology can be used to liberating effect, producing series that harness 'the cumulative intelligence' of type, while 'surpassing both its idea and its deep structure'.

Where does architecture stop and urbanism begin? What are the disciplinary tools of the architect that will enable his or her sustained engagement in the larger scale of the urban plan? And in a climate where any shape and form can be sold as a building type or, worse, as a whole city – in search of novelty and in service of the spectacle – how do we imagine, produce and discriminate between a relevant inventive solution and another iterative cliché?

For three years, Diploma Unit 6 has speculated on the possibility of a renewed relevance of typology as a tool for reasoning and producing an urban plan. At the heart of this investigation is the rethinking of the effect of types beyond their immediate architectural scale, by understanding types as a collective urban entity that holds the potential to seed, differentiate, regulate and administer the urban plan. To work typologically is also to work in a series, harnessing the cumulative intelligence of the type in question and surpassing both its idea and its deep structure.

This attempt also marks a return to a more critical approach in projecting new ideas for the city, via dominant types. The role of typology here is both to question, and reason through, the transformative pressure that is exerted on the city through its building types and to find an alternative way of approaching the debate of its sustainability through a critical lens rather than from a technological point of view. The growth and transformation of cities are affected more by social and economic pressures and political impetus than by technical innovations in building products and components. Thus our assumption is that if urbanity is the composite effect of dominant types, investigation on the nature and potential of 21st-century types – as elemental parts of an urban plan – is critical in any attempt to stage alternative visions for our cities.

Our findings so far are pointing to two trajectories of development of dominant types as renewable types: they can be envisioned as either 'punctuators' or 'dispersers' in an urban plan. They both share the characteristic of a type that indexes the organisational imprint of its precedent types and attempts to elude its own expiry by harnessing the cumulative intelligence of its evolution.

Punctuators

Exploring the issues of control and difference in a sustainable urban plan, Yi Cheng Pan's Resisting the Generic Empire challenges Singapore's addiction to the ubiquitous high-rise type and confronts the state's inability to conceive of any new development that is not populated by high-rises. Marina Bay is a 139-hectare (343-acre) reclaimed site originally earmarked for development under the state's ambitious 1996 master plan, but the 1997 Asian economic recession left it barren for over a decade. Recently, under a new leadership, the state has decided to reapply the failed master plan, this time repackaged with

Yi Cheng Pan, Resisting the Generic Empire, Marina Bay, Singapore, 2005–06
The clustering of the inverted high-rises captures and defines public volumes in the intersections.

The liberated ground for the cultivation of a more diverse constituency of stakeholders.

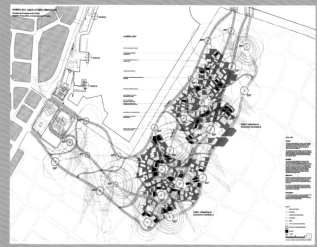

The network of continuous shaded open space.

Max von Werz, Open Source Fabric, Zorrozaurre, Bilbao, Spain, 2006–07
The open-source menu of urban blocks.

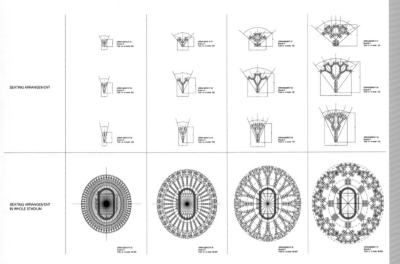

Kelvin Chu, Perforated Hill, Lea Valley, London, 2004–05
The closed bowl structure evolved to a perforated bowl.

The Olympic phase.

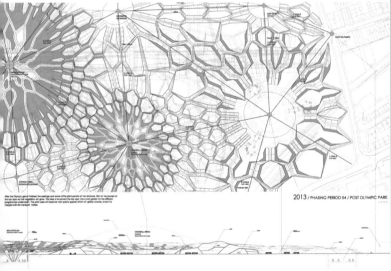

The post-Olympic phase.

iconic structures that promise to deliver a plane of spectacular skyscrapers. Yet a master plan that is homogenously structured for the mass production of these high-rise structures increases the city's dependence on the precarious global market. It takes away its ability to respond quickly to change, as each plot can only be developed through massive economic investment.

To wrest control of the ground plane from the endlessly proliferating skyscrapers, Pan inverts the skyscraper's massing through the cultivation of multiple urban plans within the skyscraper type. This strategy not only releases the ground plane for immediate activation by smaller building types, but also creates multiple 'clustered' volumes for increased public and private partnerships. The project, in this way, resists the formation of the state-engineered Generic Empire – a city entirely subjugated to the whims of large corporations – by providing a typological framework that cultivates difference through the coexistence of multiple types. The released ground plane is further articulated with a fabric that creates a continuous surface of shaded open spaces suited to the tropical climate and to occupation by smaller and more diverse stakeholders. For Pan, the best way to promote difference and participation in a city-state like Singapore is not to relinquish control, but rather to intensify it, forcing a typological change that encourages the participation of the wider population.

Dispersers

As part of Diploma Unit 6's 'London 2013' brief, Kelvin Chu's Perforated Hill challenges the conventional conception of an Olympic stadium as an architectural artefact impregnated with iconic powers (which unfortunately fade after 16 days of frantic use and devoted veneration). These large types are commonly placed on the fringes of the city, surrounded by tarmac and completely closed off from their context. They contribute as much to the urbanity of the surroundings as the average Ikea superstore. The organisation of the stadium is strictly governed by pedestrian escape routes and seating angles. Chu's project takes the inclined escape routes and raked seating as the deep structure of the type, and fixes the capacity of the stadium at 80,000 spectators. It differentiates the type by decreasing the number of routes while increasing their overall bifurcation. As the routes branch out and reorganise the spectator seats, the stadium incrementally evolves from a conventional closed bowl into a porous structure. This typological change then opens up further urban possibilities. At the close of the London 2012 games, the stadium can be turned into a perforated hill, with its top layer and the field around it becoming a public park, and the perforated volumes below seeding a fully functional post-Olympic neighbourhood. Overall, Chu's project seeks to replace the traditional Olympic Park dotted with defunct stadiums with a new city fabric that is able momentarily to absorb the games, yet is biased towards the long-term cultivation of a cohesive urban fabric.

Max von Werz, Open Source Fabric,
Zorrozaurre, Bilbao, Spain, 2006–07
Cultivation of diverse public voids.

Multiple Technopole centres
dispersing towards Technoparks.

Max von Werz's Open Source Fabric speculated on the possibility of type as a permissive fabric. The differentiation of urban blocks and their collective voids is utilised to absorb the relentless shifts in the knowledge industry that is to occupy the peninsula of Zorrozaurre in Bilbao, Spain. Following a typological investigation into research buildings, the project set out to create an 'open-source menu' of urban blocks acting as a toolbox from which anyone could generate a diverse yet coherent urban fabric. The stringing together of the exterior void offered the possibility of a coexistence between the two models of knowledge environments: the suburban-like Technopark and the city-like Technopole. Resisting the tendency for singular types, his project introduced the heterogeneity of diverse type-specific environments capable of consolidating leisure networks to attract a lived-in population within the peninsula. The array of endless options, however, also created a condition of democratic paralysis and von Werz concluded that a certain degree of top-down strategic control is necessary to regulate this typological difference. Thus, the potential of a polycentric radial grid was exploited, establishing multiple dense Technopole centres, each catering for a different industry and dispersing outwards towards loose Technopark peripheries. This mediation attempted to reinforce the resilience of the urban plan by facilitating unforeseen fluctuations in the leisure and knowledge industries.

The common misunderstanding when reading and understanding highly differentiated and articulated urban plans such as these is to confuse the urban plan with a gigantic piece of finished architecture. These projects instead should be read – despite their scale and representation of seeming completeness – as a set of typological guidelines that primarily exist as diagrammatic imprints of typological performance for the enactment of a new pliant urban plan. ∆+

Christopher CM Lee is a principal of Chris Lee Architects, whose completed projects include the Thanks Boutique and Jewel Tech factory. Current projects include V-Office and Birla International School and a new environmental township master plan for Pune. He is the co-author of *Typological Formations: Renewable Building Types and the City* (AA Publications, 2007). He lectures internationally and has been awarded the RIBA President's Medal Commendation and Architectural Record's Design Vanguard 2005.

Sam Jacoby graduated from the AA and is an architect in private practice. He previously worked for offices in the UK, Germany, US and Malaysia, and also trained as a cabinetmaker with Erich Brüggemann. He has been teaching at the AA since 2002 and is currently a doctoral candidate at the TU Berlin in Germany.

Unit Factor is edited by Michael Weinstock, who is Academic Head and Head of Technical Studies at the Architectural Association School of Architecture in London, and also a visiting professor at Yale University and at ESARQ Barcelona. He is co-guest-editor with Michael Hensel and Achim Menges of the *Emergence: Morphogenetic Design Strategies* (May 2004) and *Techniques and Technologies in Morphogenetic Design* (March 2006) issues of *Architectural Design*. He is currently writing a book on the architecture of emergence for John Wiley & Sons Ltd.

In Praise of the Blur

Neil Spiller produces a paean to the instinctive sketch, yearning back to a time that the advantages of being 'vague, noncommittal and ill defined' were well understood.

I have fond memories of presenting one of my drawings to Prince Charles. It was 1987/8, at an Art and Architecture exhibition at the RIBA, and a difficult time for the Prince (he was in the final stages of his first marriage, I subsequently learnt), and being presented with a Spiller black-and-white drawn pizza didn't really help. I think the project was for Milwaukee. Space and decoration billowed out of the drawing in a cacophony of line and form: 'Its an interstitial drawing – between art and architecture,' I offered helpfully. He muttered 'Terrific,' his eyes glazed over and then he moved on.

Twenty years on, I still use the interstitial tactic. It is vitally important for an architect at the beginning of a design to reserve the right to be intuitive, instinctual and expediently vague. This may all seem like common sense to our older readers, but to the computer-dexterous young it is not so obvious. Many are the times when I have sat in front of a creatively blocked student and implored them to sketch. Once the sketch is done, it needs to be reread, resketched or discarded. One of the great things about sketches is that they are spontaneous. Working with a computer demands specificity too early in the process and also denies the possibility for an architect to experience his or her proposal with the visceral feeling so immediate as one draws.

As we have raced to embrace the advantages of the computer and have aided its electronic coup within our offices, we have also embraced its manifold disadvantages.

Spiller Farmer Architects' Sub Urban Fringe interstitial drawing exploring the potential of Rust Belt moated housing, 1986.

A late 1990s computer-generated field drawing by Kevin Rhowbotham concerning itself with the relationship between pattern and dwelling, town and country, figure and ground.

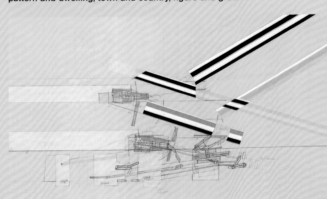

Smout Allen's Retreating Village East Anglia drawing (2005–06) explores the conceivable movement and erosion of dwellings in a coastal area.

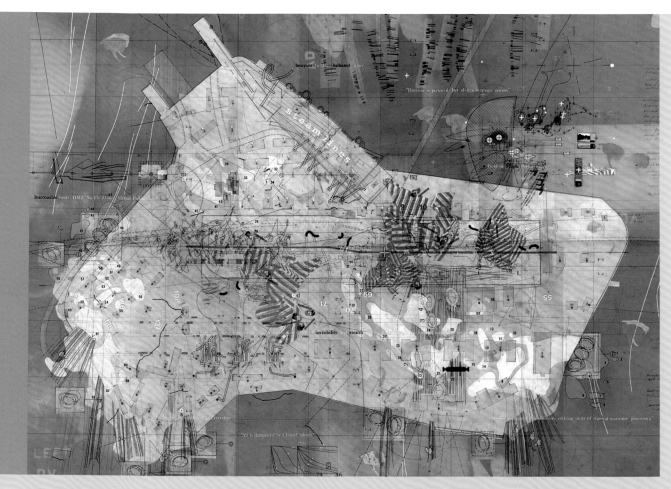

Davids Island Strategic Plot: Perry Kulper's drawing investigates the co-relationship between field, intervention, moment and event.

The ability, as Cedric Price would have told us, to be vague, noncommittal and ill defined is crucial to our ability to create architecture that is liberating. I often ask myself: Is it because so few young architects sketch that so much architectural rubbish is being built? I'm sure it is not the only factor. Indeed, learning to sketch and, more importantly, learning to reread sketches as a means to unleash a cascade of creative architectural ideas is vitally important.

I admire architects who use the sketch and the drawing as tools for pushing the boundaries of their work into non-preconceived architectural solutions or opportunities. There seem precious few out there compared to the 1980s when I was a lad. Some of this small coterie are Smout Allen, whose exquisite work has just been published as a Princeton Pamphlet, as well as my friend Perry Kulper (from the University of Michigan) and Kevin Rhowbotham.

Smout Allen's work is about unstable terrains, untouchable horizons and fleeting perceptual events. The drawings are beautiful, but equally are barometers that register the relative importance of parts of the project and their impacts. Perry Kulper's work deals with erasure, with cyborgian landscapes where histories and technologies collide with augmented space. During his 'Field/Event' period in the late 1990s, Rhowbotham created scalar field geometries that could suggest master plans, individual dwellings, wallpaper and urban connectivity. All three use drawings expediently when reread.

So as a conclusion in a world where all is transparent, defined, quantifiable and nailed down, where little that does not comply to some sort of universally acknowledged fashion or benchmark is ever taken seriously, I say embrace the blur and the multivalences of the sketch – it is another example of a baby thrown out with the nondigital bathwater. The creative vitality of our profession depends on it. In a world obsessed with data it is important sometimes to ignore all the information that an architect has access to in order to eventually create a better product. It is through the full utilisation of the sketch and its approximations that this is possible. Be smart – allow yourself to be dumb and unfocused. Δ+

Neil Spiller is Professor of Architecture and Digital Theory and Vice Dean at the Bartlett, University College London.

Recharging your Bio-Batteries with a Can of Coke

A quiet revolution has taken place in the way we make and use batteries. Ken Yeang highlights the new ground that is being broken in the production of eco-friendly batteries.

Our lifestyle is heavily dependent on batteries – the little electrochemical cells such as the standard indispensable 1.5-volt AA battery found in every household, in our torches, TV remote controls, alarm clocks, radios, etc. These small items power our portable electronic appliances by creating an electromotive force and electrical current, derived from chemical reactions within their cylindrical metal containers where the electric current is caused by the reactions releasing and accepting electrons at the different ends of a conductor inside. As throwaways, they not only become wastes, but thrown into landfills can result in ground-water contamination.

Can we develop ecologically friendly batteries to replace the currently dominant lithium ion cells as an environmentally clean power source for our portable electronics?

Rechargeable batteries have been around for some time, but have not found widespread acceptance, with many still in favour of disposables because of the inconvenience of recharging.

The future of an environmentally friendly battery may lie in fuel cell technology. Fuel cell currently in development boast the ability to extract energy from virtually any sugar source. The new technology is expected to be biodegradable, environmentally friendly and more energy efficient than current options, providing a green alternative to lithium ion batteries.

While hydrogen-based fuel cells have taken off for home or automobile use, the methanol-based versions for use in electronics have yet to be commercialised. Toshiba and NEC have promised methanol fuel-cell-based laptops in previous years, although technology launches have been delayed.

While using sugar for fuel is not a new concept, scientists have only recently learnt how to produce electricity from sugar. Sony has now succeeded in creating a battery that produces electricity by breaking down sugar. It works by breaking down carbohydrates with enzymes, in much the same way as us humans do. Power is produced through a flow of electrons between a cathode and an anode. In the biocell, sugar-digesting enzymes at the anode extract electrons and hydrogen ions from the glucose. The hydrogen ions pass through a membrane separator to the cathode where they absorb oxygen from the air to produce water as a by-product. The enzymes oxidise the sugars to generate electricity.

The Sony biocell is shaped like a cube, 39 millimetres (1.5 inches) in width, and delivers 50 mW (milliwatts) of electricity, the highest output generated to date by a passive-type bio battery. In a demonstration, four of such cells connected in series deliver enough energy to power a Walkman music player. The battery uses glucose solution as a fuel and can use, for instance, a glucose-based sports drink as the fuel. Even the battery's casing, made from a vegetable-based plastic, is environmentally friendly.

Ecologically, sugar is naturally occurring so the technology could be the basis for an ecologically friendly energy source. The sugar cell can operate at room temperature, and researchers have so far run the batteries successfully on glucose, flat soft drinks, sweetened drink mixes and tree sap.

Despite the new batteries only attaining a maximum of 20 per cent efficiency in the conversion of sugar to electricity, researchers say they will operate three to four times longer on a single charge than current battery technology, as employing sugar as a fuel can lead to three to four times the energy density (of metal-based batteries). Although only partial oxidations have so far been achieved, improvements are in progress.

The sugar battery can be used as a stand-alone battery replacement in a wide range of portable electronic devices. However, there will need to be modifications to the electronic devices, with battery compartments being redesigned to accommodate the new eco battery. For example, with fuel-cell batteries, the battery (and the portable device) may need to contain air holes to allow oxygen into the cell. The devices could then be recharged by adding virtually any convenient sugar source, including plant sap or a soft drink

Could the homes of the future be powered by a few cans of Coke?

Ken Yeang is a director of Llewelyn Davies Yeang in London and TR Hamzah & Yeang, its sister company, in Kuala Lumpur, Malaysia. He is the author of many articles and books on sustainable design, including *Ecodesign: A Manual for Ecological Design* (Wiley-Academy 2006).

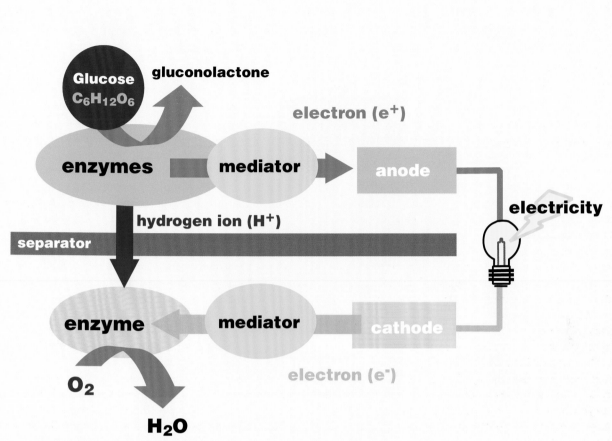

Sony's new bio battery generates electricity from carbohydrates (sugar) using enzymes as its catalyst, through the application of power-generation principles found in living organisms.

Other Batteries

- Moixa Energy Holdings Ltd of London recently unveiled a line of batteries with built-in USB connectors that turn every PC into a battery charger. This makes rechargeable batteries even more convenient than disposables in eliminating the need to keep going to the store to buy new ones. They are also cheaper, paying for themselves over time.
- ScottEVest makes a range of solar-powered jackets, including the Tactical 4.0, a waterproof jacket with lots of pockets and detachable solar panels for charging mobile phones and iPods. So instead of having to charge electronic devices at home, they can be charged on the run.
- Fraunhofer Institute (Germany) and NTT DoCoMo (Japan) have already demonstrated the prototype solar-powered mobile phone. The provision of solar-power technology will extend talk time and eliminate charging altogether.
- EEStor (Texas) claims to have invented a fast-charging ceramic 'ultracapacitor' that provides 10 times the power of conventional batteries at half the cost and without toxic chemicals for use in hybrid cars. The EEStor battery charges in minutes, rather than hours, and will have many times the range of current electric cars. Cars running on EEStor batteries may be as powerful as cars running on gasoline, and cheaper and easier to run than gas/electric hybrids. The new battery technology is reportedly applicable to laptops and other consumer devices too.
- Rensselaer Polytechnic Institute (New York) has devised a paper battery that contains carbon nanotubes, each of which acts as an electrode. These are embedded in a sheet of paper that is soaked in ionic liquid electrolytes, which then conducts the electricity. Ð+

Text © 2008 John Wiley & Sons Ltd. Diagram: adapted from
www.sony.net/SonyInfo/News/Press/200708/07-074E/index.html

McLean's Nuggets

Punctuated Delivery

The pianist Artur Schnabel, when asked what made him a great pianist, said: 'The notes I handle no better than many pianists. But the pauses between the notes? Ah, that is where the art resides!'[1] More recently, author and now professor of creative writing at the University of Manchester, Martin Amis made an elegantly timed appearance on *Newsnight* (19 September 2007), where he pre-empted an answer to the impatient inquisitor Jeremy Paxman with a self-assured silence followed by 'bear with me ...', thus affording (in televisual terms) some uninterrupted air time to express a thought. This control of information delivery is not new, but the impact of a punctuated delivery, deliberate or not, has been previously thought a less than effective communication tool. Recent research by Martin Corley and Lucy J MacGregor from the University of Edinburgh in collaboration with David I Donaldson of the University of Stirling argue that 'disfluency' in spoken language with ums and ers occurring before little-used 'low frequency and unpredictable words'[2] may actually increase comprehension, and that words proceeded by disfluency 'were more likely to be remembered'. That this interesting new research may immediately be dismissed by the voice coaches of politicians may make sense. If the public allegedly trusts fluent speakers, this 'trust' may not necessarily include comprehension.

Former MP Tam Dalyell, writing about the speaking style of Labour politician and shadow foreign secretary Aneurin Bevan (1897–1960) talks about his 'timing' and 'the use

Roy Marchant, Dinner Defence, 1990
Part of a set of designed books by artist Marchant to control physical proximity and thus the conversational possibilities at the dinner party. We may begin to speculate on the equivalent device or devices for the mediation of conversation and speech at the political party.

of his stammer to huge effect'.[3] Another report of Bevan's famous Suez speech of 1956 talks about his 'trick of brushing back a fallen forelock from his brow' and 'the mannerism of driving an argument home by stabbing the air with an index finger'.[4] This control of conversation through timing, syntax, gesture, physical ticks and general body language may be further extended through the use of the occasional 'prop'. Witness architect Will Alsop at a presentation, where the strategic 'chess-like' deployment of very specific pocket-sized accoutrements, such as his modular 'golden section' box of Benson & Hedges, a cigarette lighter disguised as a scale model of the Cardiff Bay visitors' centre and/or eye glasses, glass cases, architects' pen, etc. If all this seems distracting, that may be the point; he now ... has our full attention.

Monumental Disaster

A recent report in the *London Evening Standard*[5] detailed the concerns of Councillor Robert Davis that certain areas of the borough of Westminster were reaching 'monument' saturation point, with more than 300 statues and memorials in the borough celebrating the diverse talents and/or memories of Admiral Nelson, Winston Churchill, all the animals lost in conflicts and, more recently, the very much alive Nelson Mandela. Councillor Davis explained: 'We are proposing to limit the number of statues in Westminster, which we hope will encourage a greater distribution in other parts of the capital and the UK.' This might be a polite way of saying that in a London borough up to its cast-bronze neck in plinth-based heritage, why not force a more equitable distribution of memory reliquary across the capital? Meanwhile, the Public Monuments & Sculpture Association (PMSA) chaired by celebrity food critic and television presenter Loyd (who could possibly live in a house like this?) Grossman has launched the Save Our Sculpture (SOS) campaign, which aims to highlight the neglect of public sculpture. Redressing the overcrowded art landscape is the recent theft of large public sculptures by Henry Moore (stolen 2005) and Lynn Chadwick (stolen 2006). Perhaps we need to return to the collaborative efforts of Messrs Wren and Hooke (Christopher and Robert) who, as two not insignificant employees of the City of London, combined the monumental purpose of the Monument to the Fire of London with a huge piece of scientific instrumentation. At the time of its construction between 1671 and 1677, Hooke envisaged this 61.5-metre (202-foot) edifice as a huge zenith telescope. It was unsuccessful as a telescope due to its lateral movement, but it was certainly utilised by Hooke for pendulum and barometric experiments. In Lisa Jardine's paper 'Monuments and microscopes' she describes how 'Wren and Hooke ... naturally regarded the large man-made monuments they were involved in building as linked projects, offering tremendous possibilities as purpose-built "heights" for practical scientific activities.'[6] Also collaborators in the building of St Paul's, one wonders whether the cathedral's whispering gallery is more of a divers [sic] instrument[7] than a happy acoustic accident.

Bruce McLean, Fallen Warrior, 1969
McLean's live-action sculpture objectifying a posed form with the aid of the ubiquitous and not always helpful mediator, the 'plinth'.

What Cost Building?

In a culture where the economics of the consumer durable, clothing and to some extent food continue to polarise between exploitative cheap and superannuated luxury, the cost of building often remains unfathomable. Finitely, there are the materials: bricks and blocks with unit prices, *in situ* concrete by the square metre or fabricated steelwork by the tonne. However, in relation to a given project this definitive (albeit with local variation) set of book prices for such building stuffs bears little or no relation to the total cost of construction.

Ian McPherson's recent article in the Royal Institute of Chartered Surveyors journal *Building Control*[8] presents a concise analysis of UK building costs in relation to Europe and the US. Using *Building* magazine's annual analysis of international costs provided by Gardiner & Theobald, McPherson's synopsis contains some interesting comparisons. The price of building high-rise apartments in the UK and US is broadly similar, costing an estimated £1,160 and £1,261 per square metre respectively. The materials for such a job cost more in the UK with structural steelwork at £660 per tonne (£504 in the US), concrete at £137 per cubic metre (£61 in the US), and carcassing timber at £288 per square metre (£115 in the US). However, wages in the US are substantially higher with a skilled worker in New York paid up to £49.48 per hour (with benefits) versus £12.71 in the UK. Thus while the cost of building in the UK and US is similar, the wages are not; so where is the difference absorbed? By way of explanation, McPherson suggests that fittings in the UK are increasingly imported, and there is also an argument that construction has become more complex, which in some cases may mitigate inflated costs, but are we simply in thrall to

hugely profitable contractors? The increased costs are most certainly not being passed on to specialist firms such as steelwork contractors who have mostly had to absorb increases in raw material costs. It can only be the increasing murkiness between the designer and professionalised builder that accrues cost, which might be considered construction shenanigans buried deep in the gant chart or the dereliction of duty by the unengaged design professional.

Incidentally, one area where the UK excels is in the economic fabrication of large sheds or warehouses at £290 per square metre, which is less than half the cost in the US. 𝔻+

Notes
1. A Schnabel, *My Life and Music*, Dover Publications (Mineola, NY), reprinted 1988.
2. M Corley, LJ MacGregor and DI Donaldson, 'It's the way that you, er, say it: Hesitations in speech affect language comprehension, *Cognition*, Vol 105, No 3, December 2007, pp 658–68.
3. Great Speeches of the 20th Century, *Weapons for Squalid and Trivial Ends, Aneurin Bevan, December 5 1956*, No 13 in a series of 14, Guardian News & Media, 2007.
4. 'Mr Bevan indicts the "synthetic villains"', *Manchester Guardian*, 6 December 1956.
5. Valentine Low, 'That's quite enough statues thank you, says Westminster', *London Evening Standard*, 1 June 2007.
6. Lisa Jardine, 'Monuments and microscopes: Scientific thinking on a grand scale in the Early Royal Society', *Notes and Records of the Royal Society of London*, Vol 55, No 2, May 2001, pp 289–308.
7. Francis Bacon, *Francis Bacon*, Oxford University Press (Oxford), 1996, pp 480–9.
8. Royal Institute of Chartered Surveyors, *Building Control*, Issue 179, May 2007.

'McLean's Nuggets' is an ongoing technical series inspired by Will McLean and Samantha Hardingham's enthusiasm for back issues of *AD*, as explicitly explored in Hardingham's *AD* issue *The 1970s is Here and Now* (March/April 2005).

Will McLean is joint coordinator of technical studies (with Peter Silver) in the Department of Architecture at the University of Westminster.

The Social Call

Every time you text or call from your mobile phone, you may be unknowingly providing essential data that is being captured for public or commercial research. **Valentina Croci** describes how The Sense*able* City Lab at MIT and the Estonian group Positium LBS with the Department of Geography at the University of Tartu have been developing projects that enable us to sense the city, dynamically mapping social movement.

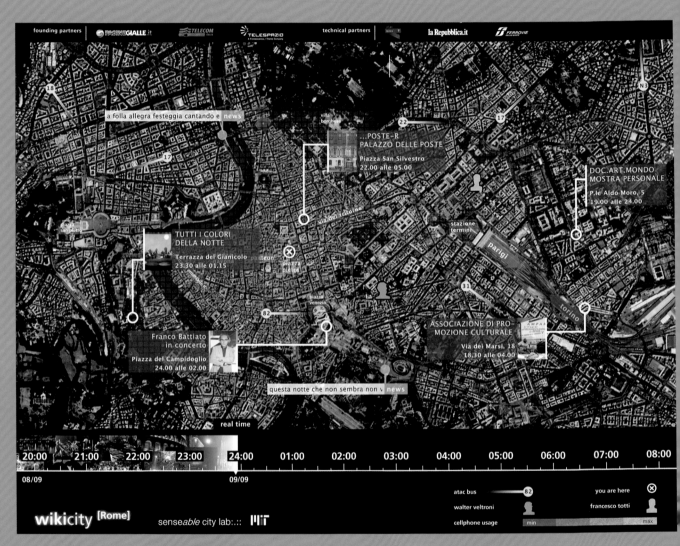

Sense*able* City Lab, Wiki City Rome, La Notte Bianca, Rome, 8 September 2007
The interactive 2-D interface permits any digital device running Web 2.0 to connect, search for, modify and add new information. The map thus becomes a flexible tool, capable of providing real-time data related to services and user density in a given part of the city.

Mobile telephone technologies are now being used to draw territorial maps and as research tools that complement the existing instruments available to traditional urban planning processes. Cellular phones can provide data related to population densities in urban areas and the movement of individuals in space. This information has been used to create synthetic images – digital territorial maps – that allow for a consideration of variables that are both quantitative and temporal (time of day, activities carried out, mobility, etc), and not generally registered by traditional mapping systems. These variables are of significant importance as they allow us to differentiate the various uses of the urban fabric by different inhabitants. In fact, the overlapping of the data

mapping with real-time updates. The images represent a synthesis of data collected from GPS transportation networks, provided by the Roman Public Transportation Authority (ATAC), the Samarcanda Taxi Company and local telecommunications antennas (Telecom Italia's Lochness platform). Cellular phone activity from 169 towers was monitored every 15 minutes. In order to differentiate the intensity of mobile-phone traffic with respect to urban areas, the city was subdivided into various zones. By applying Voronoi diagrams to the relationship between telephone signals from the antennas and geographical areas, it was possible to draw polygons that are equivalent to an urban map, subdivided into zones. Telephone activity was measured

Senseable City Lab, Real Time Rome, Venice Architecture Biennale, September–November 2006 Image of the Senseable Lab installation presenting synthetic images of the Real Time Rome project and other projects related to urban mobility.

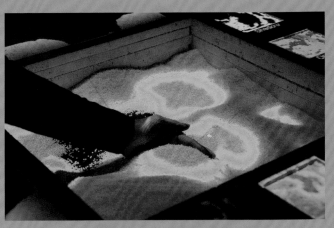

Detailed image showing a possible TUI (tangible user interface) for accessing information.

Installation by Senseable Lab showing two synthetic images of cellular phone activity, correlated to the time of day and data related to urban mobility.

in 'erlang' (the intensity of occupation in a given period of time) and interpolated with traffic data, allowing for the identification of concentration levels and the number of vehicles within the reference polygon. This collection of data provided quantitative information about density, the speed of flows in a given zone and at various times of the day. This in turn made it possible to generate visual representations of the movement and concentration of people during extraordinary events – for example, the Madonna concert at the Olympic Stadium, or the final of the World Soccer Championship, broadcast at the Circus Maximus.

However, if this information is not analysed in terms of broad temporal statistics, it remains exclusively quantitative and does not qualify the different uses of urban areas by its inhabitants – for example, tourism, work and entertainment. Recognising the patterns of user activity with respect to urban areas was the logical next step for Senseable Lab. The temporal profiles of cellular phone usage (known as 'electronic signatures' – graphic charts that show how many megabytes cross each antenna throughout the day) were linked to information from the Seat Yellow Pages, highlighting the number of professional offices or services located in various parts of the city. This comparison allowed

captured from cellular phones on the fixed topography of the city highlights the divergence between fluid components (mobility and population density) and the static qualities of the urban landscape (the built environment and infrastructural elements). This difference determines the general quality of the urban environment, as experienced by those who inhabit it.

The Senseable City Lab at MIT, directed by Carlo Ratti, has been working in this field since 2005, producing applications such as Real Time Rome, presented at the 2006 Architectural Biennale in Venice, and its evolution, Wiki City Rome (September 2007). Real Time Rome is an example of digital

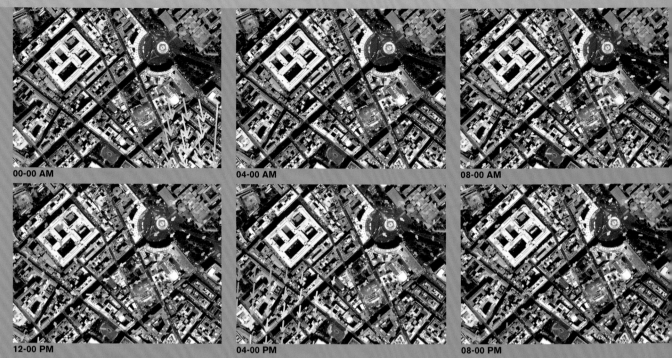

00-00 AM   04-00 AM   08-00 AM

12-00 PM   04-00 PM   08-00 PM

Real Time Rome project. Visualisation of cellular phone activity at the scale of an urban neighbourhood and at different times of day. The detail shows the area defined by San Carlo alle Quattro Fontane to the west, the Baths of Diocletian to the north, Piazza dei Cinquecento to the east and Piazza del Viminale to the south.

for a deduction of user activities in specific areas and, if related to vaster units of time (weekly or bimonthly), the construction of 'activity coefficients'. In other words, this information was used to determine patterns during different periods of the year, linked to variations in the temporal parameters of cellular phone activity and functional urban typologies. The resulting maps thus indicate how and when the city is used by its inhabitants.

Wiki City Rome is an urban map whose variable functions are based on the actions and decisions of its users. The map uses a descriptive rhyzomatic model: the organisation of its elements does not respond to a hierarchical and preferential subordination or set of rules, but rather to a spontaneous process of association where each operation modifies the entire system. In simpler terms, the interactive interface of the map is the real-time result of the individual actions of those using it. Wiki City uses *sensing* instruments (smart phones, PDAs or interactive platforms using Web 2.0) and satellite maps such as Google, which combine aerial images with sophisticated zooming-panning software. Users can thus connect to a map with their handheld device and search, modify or publish information. The user data is collected and synthesised by a central database that modifies the Wiki Rome interface in real time. This allows for the creation of a 'location and time sensitive' system and the dissemination of information related to a specific situation: by accessing specialised services users can, for example, decide to leave comments to be shared with other users.

At present the project features a 2-D interface that uses a keyboard or touchscreen, similar to existing smart phones. However, plans call for the development of multimodal or TUI (tangible user interfaces) located within the urban fabric. The difficulties related to the creation of these interfaces lies in the resolution of duplicate processes of data extraction and composition and, in more general terms, in the condensation of large amounts of data in devices with limited bandwidth.

While Real Time Rome allowed for a mapping of the activities of the city's inhabitants with respect to the specific conditions of the urban fabric, Wiki City Rome allows for the correlation of the same activities with services offered in a precise area, offering real possibilities for user interaction. The map thus becomes an active and dynamic instrument for everyday use, a role already played by mobile phones and the Internet.

Since 2001, the Estonian group Positium LBS has been collaborating with the Department of Geography at the University of Tartu on the creation of a digital map based on the Social Positioning Method (SPM). Beginning with the collection of data from cellular phones in roaming (all non-nationally registered phones) over the course of a year, the group created a map that allows for an analysis of seasonal tourist flows and the use of the Estonian territory in relationship to its services and infrastructures. The maps consider the 'social utilisation' of the landscape in reference to space-time variables and user nationality.

The anonymous roaming data gathers cellular phone activity (calls made and received, SMS text messaging, Internet and GPRS service usage) and passive information, in this case the position of the phone when it is turned on, though not used. Once again in this case, cellular phone activity is monitored in relation to areas defined by Voronoi polygons, subdividing 900,000 square miles into more than 900 reception points. The fact that the positioning of the antennas does not depend as much on administrative circumstances as on territorial infrastructures of connection has allowed for the capturing of information related to the speed of flows of persons and the quality of transportation. Roaming data is related to national access codes (not personal numbers), the time of day, the duration of phone activity and the spatial coordinates of the antenna – the position and time of the call make it possible to develop statistics regarding the movement of people. This information is then correlated with those of the Estonian board of tourism, which keeps track of visitors to various hospitality structures.

With respect to the latter data, the tracking of cellular phone activity has allowed for a reconstruction of the daily movement of users – a very important factor in Estonia, where it is possible to move through its various provinces in a day. The interpolation of roaming data in relationship to national holidays or climatic variables allows for a qualification of seasonal or weekly patterns of tourism, as well as the cultural differences between foreigners – information that can be used by municipalities, tourism entities and transportation companies. The periodic nature of flows of people, in fact, is a phenomenon that weighs on the local economy given its close ties to climatic conditions. Finally, the temporal nature of tourist flows is important for qualifying the type of visit with respect to a given area (tourism or business) and the type of activity (thermal baths, natural excursions, shopping or sightseeing). This is important, above all, for geographically remote areas, where it is difficult to gather statistics using traditional methods.

The above examples demonstrate that maps are no longer static representations of a given territory, but an open and dynamic source that is both qualitative and quantitative in terms of the development of the economy and the service industries. Such mapping systems constitute a strategic instrument of territorial management, as well as being useful for sociological studies of the movement of people. The ability to gather real-time data, correlated to territorial uses, highlights the possible repercussions on the urban economy, in addition to modifying traditional systems of urban planning. ᗪ+

Translated from the Italian version into English by Paul David Blackmore

Valentina Croci is a freelance journalist of industrial design and architecture. She graduated from Venice University of Architecture (IUAV), and attained an MSc in architectural history from the Bartlett School of Architecture, London. She achieved a PhD in industrial design sciences at the IUAV with a theoretical thesis on wearable digital technologies.

Positium, Seasonal tourism spaces in Estonia: Research project on mapping with mobile positioning data, 2003–06.

Changes to tourist visits to Estonia.

Path of tourists in Estonian locations.

Tourists visiting Tallinn's city centre.

3-D visualisation of tourists visiting Tallinn's city centre.

Distribution of tourist flows.

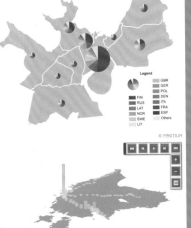

Graphs representing call activities during the Metallica concert in Tallinn (13 June 2006).

Making Waves at East Beach Café

Howard Watson describes how Littlehampton on the Sussex coast has become the unlikely home to a cutting-edge structure. The 'rippling, ribbed, brown steel mollusc' form of this year-round café-restaurant, realised by Heatherwick Studio and Adams Kara Taylor, celebrates its fresh seafood menu and beachside site.

View of the building from the seafront car park. The mild steel has been finished with an oil-based coating, allowing for a rust-like patina without structural degradation.

Terence Conran recently compared Thomas Heatherwick to Leonardo da Vinci, heralding him as one of the great thinkers of our times, but he also mentioned his great modesty. The latter is borne out by Heatherwick choosing East Beach Café, a £500,000 beachfront café, as his first completed building project; the da Vinci comparison has some weight as this young British designer manages to combine aesthetics, form and function in his creations such as the Rolling Bridge (London) and the sculptural Longchamp retail interior (New York). Clever, precise engineering lies at the heart of his ideas, no less so for this humbly financed café. Packman Lucas helped with the structural concept of the café and Heatherwick turned to Adams Kara Taylor, a London-based, design-led engineering consultancy that has established a reputation working with challenging architects such as Zaha Hadid and Will Alsop, to engineer the unusual structure.

The stand-alone building replaced a beach kiosk and had to incorporate café, restaurant and takeaway kiosk functions on a very narrow (just 7 metres/23 feet at its widest), 40-metre (131-foot) strip between a beach and a car park in the rather old-fashioned resort town of Littlehampton on England's south coast. The clients, mother and daughter Jane Wood and Sophie Murray, regarded earlier plans for a replacement kiosk as an eyesore on an extremely visible and sensitive site. They turned to Heatherwick, who was given licence to resist the conformity of seaside architecture and has created a rippling, ribbed, brown steel mollusc.

The exterior shell is made up of 36 ribbons of 8-millimetre (0.3-inch) mild steel stretching along the length of the building. The weathered, Owatrol-oiled ribbons step down and outwards from the highest, longest point of the roof, entirely encasing one long side and curving under to form the narrow backside of the building. The other long side is the restaurant entrance, mostly comprising shutters and glazed doors that face the sea. The rhythm of the ribbons topically evokes the contours of tide-washed sand and the motion of the sea, but the beauty of the structure is that the aesthetic is also functional. The ribbon structure allows the shape to step inwards as the footprint narrows, while the ribbons themselves are 30 millimetres (1.2 inches) wide, precisely allowing the protective metal shutters to recede into the shell structure. Furthermore, Adams Kara Taylor used finite-

Heatherwick Studio and Adams Kara Taylor, East Beach Cafe, Littlehampton, West Sussex, 2007
The front of the café, seen from the beach. The left-hand end of the ribbons forms a canopy for the takeaway kiosk. Inside, white plasterwork follows the contours of the exterior shell.

element analysis of the shell structure, inputting the designer's digital 3-D model, to prove that it was easily supportable through columns only along the glazed side: to some extent, the shell is self-supporting, allowing for the fullest use of the interior space.

The final design was fabricated off site, but literally a stone's throw away, by local steelwork firm Littlehampton Welding, who worked on Heatherwick's Rolling Bridge and Future Systems' West India Quay Floating Bridge.

The exposed building is situated on sand, and the close proximity of a high-pressure sewer did cause concerns, but a strip footing proved suitable for the one-storey load. Hanif Kara of Adams Kara Taylor says the biggest challenge 'was to make a connection between what is a very low-tech material of flat steel plate with the most advanced high-tech design tools available for drawing and forensically analysing the form to create a complex "whole" with very simple "parts".' The engineers unfolded the design using Digital Project/CATIA, while running SOFiSTiK software for the analysis. Kara adds that the firm was glad 'to get these tools to talk to each other and develop the ingenuity of Heatherwick's initial idea and Littlehampton's appetite to push the fabrication further beyond just an image ... with the client's encouragement.' The local community and council were extremely positive about

having this extraordinary, nonconforming building posited in such a visible place on the shoreline.

Kara concludes: 'Such projects are critical and push essential collaborative tensions to the limit in an age where creativity and "boldness" are often eroded in the shadows of production and "buildability".' Irrelevant to the design's topicality, there is a question mark as to whether a structure such as this could have found a place in London, or whether Jordan Mozer's contoured, metal-clad restaurant buildings in extremely unlikely suburban settings in the US could have found sites, and support, in New York. It seems that there is a place for mid- to low-budget design experimentation many miles from the cities that regard themselves as the epicentres for both architectural and culinary innovation, and that there is a burgeoning certainty of the benefits of innovative design in provincial environments. East Beach Café, which specialises in seafood, is packed to the gills. ᗪ+

Howard Watson is an author, journalist and editor based in London. He is co-author, with Eleanor Curtis, of the new 2nd edition of *Fashion Retail* (Wiley-Academy, 2007), £34.99. See www.wiley.com. Previous books include *The Design Mix: Bars, Cocktails and Style* (2006), and *Hotel Revolution: 21st-Century Hotel Design* (2005), both also published by Wiley-Academy.

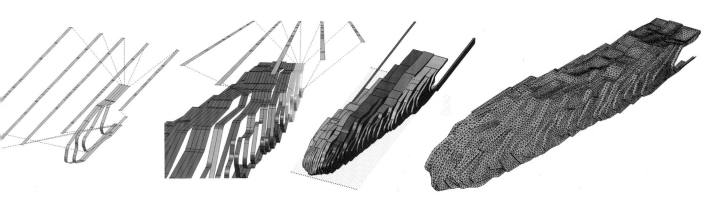

Adams Kara Taylor unfolded the design shape using CATIA and analysed it with SOFiSTiK software.

Subscribe Now

As an influential and prestigious architectural publication, *Architectural Design* has an almost unrivalled reputation worldwide. Published bimonthly, it successfully combines the currency and topicality of a newsstand journal with the editorial rigour and design qualities of a book. Consistently at the forefront of cultural thought and design since the 1960s, it has time and again proved provocative and inspirational – inspiring theoretical, creative and technological advances. Prominent in the 1980s and 1990s for the part it played in Postmodernism and then in Deconstruction, in the 2000s ⚠ has leveraged a depth and level of scrutiny not currently offered elsewhere in the design press. Topics pursued question the outcomes of technical innovations as well as the far-reaching social, cultural and environmental challenges that present themselves today in a period of increasing global uncertainty. ⚠

SUBSCRIPTION RATES 2008
Institutional Rate (Print only
or Online only): UK£180/US$335
Institutional Rate (Combined Print
and Online): UK£198/US$369
Personal Rate (Print only):
UK£110/US$170
Discount Student* Rate
(Print only): UK£70/US$110

*Proof of studentship will be required when placing an order. Prices reflect rates for a 2007 subscription and are subject to change without notice.

TO SUBSCRIBE
Phone your credit card order:
+44 (0)1243 843 828

Fax your credit card order to:
+44 (0)1243 770 432

Email your credit card order to:
cs-journals@wiley.co.uk

Post your credit card or
cheque order to:
John Wiley & Sons Ltd.
Journals Administration Department
1 Oldlands Way
Bognor Regis
West Sussex PO22 9SA
UK

Please include your postal
delivery address with your order.

All ⚠ volumes are available individually.
To place an order please write to:
John Wiley & Sons Ltd
Customer Services
1 Oldlands Way
Bognor Regis
West Sussex PO22 9SA

Please quote the ISBN number of the issue(s) you are ordering.

⚠ is available to purchase on both a subscription basis and as individual volumes

○ I wish to subscribe to ⚠ *Architectural Design*
at the **Institutional rate of (Print only or Online only** *[delete as applicable]*)
UK£180/US$335

○ I wish to subscribe to ⚠ *Architectural Design*
at the **Institutional rate of (Combined Print and Online) UK£198/US$369**

○ I wish to subscribe to ⚠ *Architectural Design*
at the **Personal rate of UK£110/US$170**

○ I wish to subscribe to ⚠ *Architectural Design*
at the **Student rate of UK£70/US$110**
⚠ *Architectural Design* is available to individuals on either a calendar year or rolling annual basis; Institutional subscriptions are only available on a calendar year basis. Tick this box if you would like your Personal or Student subscription on a rolling annual basis.

Payment enclosed by Cheque/Money order/Drafts.

Value/Currency £/US$ [   ]

○ Please charge £/US$ [   ]
to my credit card.
Account number:

[ ][ ][ ][ ][ ][ ][ ][ ][ ][ ][ ][ ][ ][ ][ ][ ][ ][ ]

Expiry date:

[ ][ ][ ][ ][ ][ ]

Card: Visa/Amex/Mastercard/Eurocard *(delete as applicable)*

Cardholder's signature [   ]

Cardholder's name [   ]

Address [   ]

[   ] Post/Zip Code [   ]

Recipient's name [   ]

Address [   ]

[   ] Post/Zip Code [   ]

I would like to buy the following issues at £22.99/US$45 each:

○ ⚠ 192 *Versatility and Vicissitude: Performance in Morpho-Ecological Design*, Michael Hensel + Achim Menges

○ ⚠ 191 *Cities of Dispersal*, Rafi Segal + Els Verbakel

○ ⚠ 190 *Made in India*, Kazi K Ashraf

○ ⚠ 189 *Rationalist Traces*, Andrew Peckham, Charles Rattray + Torsten Schmiedeknecht

○ ⚠ 188 *4dsocial: Interactive Design Environments*, Lucy Bullivant

○ ⚠ 187 *Italy: A New Architectural Landscape*, Luigi Prestinenza Puglisi

○ ⚠ 186 *Landscape Architecture: Site/Non-Site*, Michael Spens

○ ⚠ 185 *Elegance*, Ali Rahim + Hina Jamelle

○ ⚠ 184 *Architextiles*, Mark Garcia

○ ⚠ 183 *Collective Intelligence in Design*, Christopher Hight + Chris Perry

○ ⚠ 182 *Programming Cultures: Art and Architecture in the Age of Software*, Mike Silver

○ ⚠ 181 *The New Europe*, Valentina Croci

○ ⚠ 180 *Techniques and Technologies in Morphogenetic Design*, Michael Hensel, Achim Menges + Michael Weinstock

○ ⚠ 179 *Manmade Modular Megastructures*, Ian Abley + Jonathan Schwinge

○ ⚠ 178 *Sensing the 21st-Century City*, Brian McGrath + Grahame Shane

○ ⚠ 177 *The New Mix*, Sara Caples and Everardo Jefferson

○ ⚠ 176 *Design Through Making*, Bob Sheil

○ ⚠ 175 *Food + The City*, Karen A Franck

○ ⚠ 174 *The 1970s Is Here and Now*, Samantha Hardingham

○ ⚠ 173 *4dspace: Interactive Architecture*, Lucy Bullivant

○ ⚠ 172 *Islam + Architecture*, Sabiha Foster

○ ⚠ 171 *Back To School*, Michael Chadwick

○ ⚠ 170 *The Challenge of Suburbia*, Ilka + Andreas Ruby

○ ⚠ 169 *Emergence*, Michael Hensel, Achim Menges + Michael Weinstock

○ ⚠ 168 *Extreme Sites*, Deborah Gans + Claire Weisz

○ ⚠ 167 *Property Development*, David Sokol

○ ⚠ 166 *Club Culture*, Eleanor Curtis

○ ⚠ 165 *Urban Flashes Asia*, Nicholas Boyarsky + Peter Lang